THE UNDERTAKER'S DAUGHTER

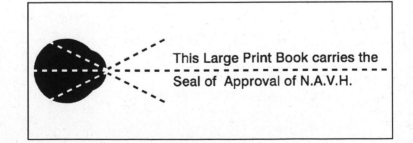

This Large Print Book carries the
Seal of Approval of N.A.V.H.

THE UNDERTAKER'S DAUGHTER

KATE MAYFIELD

THORNDIKE PRESS

A part of Gale, Cengage Learning

Farmington Hills, Mich • San Francisco • New York • Waterville, Maine
Meriden, Conn • Mason, Ohio • Chicago

LIBRARY OF CONGRESS CATALOGING-IN-PUBLICATION DATA

Mayfield, Katherine, 1958–
    The undertaker's daughter / by Kate Mayfield. — Large print edition.
        pages cm. — (Thorndike Press large print biographies and memoirs.)
    ISBN 978-1-4104-7894-8 (hardcover) — ISBN 1-4104-7894-7 (hardcover)
    1. Mayfield, Katherine, 1958– —Childhood and youth. 2. Authors—United
States—Biography. 3. Large print books. I. Title.
CT275.M465173A3 2015
920.72—dc23
    [B]   2015000790

Published in 2015 by arrangement with Gallery Books, a division of Simon & Schuster, Inc.

Printed in Mexico
1 2 3 4 5 6 7 19 18 17 16 15

For my father

In Memoriam

And for my mother

AUTHOR'S NOTE

The names of places and many people in this book have been changed, including those in the author's own family.

To Be Sure

I wouldn't want to bring him back
from his permanent interment
even if I could
but I wouldn't mind a visit now and then,
a trip down
to keep each other company.
I could push back the top of the concrete
  liner,
pull up the half lid of that quite tasteful
  furniture
that is now his home
and fill him in
on the news of the business and my life
since he's been gone.
He's easier to talk to now
and I miss him
more than I thought I would,
more than I thought I could.
Always expected his going
would set me free
and now I am
surprised really
that his new silence
and contained grace
leave me finally free
to love him and to grieve.

LARRY SORKIN

PROLOGUE

"Mayfield and Son Funeral Home." My father answered the phone using his undertaker voice.

My mother stopped fiddling with her gloves and strained to hear his responses.

"Who is it?" I asked.

"Shh!" She put her finger to her lips, clearly annoyed.

He placed the phone back on the receiver and met her worried eyes with a somber look.

"Frank?"

He didn't answer her.

"Okay." Defeated, she threw her gloves down on the table. "Who died?"

He tilted his head back and laughed. "Got you, didn't I?"

"That is not funny. It's just not funny at all."

He winked at me. "I got your mother real good."

"Yeah, you sure did, Daddy!"

When your house is a funeral home, you spend a lot of time sitting around waiting for someone to die. But there were days, like this one, when we'd rather they didn't.

My mother frowned at me. "I'm going to Mildred's to get my hair done. I want you to stay up here and out of Belle's way. Don't go downstairs, do you hear me? I don't want you underfoot bothering your daddy."

"Okay."

"What?" She looked up from rummaging through her handbag.

"I mean, yes."

"Yes what?" she snapped.

"Yes, ma'am."

"That's better."

"What's the matter with her?" I asked my father when my mother left the room.

"She's a little tense. She's afraid she'll have to cancel the bridge party if we get a body." He went to the kitchen counter and downed his second double Alka-Seltzer of the day.

It had happened before. On the eve of a long-planned bridge luncheon, the phone rang during supper. Its distinct, long tone was a sound I would never forget. After a short conversation, my father looked at my mother and said, "I've got to go pick up

Mr. Rayner."

She threw out most of the deviled eggs that night. What a mess they looked in the garbage: a mound of shiny egg whites smeared with pale yellow yolks all smashed together, the whole lot spattered with deep red paprika, as if they'd been murdered.

Today we monitored my father's expression with apprehension as he spoke into the phone again; his eyes and a slight shake of his head told us no, this was not a death call. Our housekeeper, Belle, who'd grown accustomed to these pauses, shifted quickly back into gear with the food preparations.

Bridge-party food was like no other sort. Belle spooned wiggly, lime-green, congealed salad onto iceberg-lettuce leaves, then placed them with precision on paper-doily-lined plates. Chicken Surprise was a concoction of chicken, grapes, Miracle Whip, nuts, and unidentifiable morsels that made my eyes water when I tasted it. Belle rustled around with crackling sounds in a stiff, shiny black dress accented by a white collar and white-cuffed sleeves. She wore a fancy white apron with a ruffled border. The dress made her look like she worked for us, and I didn't like that, even though she did.

"Why are you wearing a costume, Belle?"

"Not a costume. It's jest a nicer dress

13

'cause yer mother's havin' comp'ny."

I snuck around behind her and untied her apron. It delighted me to see it fall to the floor.

"I ain't got time for this today. I'm gonna git a switch after you if you don't behaves yerself." An empty threat.

"Who told you to wear that dress, Belle?"

"Nobody. I wears it myself. I owns it. Now run along and leave me be. Come back later and I'll fix you some lunch. And takes them trousers off and puts on a dress, ya hear?"

After my mother returned from the beauty parlor, she and Belle focused on preparing the dining room. The funeral-home phone rang all morning in spurts, as usual, but on bridge-luncheon day it was like watching a game of musical chairs. My mother and Belle scurried around working to make things perfect; the phone rang, they froze, waited for a sign that all was well; and then resumed a new position. Good Lord, I thought, who would have the bad grace to depart this life at such an inconvenient time?

Just before noon, the first of the seven hat-wearing, glove-toting ladies paraded through the front entrance to the funeral home. My father held the door open for them.

"Afternoon, Becky Lou . . . Mrs. Apple-ton . . . Mary Daley." He nodded to each of them in turn.

"Frank, how are you?" they chorused.

"You ladies are well turned out today, but I think there must be some misunderstanding. The luncheon is tomorrow," he said amiably.

Their eyes froze in horror.

"But . . . I'm sure . . . isn't today Tuesday?"

He burst into laughter. "Oh, I'm just kidding you! You all go on upstairs, now."

"Well, Frank, I swanee."

My father was comfortable around women. He always seemed to know just the right thing to say. Flattered by his teasing, the ladies glowed as they climbed the stairs to our living quarters.

The odor of their hairspray preceded them as they entered the dining room and remarked favorably on its transformation. They might even forget they were in a funeral home. The room felt spacious in spite of the toile wallpaper. A small, tiled fireplace framed by a wooden mantelpiece, normally a focal feature in other homes, stood tucked away in a corner of the room. On the other side of the room was one of my father's recent finds — a seventy-five-year-old child's coffin. He had commissioned a carpenter to attach four tall,

15

elegant legs to support its tender weight. The lid was propped open to expose an empty space from which the lemony color of the pine glared back at those who were brave enough to peek inside. He looked upon it as a piece of art, or an antique to be treasured. I once placed a doll in it and pronounced it dead. He insisted I remove it. "It's not a toy, so don't treat it like one."

The card tables were set up in the center of the room, covered by starched white tablecloths and napkins, which offset the good china and silver laid out to perfection. Brand-new packs of bridge cards, score pads, and jeweled pencils sat ready on each of the card tables. The ladies brimmed with excitement at the prospect of an afternoon filled with food, bridge, and gossip.

I spied on the women from the kitchen; the doorway offered a clear view of their manicured hands already fingering the glass bowls filled with Bridge Mix. The chatter began and would not cease for hours. I heard the china clinking and the silver clanging in concert with the women's voices, while Belle swished around as efficiently as a worker bee. The dining room began to smell like a restaurant, thick with food, perfume, and — wait. What was that scent that cut through? Mothballs.

"Belle, one of those ladies in there smells like mothballs. I think it's Mrs. Appleton."

Belle gave me a rapid-fire piece of her mind. "Hush up, that's not polite. Maybe she does. I don't cares if she smells like a pair of nasty ole boots. She mightn't gets out much. This might be a real treat for her. You be nice, ya hear?"

Duly chastised, I watched as the ladies demolished the last of the celery sticks stuffed with pimento cheese and moved on to the next course.

"Mmm. Delicious! Why, Lily Tate, this is the best congealed salad I have ever had. Does it have a name?"

Everyone called my mother by both of her names. My father first among them. He addressed most people by their first and middle names, as if to remind them of their whole selves, a habit that seemed to cozy up nicely with our new territory. Jubilee's old Southern aristocrats took pride in their family surnames and used them to clarify well-used first names about town: Mary Paige, Mary LaRue, Mary Blythe; and no one thought it at all strange that one of my mother's friends was called Mary Pillow.

"Oh, I don't know what it's called, Mary Daley, but I'm happy to pass on the recipe. I got it out of *Southern Living Classics*."

17

"Well, I hope you don't mind, but I just have to have it." Mary Daley's deep drawl rose above the others.

"Colonel Leonidas L. Polk," Mrs. Appleton announced.

Mrs. Eunice Appleton, a retired schoolteacher who regularly erupted with bits of information without explanation, enjoyed being coaxed.

"What about Colonel Polk, Eunice?" Becky Lou asked.

"Founder of the *Progressive Farmer* newspaper, 1886. Eventually became *Southern Living Classics.* Delicious salad, Lily Tate."

My mother was genuinely grateful for the approval. Jubilee represented a fresh start in a new town, a new business, and, I was to learn, a fresh start in her marriage. The flattery was nice, but relief was the primary emotion, because it was important to break ground in Jubilee's society when your roots didn't sprout from Beacon County soil. Bridge playing was serious social business. The ladder of acceptance was tall, and to climb it playing bridge ranked right up there after churchgoing and a spot of charity work. My mother knew nothing about the game until we moved to Jubilee. One of the women from our new church invited her to come along one day and watch a group play.

18

She picked it up quickly and soon became a somewhat formidable player. I, too, would one day have to learn to make my way among the coteries of Jubilee society.

Belle wouldn't let me help serve the food, but allowed me to collect the empty plates while she topped up the sweet iced tea in the crystal glasses, which she pronounced *chrishtal.* I sensed my mother holding her breath, waiting to see if I could manage the task without spilling anything in the ladies' laps, or saying something wildly inappropriate. At the last bridge party, I'd asked, "Isn't it lucky that no one died yesterday?" — and my mother wanted to fall through the floor. But today I followed Belle's instructions to the tee.

"Now you jest waltz in there and gives each of them ladies a big smile. Jest like it's Christmas mornin' and you gots everything on your extry long list."

"May I take your plate, ma'am?" My cheeks almost burst with the plumpness of my smile.

Back in the kitchen, Belle wrapped up a plate of food in foil.

"What are you doing?" I asked.

"Mrs. Hargrove, she's takin' it home with her."

"She have a dog or something?"

"No, she keeps skin and bones on her by jest eatin' half of everything. Saves money, too."

"Is that polite, Belle?"

"Not fer me to say. It's jest the way she is. Yer mama says she does it ever'where she goes. They sees Mrs. Hargrove a'comin', they gets out they's foil."

After lunch the first progression of bridge began. I was no longer welcome in the dining room and Belle shooed me out of the kitchen. But our big old house was so full of doors and stairways and nooks and crannies that I was able to race down the stairs, run around the outside of the house to the front entrance of the funeral home, and sneak up the front staircase. The dining room where the ladies played was sandwiched between the living room and the kitchen, which provided two perfect aspects from which to spy. I tiptoed into the living room, and listened undetected to the conversation next door.

After the opening bid, the harmless talk of children, church, and school trickled back and forth between the tables. These women were adept, the cards an extension of their fingers. They chattered like a tree full of birds as they played their hands, yet remained watchful as the game unfolded before them.

"Have ya'll been busy, Lily Tate?" asked Mary Daley.

"Fairly. We buried Mr. Jessup last week."

"I stopped by for visitation," said Becky Lou. "Frank sure did a nice job on him."

"He was a very . . . large man," said my mother. "His casket was specially made."

Snap, snap, snap. The sound of the cards hitting the tables merged with their voices.

Then, Becky Lou tossed out a concept I knew I would never learn in school: "People from The North don't play like we do."

"Why, what do you mean?" asked Pearline, the group's newest player.

"They have different rules."

"Good God A'mighty, that's an understatement if I ever heard one," piped up Mary Daley.

"They don't bid like we do and they question everything," Becky Lou said. "They go on all day with 'What does this mean, what does that mean? We don't play this way where we're from.' Lord, it felt like she was accusing us of cheating."

"Good heavens. Where's the poor thing from?" asked Pearline.

"Ohio." Becky Lou paused for emphasis. "There's *nothing* Southern about *her.*"

"That is the truest thing I ever did hear.

When you cross the Ohio River, it's just a different world, now I mean to tell you it is." This from my mother.

*Mmm-hmm*s all around the room.

"They were talking about the Ohio." Mrs. Appleton came alive again.

"Who was, Eunice?" asked Mrs. Hargrove.

"The expression *sold down the river* originated from the mouths of Kentucky slaves. They rode the Ohio River further south to the plantations when they were sold on."

"Thank you, Eunice," the chorus patiently replied.

By the second progression, a palpable tension entered the room. When Pearline excused herself to the restroom, each woman leaned into the center of her table as Becky Lou, Pearline's current bridge partner, vented her frustration amid the shuffling of the next hand.

"For heaven's sake. You'd think anyone could count to fourteen. Why did she bid so low? She always does that." Becky Lou's temper could be as flammable as her hair.

It was truer than the truth that Pearline was a terrible bridge player. She'd learned nothing from Mr. Ferco's evening bridge class out at the high school. Each time Pearline placed her cards down at the end of a hand, Becky Lou bit her fuchsia-painted lip.

But the real trouble wasn't the bid, or the count, or even Mr. Ferco's inability to teach the game of bridge to Jubilee women. No, the real reason for the seething atmosphere between these two women was their husbands. The beauty-parlor prattle was that something had happened between Mr. Farmer and Mr. Peyton. No one knows what it was, but rumor had it that one owed the other money, and it all blew up, and the result was an obvious coolness between Becky Lou and Pearline.

When Pearline sat down again and arranged her swishy skirt, Becky Lou quickly changed the subject. "I can't wait for Belle's pecan pie. It's better than my own mama's. Isn't it the most marvelous pie you ever tasted?"

"Mmm-hmm," everyone agreed. More shuffling.

The rich, dark smell of freshly brewed coffee and the resumed clatter of dishes meant one thing: Time for dessert. Down the steps I tiptoed and bumped into my father. He was familiar with my detective routine and laughed as I made my way out the door and around the house again.

I avoided a near collision in the kitchen with Belle as she balanced a gigantic tray of

23

cups and saucers and a steaming silver coffeepot. The phones were ringing off the wall, but the bridge party was in the clear now. We could get a truckload of bodies and it wouldn't disrupt the third progression, no, sir. As my father would say — play on, ladies, play on.

After the voracious eight swooned over Belle's gooey pecan pie and stained the coffee cups with their lipstick, Belle finally gave me some food. I was starving after being subjected to the cruelty of two hours of heaping plates that drifted past me. I wasn't allowed bridge-party food, but instead quietly enjoyed a cheese sandwich and was deep into a bowl of soup when I heard Mary Daley clear her throat.

"You will never believe what Sophie May told me."

Immediate silence. Mary Daley's maid was the equivalent of a news editor who reported only the best kind of gossip. Positioned near the open kitchen doorway, I had only a thin wall between the ladies and me. I felt as if I were sitting right next to them.

"You know those parties the doctors and lawyers throw in the big house out there on the Sugar Lick Road? Well, Sophie May said that . . . well, you know, that the husbands and wives got . . . mixed up."

"Well, for heaven's sake. What are you talkin' about?" asked Becky Lou.

"Well, you know . . ." She couldn't quite get it out.

"Now, Mary Daley, this is not the time to be —"

"Wife swapping," Mrs. Appleton perked up. "That's what she's sayin'."

Audible gasps.

"What?"

"Not in Jubilee!"

"No. I don't believe it. Sophie May made that up."

"Sophie May has been working for me for over twenty years and she does not make up stories," Mary Daley said. "She used to work at those parties. She told me they think the coloreds are invisible and don't hear, think, or speak. Those country-club people aren't a bit worried about the talk. Every one of you knows how they are. Sophie May said that Dr. Benson was on top of Peg Carlton so quick it would make your head spin."

Belle came toward me like a rushing wind and slapped her hands over my ears.

I squirmed out of her reach. "Belle, what's wife swatting?" I whispered.

"You better git yerself out of here right

25

now." She chased me out of the kitchen with a serving spoon.

"But I haven't had any pie yet."

"Go on, now. Don't be comin' back in this kitchen for the rest of the day. You gots no business in here listenin' to them ladies. They's adults, and you ain't, so you best be gittin' to yer room and play or read one of yer books. Lawd knows you gots plenty of things to do 'sides sittin' in here spyin' on yer mama's friends. Lawd, lawd, lawd. I never *seen* such a nosy child."

Like a disturbed hen, she clucked back to the kitchen.

I left as Belle asked, but I didn't go to my room. The floor in the laundry room felt cool. I rested my back against the paneled wall and listened to Belle washing the dishes. The ladies' voices added a faint song above the hiss of the running water as it hit the porcelain sink. There I stayed, cross-legged on the floor, until the group broke up and one by one descended the stairs. I often gave the appearance of obeying, when in reality I found ways to skirt the rules. I learned that to live in an environment that cared for the needs of a constant flow of people — both living and dead — it was necessary to steal an ounce of personal freedom wherever and whenever I found it.

CHAPTER 1
WE'VE GOT A BODY

One of the opening shots of my family's 8 mm home movies was of massive funereal flower arrangements, flowers so plentiful and so flawlessly arranged that they did not look real. The camera slowly panned over a casket in which a young woman lay in perfect stillness. I'll never forget how she looked. Her coal-black hair spread over a white satin pillow; her lips, painted a bright cherry red, contrasted brazenly with her gypsumlike skin. She looked like the Disney version of Snow White, except that her thick, black glasses revealed the era of her death to be the 1950s, the grainy film already at least ten years old. Her glasses looked out of place — why did she need them now? She didn't, but her family needed them. Their last memory of her required familiar and, therefore, comforting details. The first time I saw a close-up of her face, even with her eyes closed she

27

looked so alive and vibrant that I asked, "Is she really dead, or were you all just fooling around?"

I have tried to remember the first time I saw a dead body. There have been many odd firsts in my life, like the first time I touched a dead person. I was too short to reach into the casket, so my father picked me up and I leaned in for that first empty, cold touch. It was thrilling because it was an unthinkable act. But I recall no first viewing because from the time I entered the world there were always dead bodies.

When I was old enough to understand what they meant, people told me they felt decidedly creepy about funeral homes. I knew a woman who always ran to the other side of the street whenever she happened upon ours. She gave a little shudder when she saw me seated in the swing on the veranda. I nodded to her and remained silent, having no need to defend my position, and anyway, sooner or later she, too . . . But I could understand how one would think it a bit unnatural to spend day after day, year after year, entertaining the grieving and caring for their dead.

It could have been a gloomy existence were it not for my father. Whenever I mentioned "undertaker" or "mortician" to people who'd never met him, I saw in their eyes what they thought. They pictured a dour man, a Uriah Heep sort who wore black, scratchy suits with dull white shirts fading to yellow. Nowadays, people raise their brows when they think of the modern undertaker, who burrows down in courses such as General Psychology and Dynamics of Grief, Mortuary Law, and Death and Human Development. These men are thought of as exploitive, nothing more than ruthless businessmen. My father would have squirmed at being compared to them. Each funeral was an opportunity to imprint his stamp, the details of which bore his personal touch. Not one strand of the corpse's hair should go astray, not one of a family's requests should go unheeded. A final per-fected image, a memorable experience, was his unwavering goal.

He never had to work too hard at being different, he just was.

Frank Mayfield was a clotheshorse, an undertaker with flair that verged on dandy-ism. He thought nothing of driving miles to hunt down a better-quality suit, no easy task given that our little, rural town did not border any large metropolis.

My father allowed me to observe as he groomed his dark brown, wavy hair into a matinee-idol sweep. I sat on the sink or stood in the claw-foot bath to gain a little height and squirted the Brylcreem into his palm, but the stuff did nothing to tame the dramatic widow's peak that marked his forehead. Long, curly, black lashes accented his hazel eyes, and a prominent swath of dark eyebrows ran across his forehead. I swear he looked like a movie star.

He never struggled when dressing. His fingers and hands played with his diamond cuff links as I imagined they might have swept up jacks and a ball, nimbly and quickly. The eye-catching ties did not demand extra time or attention, but magically knotted themselves into place as if he were only there to assist. He had leaned over hundreds of men as they slept the deep sleep of death, slipping their ties under their collars and knotting the fabric one last time. His reputation depended upon the perfection of such a task.

On the last day of 1959 my father, the Beau Brummell of morticians, piled us into his green-and-white DeSoto and drove away from Lanesboro, the city in which my older brother and sister and I were born, and toward a small town on the Kentucky-Tennessee border. Though only a ninety-

30

minute drive, it might as well have been to Alaska.

Gliding into Jubilee, our big boat of a car circled the town square and headed toward the residential section of Main Street. My father pulled over, and our five dark heads turned to face a huge, three-story, slightly run-down house. In this old house he would finally realize his dream of owning his own funeral home.

Back in Lanesboro, I had been the first in our family to be carried as a newborn from the hospital directly into a funeral home. Birth and death in almost the same breath. My brother and sister, Thomas and Evelyn, had enjoyed living in a normal house until my father's employer forced him to move into the funeral home in Lanesboro so that he could be available at any time of the day or night.

"Well, if we're going to live in a funeral home, it might as well be one that I own," he'd said upon deciding to move.

My mother told me that the first week after our move to Jubilee, I held on to the hem of her skirts and would not let go. Where she went, I followed. "You wouldn't let me out of your sight," she said. Then I turned a corner, let go of that familiar fabric, and slowly became fascinated with the funeral home.

The front door opened into the office, a space from which traffic seemed to want to flow and not linger. My father kept it simple; he thought a plush office would appear pretentious. His hefty wooden desk nearly dwarfed what was barely a room at all. In front of the desk and against a windowed wall, several wooden folding chairs formed a row into which family members sat to make funeral arrangements. In this room the families of our town made difficult decisions, sometimes numbly asking how this event came about so quickly. "Why, just the other day Truman was mowing the lawn . . ." My father would gently steer them back to reality.

When a death occurred, an entire series of rituals shifted into gear. My father led each grieving family on a journey as they completed the necessary funeral arrangements. From the office, they first approached a large foyer. On the right, the Hammond organ loomed in a small corner, and on the left, they walked past the large, open entry that led directly into the chapel, where their recently departed would be on view in a matter of hours. Opposite the chapel's doorway, a tall staircase flanked by a wooden banister led upstairs to our private rooms.

Most people respected the boundary and resisted the temptation, but something about a nice staircase beckons.

One night while the people downstairs milled about during a visitation, I lay sprawled on my stomach upstairs leafing through a coloring book. Crayons were scattered on the carpet. I heard the familiar creak of the stairs, which I assumed was my mother making her way up for the evening. I quietly walked toward the top of the stairs, where, in a dull glow that emanated from the lights downstairs, stood a beanpole of a man wearing overalls and a suit jacket. Shocked and suddenly vulnerable in my nightgown, we stared at each other.

"Who are you?" he asked, his mouth agape.

"Who are you?" I took a step back.

Then I heard my father racing up the stairs. "Mr. Granger, the bathroom's downstairs."

"Who's that, Frank? Do you see a child?"

"Well, of course. She's one of my daughters."

"You mean you and your family live up here?"

"Yes, sir, we do. Now if you'll just step down here with me, I'll direct you to the restroom."

"I ain't never heard the likes of that, Mr. Mayfield. I'da never known if I ain't seen it with my own eyes, a family on top of a funeral parlor. I swear, I thought I seen a ghost."

That happened occasionally, when the rooms downstairs were full of people and it was hard to keep track of everyone. Beyond the staircase, the foyer narrowed into a hallway so dim that a ceiling light burned throughout the day. To the left, a small, humble hospitality room was comfort enough for those who came to visitations and funerals. Here families and their friends paused for a hot or cold drink and murmured in low whispers. An old-fashioned snack machine stood against the wall filled with packs of Planters peanuts, Nabs crackers, and candy bars that dropped into the tray after the money rattled down. Bright red knobs protruded from the cream-colored frame, and I could almost hear the old machine asking to be touched. "Not so hard," my father would say when I pulled with all my might.

Farther down the hall to the left was a door that always remained closed. This room pressed upon my childhood, possessing the power to scare the bejesus out of a grown man, conjuring the stuff of nightmares. This room housed the monstrous white porcelain table, the knowledge of which hastened my step when I walked past each day: the embalming room.

My father ushered family members past the embalming room where their loved one lay under a crisp white sheet, to the door facing them at the end of the hall. This was "the showroom" where they would choose the casket. One of the last choices the family made with my father took place in the casket room, my room of cold comfort, the only room downstairs spacious enough to accommodate a large array of caskets. It was, as if by design, the end of the journey. This journey from the front of the funeral home to the back, made with countless families over the years, became the rhythm of my childhood.

One of the first things my father did when we moved to Jubilee was to contact Southern Bell to make sure we had enough telephones. The telephone, which brought news of tragedy and death, was our lifeline. At that time funeral homes also operated as an emergency service. As the world's surgeons became more skilled, the reasons to bring doctors' patients to the hospital increased. Funeral-home ambulance service began as an outgrowth of their need to transport human bodies supine in their long hearses. When a citizen needed to go to the hospital, or just wanted a ride to the doctor's office, they called the funeral home of their choice. The telephones in our new house were sacred objects, and one could be found in almost every room downstairs and up-stairs. They rang at all hours of the day and night, the volume cranked as high as it could go. Every time they rang, it sounded like a house full of alarm clocks going off. Two of them sat importantly on the corner of my father's desk. On each of the flesh-colored telephones a row of clear-plastic buttons lit up whenever we received a call. I couldn't keep my hands off them and played with the buttons when no one was looking, intrigued by how the light flashed first and the tone came afterward, like a warning strobe light — death calling, death calling. I still can never hear a phone ring without thinking that someone, somewhere, has died.

When a death call came the entire atmo-sphere in our home changed instantly. My father ran out to the three-car garage in the back of the property and revved up his Henney-Packard ambulance. What a piece of fast-rolling machinery. The Packard ambulance — a smaller version of our black hearse, which had the sharp, sleek lines of the later-model Cadillacs — looked like a long, fat cigar. It was known for its disturbingly named "suicide doors": the back doors were rear-hinged and susceptible to all manner of dangers. If one of them opened accidentally, the force could cause the ambulance to swerve either into oncoming traffic or onto the side of the road — and that wasn't the half of it.

"Do you remember the undertaker in Mullen County?" My father loved to tell this story, erupting in peals of laughter before he began, which anyone listening echoed. "This undertaker, Fred Bowles was his name, picked up a patient at his home to take him to the hospital. It wasn't an emergency; the man just needed a comfortable ride. Well, the patient's doctor was at his house, too, and wanted a lift in the ambulance. Fred told the doctor to sit in the front, but, no, this old crank just had to sit in the back with his patient. I remember Fred said he was pretty hot under the collar about it. You know, everybody thinks they can just sit back there, go for a ride like they know what they're doing.

"Anyway, this doctor got real hot sittin' back there and took it upon himself to open the window on the passenger side. Well, hell,

37

what did he do? He opened the damn door by mistake. I tell you what, that wind got ahold of that suicide door and it flew back, and it was like the wind just sucked him out and that old crank fell out of the ambulance. And you know what else? The door came swinging back and gave him a good smack before he hit the ground." And here, my father finished between fits of laughter, "Fred wasn't going fast, the doctor was all right, a little bruised, but he never asked if he could ride in the back again."

Whenever my father set out to bring a body home to us, my mother became the noise police. She marched through the rooms upstairs like a sergeant major, her solid frame following her headfirst walk, spreading the word to her children.

"We've got a body," she clipped. "And you know what that means, so get to it!"

I sighed. Another one? A dead body in the house meant we would be sequestered. Even though many of Jubilee's dead rested with us over the years, we were the ghosts of the house. Our family learned how to disappear with those four words: "We've got a body." From the time the family of the deceased first entered the door to make arrangements until days later when the last person left after the funeral, our family became invisible, nonexistent. We tiptoed around upstairs and whispered to each other when it was necessary to communicate. The sound of music or the television would not be heard in our house until the last mourner walked out the door. Foods that emitted strong odors were out of the question so that we wouldn't offend the bereaved with a reminder of life going on above them. The volume of the chiming phones was lowered to a softer, duller ring.

The days and evenings of visitation culminated in the funeral service. The chatter of the visitors halted, the movement of people downstairs calmed, and now, during the actual funeral service, we weren't even allowed to speak or walk upstairs. We created a hush and the house fell silent.

Funeral services were usually held in the afternoons when Thomas and Evelyn were at school. Thomas was already in junior high school and Evelyn was two years behind him at the end of a less than spectacular grade-school career. They were more occupied with new teachers and friends than the business of death. Thomas was particularly industrious and soon became familiar with Jubilee's various neighborhoods when he began a paper route. He delivered the *Nashville Tennessean,* a daily afternoon paper that occasionally reported on a few counties in Kentucky. Jubilee's newspaper came out only once a week, filled most prominently with the news of lost cows, ice-cream-supper locations, and, most important, the obituaries, which my mother proofread with a magnifying glass like Mr. Sherlock Holmes.

Kindergarten was held only in the morning and I was home by lunchtime. I was funeral-home trained from the beginning. When school closed for the summer break, Thomas and Evelyn climbed into the cloth seats of the Greyhound bus for the trip to Lanesboro, where, once there, they parted ways and visited cousins, aunts, uncles, and grandparents. So for the first few years I bore the brunt of the daytime silences alone. When death came visiting and I was forced into silence, it felt like a lock had been turned and I was shut off from the world for a period of time, isolated from any living thing. It was difficult in the beginning, like jumping high, both feet off the ground, and trying to pause in midair. With my arms folded and my face screwed up in a stew I sat quietly, swelling with resentment and irritable that yet another person had died. But as I grew older and death continued to claim our citizens, I learned why silence was necessary: Respect. This is the word I heard consistently during my childhood. When a life fades and ends, the family deserves a quiet place to mourn. I gradually made peace with a life that demanded to be lived in quantities of silence. Resentment flickered to acceptance, and boredom fell away, replaced with a curiosity about what went on downstairs.

My mother, intolerant of noise at any time, was perfectly suited to this line of work. Childish expressions of emotion irritated her. She must have invented the phrase "If you don't stop crying, I'll give you something to cry about," which she threatened whenever she spanked me.

She was the disciplinarian of the family. My parents must have agreed that her job was to relieve him of the burden of attending every scrape, fight, tug-of-war, disobedience, whine, and moan that three children were sure to muster. Although she often threatened us with "I'm going to tell your father," he rarely stepped in.

I blamed sour-faced Bretta West for my mother's ability to slip so easily into funeral-home mode. Bretta, my mother's mother, was a strict Southern Baptist. She and her husband had settled on a small farm in

41

western Kentucky, where she was a Bible-reading, churchgoing, no-nonsense woman who didn't believe in dancing or music other than hymns and who insisted on modest dress. Two things Bretta would especially not tolerate were noise in the house and sassing.

I never saw Bretta laugh, and on the few occasions when she smiled, her eyes crinkled up and narrowed as if she were in pain. I thought her face would crack from the effort.

My mother was accustomed to being on her own. By the time she was ten her older brother and sisters had already married and were living in Lanesboro, the largest city near them. No other children her age were within walking distance, so she entertained herself with a few wooden toys, a doll, and her pet squirrel, Fuzzy, who lived outside in a nest at the corner of the house.

My mother doesn't remember ever being punished.

"You never got in trouble for anything? Nothing?" I once asked.

"No, not really. Nothing serious. You don't get in trouble when you mind your parents."

We always had our evening meal together as a family, but like her mother, my mother had expectations for our behavior that were positively Victorian. She demanded our elbows off the table, polite passing of the food, napkins in our laps, and a minimum of table talk. This was exactly how her meals with her parents must have been, except for one thing: I enjoyed a good supper conversation.

"Daddy, if you were arrested right now, the sheriff couldn't take your fingerprints."

"Hush," my mother said.

" 'Cause if they did, all they would get is a picture of your wrinkled fingers."

"That's enough." A clear warning was in her voice.

"But it's true. Look how wrinkled his fingers are."

He'd just sat down to dinner having embalmed a body, and his fingers were prunelike from the tremendous amount of water he used. He never wore the ghastly rubber gloves that hung from the handle of a storage cabinet in the embalming room. They were actually old-fashioned autopsy gloves he'd bought from the hospital. They dangled in the air, an awful brown color, swollen, larger than a big man's hand. When he made the effort to work in them, they were so thick and heavy he became annoyed, pulled them off, and flung them on the floor. This was long before the fear of disease and the invention of latex gloves.

My father never interfered with my mother's constant quest for silence, but the slight lift at the corners of his mouth told me that he was sometimes on my side.

"You do not talk about this subject at the table. Now be quiet." She passed the mashed potatoes. But of course she and my father spoke of nothing else.

"It looks like Mr. Simmons will be dead by morning," my father would say.

"I don't know, Frank. Elsie told me that he should have died last month. His heart is barely thumping, she told me, but he's still hanging on."

I worked on a fried chicken leg for a while, then thought aloud, "You know, Totty has a chair what sings and —"

"That," Thomas offered. "A chair *that* sings."

"Uh-huh, Totty has a chair that sings. It's a little wooden rocking chair and —"

"You're so stupid," Evelyn said.

"That's enough," my mother intervened.

"She's so stupid." Evelyn had to have the last word.

My mother knew absolutely that children could be trained to be still and silent. Her mother wasn't the kind of woman who had the time or patience to teach her youngest how to cook or clean, nor did she invite her to sit with her at the sewing machine while she made her clothes, nor into the garden to plant beans and tomatoes. Like me, my mother turned to her father for attention, and there, too, she met lessons in silence.

Charles West, my mother's father, worked the land-based oil fields in western Kentucky during the 1930s. After the roughnecks had drilled the wells, hauled the supplies, and laid the pipelines, they relocated to the next potential oil field. Charles was a pumper, the man who stayed behind after the others moved on. He monitored and maintained all the equipment, working as a caretaker of a producing oil field.

During the summer, my mother would clamber up into his pickup truck and accompany him to work. She stood a safe distance from the heavy equipment in the humid summer heat, a solitary figure in her brown leather lace-ups. Black ringlets of hair fell to her shoulders; her homemade dress caught an occasional breeze. The air smelled nothing at all like gasoline or tar; the odor of crude oil registered as something sweeter, softer, as it filled her lungs. She followed his movements as he walked down the pipeline to the tune of a whole field full of equipment; the pump-jack sang a steady song, the cling-clang of tubing, rods, and valves its chorus. They lunched together in the shade of the truck with crinkled paper bags in their laps, biting into thick-bread, roast-beef sandwiches and sharing a thermos of iced tea.

On Saturdays her father often took her fishing, but she couldn't sit still in the small boat. She squirmed, rocked the boat, stood, and leaned over one too many times, until Charles scolded her and threatened to leave her at home in the future. She learned to sit still. She learned to be quiet.

Then she lost him to the final silence. On one of those unpeopled oil fields, surrounded by the pumping, grinding equipment, something went wrong. A piece of equipment fell. He didn't die immediately, but later, in his home, of internal injuries. It was hard to prove in those days that his death was caused by an accident on the job. There was no compensation. She was fifteen when her father died.

My mother may have been a seeker of silence, but I wasn't. Living in a funeral home was unnatural to me. During the funerals and in the evenings when the townspeople filed through the front door for visitation, I often felt I couldn't sit still for another second. Out of sheer boredom,

I crept to the landing at the top of the stairs, from where I heard the sounds of the people below. This was risky. One only need look up to see my loose hair hanging down and my nightgown floating in the air, my mischief a distraction from their mourning.

It being so vital that the scene downstairs not be disturbed by our presence upstairs, my mother grew overly sensitive to our movements.

One night I leaned over the railing and peered down at the row of ladies with violet-rinsed hair who sat just below me. Among the elderly women sat a young girl who suddenly burst into song. The song had no words; a light *la la la* rang above the ladies' low hum. The sound of her voice rose up into the air to the exact spot where I stood. My mother, convinced I was the culprit, came toward me with her lips pressed tightly together, her eyes narrowed into angry slits. She grabbed me by the arm and spanked me before I had a chance to proclaim my innocence.

In a tense whisper she asked, "What do you think you're doing?"

Before I could say anything, she clamped her hand over my mouth so that I couldn't respond. I tried to wriggle away, but she held on with a strong hand that smelled of

Jergens lotion. The child sang again and my mother knew she'd made a mistake.

"You should never have been standing there in the first place!" she hissed. The apology I awaited did not materialize. My mother didn't like to be wrong. My legs stung for a second or two from her spanking, but my feelings . . . they were bruised for days. Small, weepy hurts like this later snowballed into disagreements that ended at an impasse with my mother and drove me downstairs to my father, where I felt more accepted.

On the days when she wasn't around, I crept back to the spot, where I would close my eyes and listen to the rhythm of it all. Everyone grieved differently. Some mourned in silence; I thought maybe they cried silently inside or saved up their tears, too embarrassed to weep publicly.

The first time I heard a wailer, I jumped from my seat on the stairs. It's hard to forget the sound of someone wracked with sobs. It scared me to death — I thought she was dying. I was relieved to hear the notes from the Hammond organ. My soon-to-be piano teacher, usually chatty and mischievous, was on her best behavior as she played the mournful hymns. Totty Edwards was a musical woman who had slipped right out of her nun's habit when she found love in the form of Victor. She told me Victor was "from the plant," as if he had sprouted from the earth. An explanation from my parents revealed that he was a business executive the local toolmaking company had recruited from The North.

My mother thought she was crazy. What she really meant was that Totty was different. She was different because she, too, was from The North. "Somewhere in Michigan," my mother said, as if it were near the Arctic.

"Totty's scatterbrained and silly. How many times has she told the same old story about the time Perry Como kissed her on the cheek? And she's always late. Your daddy asks her to be here fifteen minutes before the funeral starts, but she never is, we have to call her, and then she waltzes in wearing those tall boots, all apologetic, smiling at everybody like nothing's wrong, while we're on pins and needles. He doesn't need to worry about things like that, she should just be on time."

I tried to understand what this had to do with being from The North. As far as I could make out, people from The North were bad timekeepers, wore tall boots, and played bridge quite atrociously. These things made them crazy and not to be trusted. But

49

I liked Totty's Northern accent, which sparked my imagination. She spoke so quickly, like short flashes of lightning. I imagined everyone in The North raced about their day, speaking in clipped spurts while we walked through molasses elongating our vowels.

One day after a funeral, I noticed Totty had placed a strand of beads on the organ. I asked to hold them. My mother overheard me and was furious. It was as if I had intentionally betrayed the Baptists.

"The next time you ask to see her rosary beads, I will smack you into tomorrow."

I had no idea what rosary beads were. I thought Totty's string of black and silver beads was a necklace. I didn't take the huge silver crucifix hanging from it as anything other than decorative. Good Lord, the sign of the cross jumped out from all sorts of places all over town, most prominently in the jewelry section of the drugstores, on sympathy cards, and church signs of every denomination. None had anything to do with Catholicism; how should I know that Totty's was a Catholic cross?

Despite being a Catholic from The North, Totty's music must have soothed the wailing woman downstairs because she soon caught her breath and quietly wept. As I listened to Totty's hymn playing, I waited for the clinkers. I often heard her shoes struggling with the pedals, as if she'd caught the heel of one of her tall boots in the cracks. Sometimes the music swelled when it should not. My father made concessions. Totty was available when most other musicians were not, and there weren't many in Jubilee, anyway. He forgave her shortcomings as an organist when she played his favorite hymn. He always said that Totty played a mean "Nearer, My God, to Thee."

As I sat on my secret perch waiting for the service to begin, the heady, concentrated odor of the flowers in the chapel found its way up the stairs. It took some time for the flowers to warm up; they stood in buckets in the refrigerator of the local florist and arrived with a chilled, subdued aroma. Soon the lights and the warmth of the people who filled the rooms summoned the fragrance of roses, carnations, chrysanthemums, and gladioli, and the marriage of their scents gathered strength as the day progressed. Occasionally a lady's eau de toilette drifted through the air to merge with the perfume of the flowers. These were the days and nights of mourning; the funerals I heard and smelled.

I recognized my father's footsteps during

the funerals, which wasn't difficult because he was usually the only person allowed to walk around during a service. Even so, his slow, deliberate stride was distinctive. He was in his element — master of the grand finale, directing families through the hardest, most uncomfortable forty-five minutes of their lives. My admiration teetered when I faced the world without him. One of the teachers in our school always sniffed when she passed me in the halls, as if I carried the odor of the dead. Suddenly the warmth of a blush rose from an understanding that his profession was offensive to some. Then her mother died and my father was called upon to bury her. The teacher's sniff was replaced with a little nod. Oh the glee of that comprehension, the little skip in my step, the satisfaction I felt. I was filled with an awareness of his unique duty in this little scrap of a town.

He and his employees communicated with eye contact and barely noticeable hand motions. They never spoke to each other during a funeral. If my father looked at one of his men during the service, that man knew exactly what he should be doing at that particular moment. A quick glance to one of them meant to seat the latecomer. The slightest nod of my father's head to another was a cue to move toward the front. A subtle hand motion toward Totty and he became the conductor of music. At the end of the funeral the men dared not move toward the casket without his signal.

In the beginning, my father hired a few part-time men to help out during the funerals and visitations, but he also took on a full-timer who knew nothing about the funeral business. Sonny was a Beacon County boy, hired because he had connections. He knew everyone outside Jubilee who lived on the farms and in the little one-street towns in the county. And my father badly needed a Beacon County representative.

Sonny was a big oaf of a man whose large, protruding ears looked as if they might help him take flight. He often placed his fists on his thick waist and looked down at me, frustrated by my mere presence.

Sonny and I were never going to be friends. I sensed his false civility immediately, which was easy to decipher by the way he became bossy in my father's absence.

"Leave the mail alone. Go on upstairs now," he would say.

"I don't have to. I live here." I would pretend to read the latest embalming supply catalog to solidify my existence.

Sonny lumbered through the hallways in stereophonic thuds, but somehow managed to quiet his footsteps during the funerals. He would station himself in the back of the chapel, his rounded shoulders only slightly squared by his rumpled suit.

In stark contrast, my father, immaculately dressed, stood in the front to one side of the casket, alert and present during the entire service. Whatever awkward emotions squirmed in the minds and hearts of funeralgoers, my father was at ease with them. While he conducted funerals, he was as comfortable in his own skin as he was in his beautiful clothes. And that was a thing of solace to those who were grief stricken. His task was to close the door on the messy sight of death and open another to the heavenly ever after. Some people thought their preacher opened that door, but from my balcony seat, it always looked to be the undertaker, whose smooth orchestration made saying good-bye a less difficult task, a more assured journey.

Especially when the preacher was Brother Vince. Oh Lord. After Totty attempted a couple of hymns, Brother Vince, who was today's Representative of God's Word, stepped up to the podium in front of the casket.

He began with a prayer that blessed everything from animals to tractors and finally wound down to the deceased.

Then he took his glasses off, placed them on the podium, and reached into his back pocket for his handkerchief. While he cleaned his glasses, he began his dry-bones eulogy. This funeral sermon was full of imagery of the gruesome Bible story of Ezekiel. He relied on this sermon when he didn't personally know who lay behind him in the casket. He varied it, but the basics were always there. Brother Vince was off and running and wouldn't draw breath for another fifteen minutes.

Following a long piece wherein Ezekiel walked on the bones while conversing with God, the preacher's tinny voice headed for the home stretch with a hypnotic repetition of the promise of life everlasting.

"So you see, God's gonna breathe life into that graveyard of dry bones, he's gonna create anew, and it says right here in the Bible that God put sinew and muscle and flesh on those old dry bones, and he's gonna join all these rattling, brittle bones together and create an army. God commanded old Ezekiel to prophesy and to tell those dry bones to live. Dry bones can *live*! Restored to life. Hallelujah. Praise the Lord. Restored to life. Restored to life. Do not despair; the bones can live again, as does our Hessie. She lives again with Sweet Jesus in heaven. Everything has all come together for her, just like those dry bones, and she now lives forever. Her spirit will be with us always. Let us pray."

Cue Totty's heavy foot upon the pedals as her fingers searched for the final notes.

At the end of the service my father stood in front of the casket and without uttering a word made the slightest gesture with his palms up, just a small movement right in front of his chest, and as if by magic, the congregation stood. He offered his arm to the grieving sister, which she took gratefully. His head bowed, he led her to the funeral car. He was never accused of showing false sympathy.

When it was all finally over, my father's friend Billy, who helped out during the funerals, climbed the steps to where I sat waiting, fists on cheeks.

"Is it over?" I whispered.

"Yes, you can come on down now."

I ran. I ran anywhere I could, just to feel what it was like to move again. The silence downstairs was abruptly broken, the rooms were vibrant with action all around like a circus ring with each performer soaring at the height of his or her act, an organized chaos. As my father led the cortege to the cemetery, the employees rushed around in unison. They carted flowers out, maneuvered chairs to clear paths, cleaned as they worked, loaded the flowers into the van, and rushed to the cemetery so that the flowers would magically appear at the burial site before the slow procession arrived. Totty gathered her music and tidied up the hymnals. My mother manned the all-important instruments of the trade — the phones. She raised the volume, because no one knew when, but the ritual would begin again at any moment.

I wondered why my father chose to wake up every morning to take care of dead people. But I never asked, for as the years passed, I could imagine him doing nothing else.

He grew up on farmland during the Depression, a place called Red Hill, not far from my mother's family, with fertile land that produced a bounteous supply of food and goods. They were free from worry about their next meal when so many others suffered. His mother, Katie, a statuesque, handsome woman, was quietly proud that she bought only sugar, coffee, tea, and flour at the general store owned by her sister,

Marybell, and Marybell's husband, Wallace. Everything else was at their doorstep.

My grandmother Katie was industrious and created her own little business by selling her top cream at the store. My mother said a surprise spot-check of her mother-in-law's house would produce less than a teaspoon of dirt. Katie wore dresses on the farm, great flowing things that whipped around her legs as she moved about. She loved big hats and coats with huge fur collars. Her husband's idea of dressing up, on the other hand, was a fresh pair of heavy cotton work pants, and though I never saw him wear a suit until the day he was buried, I was given photographs to prove that he did.

My father's childhood was full of noise, a completely different home life from my mother's. His brother and sister were not much older than he, and the three were a raucous trio. A slew of cousins, among them Marybell and Wallace's children, often visited the farm, where they roamed the countryside unbridled.

As quietly behaved as we were at Bretta West's house, when we visited my father's family, we were free to be as noisy and playful as he had been. Being older, Thomas and Evelyn were more accustomed to visiting our grandparents' farm. On the week-ends, with the congregation of the cousins in full session, they took turns riding the ornery horse and fished in the farm's expansive lake. They played football and cowboys and Indians. Too young to be included in such games, I was unaccustomed to farm life; to me it felt like visiting another country in which there were countless miserable tasks like cleaning the chicken coop and hauling water from the well. If not for one vivid detail, I would scarcely remember the house before my grandfather installed indoor plumbing: the outhouse terrified me. The wind whipped around the wooden shack and banged the door open and shut. It was so dark inside I groped to find the seat, which was too big for me. I closed my eyes and prayed that I wouldn't fall in and that no spiders would crawl up from the depths of the pit. I worried about splinters. *Good grief,* I pleaded, *take me back to the funeral home.*

My father was the youngest of the three, and although his father was quite straitlaced, his mother indulged him. Aware he was not inclined to work the land, his parents never forced him. He gravitated to the city of Lanesboro, which overlooked the Ohio River, originally known as Yellowbanks for

59

the color of its soil. The action of the river town spoke to him, and the buzz of people made him feel alive.

He enjoyed wearing the kind of clothes that were out of place on the farm. It was no surprise when I learned that he spent his high school vacations working in the menswear department of JCPenney's. The management placed him in the men's glove department, hardly a hub of excitement in the hot summers, but it was a natural fit and better than the fields.

On a late summer's day in 1942, Frank sat with his elder brother under the big shade tree by the lake on his family's land. Everyone called him Jimmy, but of course he was James Maple to my father. As the two skipped pebbles into the quiet water, he discovered that James Maple had no intention of being a farmer either. Sitting on a spot of land that offered so much life, James Maple told him that when he returned from Europe, he was going to be an undertaker. Frank had laughed.

My father could have told me himself that it was first his elder brother's dream to become an undertaker. But the war intervened and sent the brothers on two entirely different paths. Frank served on the ground in C Company of the 137th Infantry Regiment of the 35th Division. James Maple spent the war in the air, on the underside of a B-17 as a ball-turret gunner. When his plane was shot down over Germany, he was captured and held prisoner. James Maple never became an undertaker, or anything else. Years later his bones were sent back to Kentucky in a sealed box. My father, suffering the effect of his own war wounds, received the box on behalf of his grieving family from the hands of an undertaker.

IN MEMORIAM:
ALBERT FOXWOOD

One by one they trailed into the funeral home. Traces of lavender water lifted the air. Black hats punctuated the chapel like spots on a dalmatian. They sat in dark rows and held hemstitched handkerchiefs dotted with embroidered violets. Trimmings of black lace decorated a collar, the cuffs of a blouse. The metal clasps of their Sunday-best pocketbooks invaded the silence. Snap, click. Face powder settled darkly in the creases of their faces, and the palest lipstick stated, "We are still women, after all, and we like a little color." They wore stockings the thickness of flannel, and a cloud of Evening in Paris floated behind the footfalls of their sturdy black shoes, swollen with imprints of bunions. Cotton gloves hid brown-speckled hands.

They were the widows of Beacon County. Mourning in unison, these blackbirds offered a long line of support for the most recent addition to their clan. It was odd, but I knew from a young age, when I scarcely knew the meaning of the word, that I would never be a widow of Beacon County. I thought of the future as a blank space to fill and it existed somewhere other than this house of death, somewhere other than the streets of this town. Years later I would remember the widows with a sensation of claustrophobia, a slight fear that I had only narrowly escaped their course.

Standing slightly apart from the others was Mrs. Foxwood. She was well acquainted with each of them, but was not yet a member of their society because Mr. Foxwood was alive and, if not kicking, then still shuffling along.

Mrs. Foxwood spoke aloud to Jesus quite a lot. A trace of garden dirt was always under her nails, and I thought this made her prayers the humblest I'd ever heard. With her head tilted back, she opened her eyes wider and wider, until it seemed she strained to see the heavens right through the ceiling. Her throat lengthened, lengthened, lengthened, until it concertinaed at "Thank you, Jesus. Amen." She could beat a horse down to its knees with one of her prayers. I observed this every

Sunday for an entire year when she was my Sunday-school teacher — the longest year of my life. The Foxwoods lived frugally, remained childless, and plodded through life in our community without a fuss. Married for over sixty years, Mrs. Foxwood always included her husband in her Sunday-morning prayer: "God bless Albert." Mine was slightly different: "Please, Lord, can this be over now, for I am hungry, sleepy, and in need of a pee."

When Mr. Foxwood passed over yonder at last, his body was laid out in our chapel. His burial suit looked stiffer than his alive suits, and his back seemed straighter in repose. I wondered if this pressed-out version of her husband might bother Mrs. Foxwood. Albert in life had always seemed creased.

Sometimes . . . actually, quite often, I lingered where I should not have been. On the morning of Mrs. Foxwood's private view of her husband, I was on a raid of the snack machine when I heard the front door's jingle-jangle. My father greeted Mrs. Foxwood in his undertaker's voice. She had arrived early and I had no time to skedaddle upstairs, though I remained undetected, guiltily, with my hand on a candy bar.

He escorted her to the chapel, stood with her for a moment, then stepped away and into his office. Here was my chance to escape.

The chapel had no door, just a gaping space that I had to pass to reach the stairs. Mrs. Foxwood stood with her back to me. I'd become familiar with all of her church frocks; now she was draped in her new widow's black. I felt bad for her. Sixty years, that's a long time, I thought, practically forever. She's going to miss him terribly. I began to back away, but when she raised her hands, I knew a prayer was coming and I couldn't resist. It was the shortest I'd ever heard from her.

"O dear Lord," she whispered, "I just want to thank you today. Thank you, Lord, thank you, thank you. Thank you for allowing me to finally put this bastard in the ground."

CHAPTER 2
GRAVEDIGGERS, SHROUDS, AND LEMON MERINGUE PIES

The South is like a lusty woman who stands at the mirror and admires her own astounding beauty, a beauty that after all these years only seems to intensify with age. Even though her face has changed, she has never lost her melancholy charm.

Jubilee, the county seat of Beacon County, is a child of the South. There were no Appalachian Mountains in this town, nor coal miners, hillbillies, or holler dwellers. Neither were there white fences bordering exclusive horse farms, nor tony Derby breakfasts. It was just a sleepy, little tobacco town that fostered the illusion of self-sufficiency, even though its citizens had always abandoned it for other places where they spent money, dined in finer establishments, and generally let their hair down, free from the prying eyes of their neighbors. Sunday drivers slowly coasted through town and called it a pretty little place, but they rarely stopped. How

65

were out of towners to know they could buy a cup of coffee in the back of Perry's drugstore? No neon signs or billboards directed a stranger to Felt's Diner, or the Hilltop Restaurant, both on the outskirts of town. Despite a few stately homes positioned on the corners of tree-lined streets, when they took a closer look, they noticed that the place was a little worn around the edges, as if a fine layer of dust had settled over everything.

Life and death rolled along in Jubilee, faintly touched by those outside its boundaries. Each day started about the same. Bottles of milk sweated outside doorways so early in the morning that we thought the milkman was a phantom. We gathered around the Formica table that faced double windows. My legs dangled and my ponytail swung as a meaty aroma began to fill the air.

My mother cooked a sit-down breakfast every morning. She fried eggs, bacon, or sausage, popped biscuits in the oven, sliced juicy, red tomatoes, and sometimes made grits, my father's favorite. We drowned the thick white splotch of cornmeal in a pool of melted butter.

I begged for the percolated coffee and was usually rewarded half a cup, to which I

66

added heaps of sugar and milk to the brim. I held the cup with two hands, careful of my red-and-white candy-stripe shorts, pressed to perfection by Belle's iron.

To say that my elder sister, Evelyn, was not a morning person doesn't describe the intensity of her personality. Somewhere along the line of her development Evelyn made a sharp turn and never looked back. When she was younger, she was so active that my mother couldn't control her.

"Mama put a harness on me," Evelyn said accusingly.

"I sure did," my mother said. "You couldn't be trusted. I couldn't turn my back for a second. You'd just go wandering off no matter where we were."

But as Evelyn grew older, it was if a great magnet pulled her toward her bed, as if she needed to rest up after all the activity of her younger, wilder self.

When she arrived at the breakfast table, she sat down with a thud and a notable absence of any greeting. I was struck by her rudeness. How was it possible to sit at a table with other people and not acknowledge their presence? My mother, who never seemed to take Evelyn to task, passed food to her, so that she scarcely had the need to speak at all. We heard "Pass the salt," often enough, but other than that, not much left her lips. Of course her morning conduct fitted nicely with the morguelike silence that my mother required. Perhaps a quiet Evelyn was preferable, even if it meant sacrificing her manners.

She was strong like a boy and bossy like my mother. In her short silences between hungrily chomping her breakfast, she looked down at her food as if she dared it to leave her plate on its own accord. I usually woke up chatty, but was tamed by her sullen presence. I had the distinct feeling that cheer was unwelcome when she brought such a heaviness to our already stifled meals, a steaming volcano that constantly threatened to erupt. It was best not to disturb it. The only person who never tiptoed around Evelyn was my father.

My brother, Thomas, was kind of perfect, and despite the atmosphere, he wore a reliable smile every morning. He was going to be tall like my father, but looked more like my mother.

Thomas never got into any trouble, though occasionally my mother brought him to task whenever she thought Evelyn needed defending. Such as the time Evelyn stuck her fist through a glass pane in the back door and blamed Thomas; my mother insisted he was responsible simply because he was two years older.

Our father wasn't talkative at breakfast, either. I wondered if he couldn't wait to go downstairs and take care of a body that would never ask for salt, more sugar, or some kind of favor, all of which might be coaxed from him before his first cup of coffee.

"Daddy, can I have fifty cents?" I asked.

"May," Thomas said. "It's *may* I have fifty cents."

"What do you want it for?" my father asked me.

"The new Casper the Friendly Ghost comic book, that's twelve cents, and a pack of bubble gum, and some View-Master slides, maybe the Niagara Falls reel."

"What are you going to do to earn fifty cents?"

"Dust the caskets?"

"Leave him alone. Eat your breakfast." Too much conversation for my mother.

"Dust one and you can have it."

Every morning without fail my mother turned on the radio. This was the only sort of noise that pressed a chink in her armor of silence — to hear Whit Piper report the funeral announcements.

"Hush! Here it is," she said, and we were

69

held captive.

Forks down. Everyone except Evelyn tried not to chew loudly as we listened to Whit and breathed a sigh of relief when he announced the arrangements at our funeral home correctly. Grieving people deserved to have their names pronounced perfectly. My mother said it would be a bad reflection on us if Whit made a howler. Sometimes, he did just that.

We were anxious and hoped no one else noticed when he once said, "Mr. Kettering is survived by his husband, Mrs. Sally Kettering."

Or the time he proclaimed, "Those who wish to attend the marriage of Mrs. Laney Price may do so at the Mayfield and Son Funeral Home."

And sometimes, though both my parents swore they gave him the correct information, Whit turned it right on its head: "The funeral will be held on Thursday at three p.m."

"No!" My father jumped up. "Hatdammit. It's Friday at two. Lily Tate, call the radio station."

Twice a day, every day, even our meals included the business of death. My parents eagerly waited to hear the details of who was going to be buried by the competition.

On occasion they would vent their bewilderment and, sometimes, their anger at what they had heard.

"I don't understand. We were supposed to get Mr. Shoemaker," my father would say.

"Well, Frank, his sister was buried out in the county, too," my mother reasoned.

"But Sonny's known the family for a long time. I thought they'd come to us."

"Hm. Well. You can't always believe everything Sonny says."

I agreed with my mother on this point. Whenever Sonny settled into a conversation, he punctuated it with winks. I didn't trust him.

"I know, I know, you don't have to tell me again." Sparks of my parents' friction regarding Sonny were evident in my father's voice. "And we hauled all those chairs out to the Shoemakers' house just a few months ago. I thought that would have clinched it. Hellfire."

After breakfast I couldn't wait to follow my father downstairs. So many different things could happen in a single day in the funeral home.

For a few years I had the run of the rambling house. Thomas and Evelyn had already outgrown anything that resembled a child's entertainment. My playmates were the people who flowed in and out of the funeral home. Downstairs someone would always be around who tolerated my questions or, at the least, considered me part of the furniture.

I liked to slide down the banister early enough in the morning so that I wouldn't miss the Egg Man. The most phenomenal aspect of the Egg Man was that he actually looked like a gigantic egg. He was a huge, tall man with a shiny, bald head that was, well, egg shaped. His body swelled in his bib overalls at his middle, then dwindled down to a pair of unusually small feet for such a giant. His feet were covered by farm-worn, brown leather work boots that just barely peeked out from the faded blue denim.

The Egg Man arrived with a wire basket full of still-warm eggs, and I thought how small they looked in his plump hands. I anticipated the moment when he would sit down in a low, puffy armchair meant for delicate widows. He approached the chair by backing up to it, then slowly made his way down. He struggled to sit and struggled more when it was time for him to go. He shimmied his way out of the chair as I stood beside him and silently cheered his ascent. When this great event was accomplished, my father, the Egg Man, and I stood around smiling, rather pleased with his success.

"How in the world do you get out of bed in the morning?" I could not help but ask.

The Egg Man just laughed. "Why, honey, I just roll out."

He climbed carefully into his blue farm truck and drove away with a wave of his beefy arm.

He's going to need a really big casket some-day, I thought.

In those pauses from the dead and the dying, I lolled about in the gray wooden swing on our wraparound veranda, where the smell of strong coffee and burnt toast drifted all the way from our next door neighbor's kitchen window.

This would be the time of morning I would pester my father to take me to the Spring Farms coffee counter. When he was finally ready to go, he came outside to find me, and I grabbed his hand lest he somehow escape. I was determined not to miss out on the morning coffee klatch.

"Wait here on the front steps a minute," he said. "I'm going around back to the garage to get the car, and I'll pull up front here and you can hop in."

"But I wanna go with you."

"No, no, hold your horses a minute. Just

73

stay here."

I wondered which automobile he was going to drive this time. He bought and traded cars like livestock and absolutely flipped over antique cars.

Today he pulled up to the front of the funeral home in a convertible. I ran down the steps, set afire by the glamour. The car looked like a lemon meringue pie. I approached it in awe and ran my fingers along its pale yellow body. The interior was white leather, and I thought it was without a doubt the most beautiful car I'd ever seen.

"Did you buy this?" I asked breathlessly.

"No, it's on loan while they repair your mother's car."

My mother drove a big Buick Electra. I nagged him to trade it in for the convertible.

"This kind of car isn't practical. And your mother wouldn't want it anyway. It would mess up her hair. And we wouldn't want that, would we?"

Lord, no.

My mother's hair was sacred. Without fail, twice a week she kept standing appointments at the beauty parlor. Most of the women in our town wore beauty-parlor hair, the kind that didn't move in a stiff breeze because it was teased and sprayed with enough hairspray to kill a cat. No one touched my mother's hair except Mildred the beautician. I didn't dare and I never saw my father go near it.

I climbed to the top of the backseat and sat as tall as I possibly could, and off we went. Everything looked quite wonderful from this vantage point, and I waved to anyone I knew. I made my father honk if anyone walking the streets of Jubilee happened to miss seeing us. It was grand until a dog ran across the road and he slammed on the brakes. I went flying into the air and landed in the front right beside my father. I laughed my head off.

"Don't tell your mother, okay?"

Of course I wouldn't. Our secret.

"Pull in real slow, Daddy. So they can see me in this car."

The Spring Farms Dairy provided milk for the county, and a small lunch counter was set up adjacent to the building where the milk was bottled. We often drove up in an ambulance or a hearse, so the waitresses scarcely looked up anymore if they saw an unusual car. I took my time putting my shoes on so that everyone could get a good look at the yellow convertible.

I ran in to say hello to Paulette the waitress, who teased and tossed her light brown hair to a peak on top of her head. Paulette always had something interesting to say.

I couldn't wait for her to admire our latest ride. "Hi, Paulette! Did you see the car? We're not keeping it, though, it's a loaner."

"Yes, honey, it's mighty pretty." Paulette was just too calm about it to my way of thinking. She failed to make her usual exclamations of awe.

My father and I sat on bright, shiny chrome stools covered in fake green leather. I spun around, testing my ability to make the seat stop so that it faced the window from where I could see Jubilee's cemetery. It was a convenient location for my father; we could always go check on a grave after he had a cup of coffee. I relished these long summer mornings with him and did my best to stretch out the time we spent together. I caught the waft of his aftershave as my eye fell on the glint of his gold wristwatch, and from these things a sense of safety washed over me. We were comfortable with each other and he made me feel included. I was the only child at the counter; no other father brought his young girl or boy to shoot the breeze with Jubilee's coffee drinking men of business. My mother never joined us; she wasn't one to twirl idly on a stool. It wasn't a place for wives, but it was a place for me.

A place where I felt special.

Paulette glanced at my father when I ordered a grape Nehi and a piece of pie at ten o'clock in the morning. She was checking to make sure that it was all right and thought that I didn't know it, but I did. I nursed a bad itch to tell her, "Children do have eyes, you know. We see *everything.*"

She pointed to the pie case, where a lemon meringue pie sat temptingly uncut. I nodded. Perfect, considering the yellow-and-white convertible.

On this particular summer's day Paulette began to cry. She tried to hold it back, as she dabbed her eyes and nose with her apron, but the tears ran down her powdered face and left a shadow of lines and shiny spots on her orange lipstick.

She spoke in a low voice to my father and then moved away to get my piece of pie.

"What's Paulette crying about?" I whispered.

"Desegregation."

"What's that?"

"Her children are going to have to go to school with the colored children."

"But what's she crying about?"

"She doesn't want them to."

"Why not?" I was bewildered.

"Hush now, here she comes, don't say

77

anything else about it."

Paulette came back with a generous piece of pie. She placed it in front of me and smiled painfully with a twisted face, her eyes still brimmed with tears.

"Here, honey," she sniffed. "You tell your daddy to bring you back here tomorrow; we'll have chocolate cake, your favorite. And Miss Lucy Ann is making her chicken salad tomorrow, too."

"Yes, ma'am," I mumbled, my mouth already covered in crumbs from the flaky crust.

My father had a few quiet words with Paulette; she took a handkerchief out of her apron pocket and dabbed her eyes. I didn't know much, but I knew that Paulette would probably cry all day.

"No one wants their children to go to school with the coloreds," he told her, "but it's something we're all going to have to get used to. Not even the families who've been running this town since the Civil War can stop this."

Paulette nodded furiously, eyes down, handkerchief to her nose, as if my father had said the exact thing she needed to hear. For Paulette and for others, a smudge had appeared on the horizon. Here we were, over ten years on from the day segregation was ruled unlawful in public schools, and ours was only now preparing to comply.

The New South approached.

When we returned to the funeral home, I reclaimed my seat on the swing and waited for the Shroud Lady. My father had become aware of a woman who whipped up burial shrouds at home on her Singer sewing machine. In an admirable marketing coup he made a deal with her not to sell to any other funeral home in Jubilee, which basically meant not to Alfred Deboe, who owned the only other white funeral home in town.

She drove up Main Street in her two-tone Impala; the sun caught the green of her fenders and ricocheted off the white top. She parked, precisely, and waved to me as she opened the trunk. I opened our front door for her like a concierge, excited to usher her inside. There was work to do — shrouds to view, shrouds to choose.

She didn't have beauty-parlor hair, and that made me observe her more closely. Her hair was as black as a raven's and worn in a neat bun at her nape. Her vivid red lips stood out against her pale skin, and her thick, black glasses made her look like one of those movie librarians who takes her glasses off, shakes out her hair, and voilà —

a bombshell. She reminded me of the young dead corpse in our home movies, but my father told me not to tell her that.

Her figure, flattered by the tailored suits she wore when she delivered her goods, made me think of working women who sauntered into skyscrapers I'd seen in the movies. Just the word *skyscraper* made my imagination soar. I pictured myself at the top of one dropping a handkerchief, counting aloud how long it floated before landing on a New York City sidewalk. A return to reality brought me face-to-face with the wife of a farmer selling shrouds to a funeral home in a small town. She walked quickly in her stilettos, anxious to show her wares, which she carried in green cardboard dress boxes stacked up in her slender arms.

I followed her inside to the central hallway but the brightness of the sun did not, and our eyes adjusted to the tunnel of dim light in the foyer. The gray carpet had seen better days, the long hallway had no windows, and today, devoid of flowers and mourners, it verged on downright somber. The Shroud Lady's burial dresses transformed the dullness. I watched in wonder as she lined up the boxes on a row of chairs and opened them one by one. The chiffon billowed out of the boxes and she leaned over and smoothed out the sheared bodices. Carefully, almost lovingly, she displayed the shrouds that would only ever see a few hours of daylight.

My father turned to me. "Well, what do you think? Do you think we ought to buy some of these?"

"I guess so."

"Which ones? You choose a couple."

Oh, dear. How to choose between all of the pastel colors? Lavender, pink, mint-green chiffon, baby blue; I'd never be able to decide. I thought about all of the caskets in the showroom that matched the colors before me now.

"Can we buy all of them?"

"Do you think we can afford them all?" He winked at the Shroud Lady.

"I don't know, but maybe we can charge them." I'd heard my mother say "charge it" at the pharmacy.

"I think she might accept a check, now won't you, Mrs. Youngblood?"

I always forgot that the Shroud Lady had a name.

"Where did you learn to sew?" I asked her.

"My mother taught me," she purred. She had the loveliest Southern drawl, soft, without a hint of a country twang.

One of the strongest, most memorable images for which a mortician strived was to make the deceased appear as if he or she were at rest. If she was going to be successful, the Shroud Lady had to contribute to that image. She sat down at her Singer and imagined what she thought a negligee-type burial dress should look like. She strove to find the right balance between a dress and a nightgown. A shroud must be feminine, yet cover as much skin as possible.

"Then why aren't men buried in their pajamas? Why are they always buried in a suit and the women in nightgowns?" I asked my father.

"There's no equivalent. The shroud looks more like a dress than a nightgown. You can't camouflage men's pajamas. That's just the way it is," my father said, "and it's not a nightgown, it's a shroud. There's a difference."

Humph. Not much.

The Shroud Lady bought nylon chiffon by the bolt in sherbet colors and, eager to design something a little different from all the other shrouds she'd seen, tackled the front of the garment. She created five rows of shearing on the front of the dress, which made them nice and full. The garment was left open down the back so that it was easily adjustable.

I interrupted her right there. The image that swirled around in my mind of a dead woman's bare back lying on that satin fabric sent shivers through me. "Do you mean that it's just . . . just . . . *open* in the back?"

"No one's going to see the back of it. And it makes it easier to slip on. Here, look." She removed a pretty pink pile of chiffon from a box and gently shook it out. Two long fabric ties hung down from the back.

The "itty-bitty" buttons, as she said, were covered in her seemingly endless supply of chiffon and formed a neat row down the front. White lace trimmed the bodice and the wrists of long sleeves that hid the ravages of age and disease. The neck rose modestly high and was also trimmed in white lace. She felt these details made her shrouds special.

"How long does it take you to make one of these?" I asked.

"A *whole* day."

She sold each shroud to my father for $13.75. I wanted one for myself. They looked like something for Victorian ladies I'd seen in picture books, and I imagined dressing up in a blue or lavender shroud. Perhaps I'd pretend to be a ghost, or maybe I would play dead. I looked down at my frayed Keds and pedal pushers; it would be an improvement. My father ignored my whim, thinking it morbid.

I followed her out the front door and watched her walk down the street, empty-handed except for her small black clutch. I calculated her takings that day and considered what she might do with the extra money. Perhaps she'd buy a new hat, or a fat milking cow for her farm. I'd buy a bus ticket to those skyscrapers in New York.

She waved once more from the green-and-white Impala just as my father came out to tell me that Belle was ready for me.

Lunch. Nothing fancy, one of the many varieties of Campbell's soup and cheese and crackers, but if Belle placed it in front of me, it was food fit for royalty. My mother said she just couldn't do without Belle's help. It was the reason I couldn't understand why Paulette was so upset about her children going to school with black children. Belle was black and I thought she was exquisite. It wasn't that Belle was beautiful; in fact, she was plain and had a huge goiter in the center of her neck that moved up and down when she drank, much to my fascination.

"Here, Belle, have some ice water." I plied her with more just to watch her neck bob when she drank it.

After Belle arrived, I no longer ran around with my shirt buttoned wrong or wearing yesterday's socks. It was all right with me if I forgot to brush my hair, but Belle wouldn't stand for it. She all but spit on it to tame it. All of her own had fallen out due to an application of faulty straightening lotion that made her hopping mad at her sorry excuse for a beautician. So Belle wore a wig every day, with the stems of her eyeglasses tucked up underneath it.

One day, perched on the end of a chair as she shucked corn, she raised her dress to just above her knees to form a bowl shape to hold the corn.

"This is how I stays comfortable. I don't ever wears garters." She revealed the tops of her stockings, which were rolled up tightly around her hairless, muscular thighs.

"But how do they stay up, Belle?"

"They's rolled up real tight. Well, lookey here." She lifted the top of her stocking, where she'd formed a firm roll of nylon, then let it go; it snapped back into place, tight as a rubber band.

Every morning she tied an apron around her waist, and she squeaked when she walked in her white, rubber-soled nurse shoes. If her dress had no front pockets, she kept a fresh handkerchief wound around her bra strap.

The day had begun with Paulette's crying over something called integration. But our house had been integrated long ago. Belle knew that I was drawn to the color of her skin. Sometimes when the afternoon was quiet and she had time for me, I crawled up into her lap and ran my hand up her arm and felt her soft skin. She smelled faintly of something sweet, a combination of her natural odor and a soap that left its trace.

"Wouldn't you rather be white, Belle?" I asked her once.

"Why, Lawdy, Lawdy, no! I likes my skin color."

When the funeral home was particularly busy and day after day I was required to be silent and still, Belle took me for a walk downtown, all of two blocks, to the five-and-dime.

"Come here, Belle, I wanna show you something." I detoured to the street where, on a good streak, the movie theater remained open for weeks at a time.

"*Psycho* is playing again. Have you seen it, Belle?"

"Lawd, no, I won't watch a movie like that. And you shouldn't be watchin' it either."

"Thomas took me. You wanna go sometime?"

"No, I jest watches my stories on the TV."

I asked without thinking. Belle couldn't go with me to the movies because we'd be separated after we entered. She would be required to sit upstairs in the balcony, and I would sit downstairs. I thought this was a strange, strange rule. I couldn't understand why I could sit on her lap at home and not sit beside her in public. I wondered how it was that she could feed me and clothe me, yet be made to separate from me when we walked into the cinema.

Belle's voice seemed to ramble around corners and skip and jump through the air. Sometimes it took quite a lot of concentration to understand exactly what she was talking about.

"Well . . . it was round 'bout near eleven, no, maybe round 'bout half after eleven when Joyce, my niece, my sister Bernice's girl, comes and takes me down to my home church for they's homecoming for all the afternoon . . ." Her voice was low and deep.

"Do you mean Fifth Street, Belle?" I asked, trying to follow her train of thought.

She picked up steam and her voice became higher as she quickened her pace. "No, not the town church, down home to the home church. In the country, round 'bout an hour from here. I makes two pecan pies, one chess pie, one coconut cake, one chocolate cake, I fries me two chickens, makes some potato salad and three glass jars of my pickled cucumbers."

When Belle came close to concluding a particular topic, she sometimes clapped her hands together to accent her thoughts.

"Night before" — clap, clap — "I washes my wig" — clap — "and curls it up." Clap, clap. "I takes care of my wig." Clap.

When I became old enough to go, she walked with me to school and always insisted that I hold her hand. I was happy to do it, not for safety, but because I loved her. "I be seein' you round 'bout lunchtime" were her parting words. She was my only true friend for many years.

I visited Belle's house many times. She first shared her home with her husband, Henry, but Henry was gone. Belle told me he found a good job in another town far away and she didn't want to leave Jubilee. That was only half the truth. Belle was too polite to tell me that she caught Henry cheating on her. He and Belle became friends again after their divorce, and she always announced when Henry was in town. "I seen Henry last week. Showed me round 'bout nine" — clap, clap — "maybe ten pictures of his new house." I met Henry once when he was visiting Jubilee. He was nice enough, but I thought he'd made an enormous mistake in letting Belle go.

My parents sometimes dropped me off at Belle's house in the evening when they went to dinner out of town. I made myself comfortable in her modest sitting room and watched Friday-night wrestling with her on her small, black-and-white television. Belle became outrageously excited when her favorite wrestler, Tojo Yamamoto, appeared on the screen. She jumped up and yelled at the television as if it were a person. I'd never seen anything like it.

"Git him, Tojo!" Clap, clap. "He from Japan, or China, or somewheres like that." Clap, clap, clap. "Oh! Oh! No! Now you knows that's illegal . . . that's illegal! Blows your whistle. Blows your whistle!"

"Belle. Belle!" I yelled. "You're blocking my view! I can't see through you!"

She backed up to her seat without taking her eyes off the television. I held her chair for her to help guide her safely down.

At our house, when we didn't have a funeral or a visitation, Belle sometimes watched *The Edge of Night* on low volume while she snapped beans. *The Edge of Night* was her favorite "story," and on the afternoon Cookie, a female character on the show, was stabbed in the back with a pair of scissors, I took charge of the beans because Belle was upset and needed a moment to compose herself.

After today's lunch, Belle said she didn't have time to "mess with me," so I made my way back downstairs, where I ran into Luther and Bobby, two black men my father employed to dig graves for him.

Luther was short and quite old. His nephew Bobby was taller, younger, and often liquored up. I guess they must have been the best gravediggers in the county because my father went to great lengths to locate them. Whenever he had a hard time finding Bobby, he learned to look for him in jail and often bailed him out when he needed a grave dug. Luther was superstitious and terrified of dead bodies. Evelyn knew this and took great joy in scaring him half to death. Outside in the garage where barely a ray of sun penetrated, she would lie flat on a gurney and cover herself with a white sheet. When Luther and Bobby walked by, she slowly sat upright, the sheet still completely covering her. Luther screeched like an owl when he saw the corpse rise from the dead. Bobby tried not to show his irritation, but the theatrics put a damper on the fine buzz he had fostered with someone's bootleg whiskey.

I could see that Luther and Bobby were uncomfortable in the funeral home. They always entered through the rear door and lingered in the back, awaiting my father's instructions. Today, they looked down at the floor when I spoke to them.

"Hey, Luther. Where did you get that hat? I've never seen a hat like that."

Luther removed his flat cloth newsboy cap.

"Why, Luther, you have gray hair!"

He smiled and looked to my father for deliverance.

"Hi there, Bobby. Hey, your eyes are red today. You haven't been crying, have you?"

"No, ma'am, I haven't."

"Don't have to call me ma'am, Bobby, I'm just a girl."

"Yes, ma'am."

Last winter when a sheet of ice lay on top of the cemetery's frosty ground, my father waited for the word from Luther and Bobby. "Is she frozen, Luther?"

"Yassuh, sho is, Mr. Mayfield. 'Fraid so." Luther spoke softly and slowly.

"How long are we going to have to wait for this one, can you tell?"

"Ah" — he scratched his head — "depends on the weather. Can't rightly say."

"Well, you do your best to get that shovel in the ground as soon as you can."

Storage problems, that's what we would have if Luther and Bobby couldn't dig graves. We didn't have enough space to store more than two, maybe three bodies at the most, and they would have to lie in different rooms.

The embalming room was too small for a casket. The body, once embalmed and dressed, had to be carried into the casket room.

So, two was a crowd, and three bodies, well, we'd be on our way to bursting at the seams.

And it happened.

One quiet month, not that my father wanted one, the phone rang to bring news that Mr. Harris had died, then it rang again. Mrs. Summers was gone; and again, Mrs. Lancer, too — until we were up to our necks in bodies.

The circus began.

Mr. Harris lay on the embalming table while my father made space in the casket room on the last available cot for Mrs. Summers. Meanwhile, Mrs. Lancer lay temporarily in the hall on a gurney borrowed from the hospital. It seemed dead people were in every corner. Pulling it off involved a lot of corpse shuffling.

My father juggled each family's arrival time so they wouldn't run into each other when they came by to make arrangements.

"Move Mr. Harris and Mrs. Summers into the embalming room while Mr. Lancer is here this afternoon choosing a casket for Mrs. Lancer." My father's organizational skills burst to the fore. "We need to embalm Mrs. Lancer first, she was awfully ill."

"Now Lily Tate," my father said at dinner the first night, "I'll need you to call all the part-time boys and get them in here to help. Call the flower shops and give them the order of delivery; we'll be swimming in carnations if they deliver for three funerals all at once. Get Mildred in here for Mrs. Harris and Betty Summers. See if she can do them both at once. I'll have them ready. And get Totty on the phone. And call the radio station — no, I'll do that. I want to talk to Whit directly."

All three families knew that their deceased shared the space with the others. But when they walked into the funeral home to make arrangements, they were each made to feel as if theirs was the only bereavement that mattered, and there was no sign of any other family or, God forbid, a body. Except for one almost disastrous mishap. It became so confusing that when Mr. Summers came by to drop off Mrs. Summers's necklace, Sonny almost led him into Mrs. Lancer's private viewing. My father caught it just in time.

The next day there was an argument between the families. Two of them wanted to book the following day for the funerals. This being impossible, my father began to reason with them separately and made gentle suggestions. They couldn't agree even with my father brokering dates as if he were representing prizefighters. No one won. Both funerals were delayed a day. The third family was pushed back two days.

Luther and Bobby came by to get their instructions.

I overheard my father. "Bobby, you have got to stay sober until you get these graves ready. I don't have time to go down to the jail and get you out. Can you do that for me? Luther, will you make sure he gets to the cemetery?"

They both nodded. "Yep." "Yesser."

During this busy period, my father ate standing up. I didn't catch sight of him again until all three funerals were over.

On this summer afternoon while my father spoke with Luther and Bobby about the intricacies of a particular burial plot, I wandered out back and ran into the boy who lived next door to us for a brief period. Earlier Patrick had seen Luther and Bobby outside leaning on their shovels, and now he made a nasty remark about useless, ugly creatures. He began a chant that started with *digger* and ended with *nigger.* He sped through the back of our property on his bike and rode circles around me chanting, "The digger niggers, the digger niggers."

I lost my temper. "Stop it! Stop saying that word!" I yelled at him.

He tried to run over me with his big, red bike.

I grabbed the handlebars and twisted them. Then I gave him a lecture. "Don't you know how important gravediggers are? This is not a morgue, you know. We don't have refrigerators for dead people. We need for them to be buried. How would you like it if your father died in the middle of winter and he was stacked up in an embalming room waiting for his turn to be buried? He would turn gray and start to rot and stink. And then he'd blow up. *That's* how important gravediggers are," I said hotly.

But the boy was hateful and ignorant and nothing fazed him. He thought his father would live forever. I knew he wouldn't.

I ran into the funeral home looking for my own father. My color was high and I was eager to spill all about the wretched boy next door. But there was no time for that now. The caskets had arrived!

Casket deliveries were a big event. Not even Sonny could dampen my spirits on casket day. All hands were needed to unwrap and position the large pieces of funeral furniture. Tremendous, long boxes were rolled into the building as usual, but this delivery contained something I'd never before seen — two smaller boxes. I stood by my father's side when he opened the first one. In it was the smallest coffin I had ever seen. The pink satin box looked like a toy. I glanced at him but said nothing and watched as he opened the second one — a blue satin baby coffin. I ran my fingers along the rim of the pink one, still covered in plastic. The fabric had tufts and pleats, and inside this miniature box of sorrow a tiny pillow rested poignantly. I asked if it was for a baby girl, and he said yes, it was.

"Did a baby girl die, Daddy?"

"Yes."

"What'd she die of?"

"She was born dead."

"Oh."

He continued to take the clear plastic

wrapping off the blue one.

"What's that? What's *born dead*?"

"Well, it really just means that the baby died before it had a chance to be born, it's called stillborn."

"Will her parents leave the casket open?"

"No, they won't."

"They don't want to see her?"

"No."

"Why? Why don't they want to see her?"

"She's too small. It's just too hard on them."

"Did a baby boy die?"

"No."

"Why do we have a blue one, then?"

"Well, sometimes baby boys die, too."

"Did the baby girl's parents know when the baby was going to die? You know, a lot of times you know when people are going to die. I hear you say so, you say Mr. so-and-so is going to go sometime this weekend, and then they do."

"That's not the same. I don't know if her parents knew. It's not something I would ask them."

"Do you know when I'm going to die?"

"No, I don't."

"Where's the baby girl, Daddy?"

He glanced over at the embalming-room door.

"Is she in there right now?"

He knew where my question was headed. "We don't embalm babies."

I didn't know that babies died. I moved away from him and the baby coffins so that he couldn't see me. I felt a cocktail of sickness, fear, and sadness, but I wanted him to think that I could handle it. Otherwise, he might grow tired and impatient with me, ready to cast me off to dolls and toys in which I had no interest. And worst of all, it would prove my mother was right in her belief that I had no business being downstairs.

I felt his hand on my shoulder directing me out of the room, away from the boxes for dead people. "Come on, let's go get a Coke and some peanuts," he said as he turned out the light, closing the door on the blue baby casket.

I helped him remove the peanuts from the cellophane package, and one by one we dropped them into the bottle of Coke. Occupied with this task and the taste of salt meeting sugar, the caskets eased their way out of my mind.

I had no reason to think about dead babies again until a year later, when my mother's swollen belly reminded me. Day by day I grew secretly terrified that my baby sister, Jemma, would be born dead. Even after my parents brought her home from the hospital, I constantly checked her status.

Belle was the only person in the household who caught on. "Why is you so persnickety round the baby?"

"Well . . . Belle, I'm just checking."

"Checkin' what? She's round 'bout near perfect as she can be."

I crawled up in Belle's lap and whispered, "I'm checking to see if she's going to be born dead."

"Lawd! What you talkin' about? She done *been* born. This here baby is a'livin' and a'breathin' jest fine. What's give you cause to say such a thing?"

I burst into tears. Out poured the worries and images of pink and blue baby caskets, and talk of stillborns and born dead and dead babies in general, and when, exactly, would Jemma be out of danger, and please don't tell my parents, it might worry them.

"Lawd have mercy 'pon my soul. Child, you is all upset for nothin'. Yer sister ain't in danger of nothin' but bein' spoilt rotten."

Much to my relief, Belle was right, but I remained haunted whenever I saw a pregnant woman's protruding belly.

Just when we thought the end of this rather busy day was near, the news rang from the almighty telephone that another of Jubilee's citizens would soon be joining us.

My mother was in the kitchen almost ready to serve supper, and without a word she turned off the oven and all the simmering pots on the stove. Whit Piper's evening radio announcements kept her company while she waited for my father to complete his work.

A couple of hours later she told me to go downstairs and find out how much longer he would be. I'd done this many times, and a knock on the door would suffice. Usually, he would answer from behind the closed door, but this time the door came flying open. I'd never been in the embalming room while the deed was being done — it looked like a scene from a science-fiction movie.

Mildred, the beautician who gave my hair a permanent twice a year, stood brandishing the first blow-dryer I had ever seen. Sonny was on the other side of the table standing next to a big white pumping, sucking machine, doing God knows what.

My father stood at the head of the table with his shirtsleeves neatly rolled up, his tie still perfectly knotted, but tucked inside his shirt, and a clean towel draped around his belt loops. He held a rather nasty-looking rubber hose in his hand. Their subject lay on the long, white porcelain table. Thankfully, a sheet covered all but her head, which was suspended in the air as it rested on the black head block. Sheer luck, I guess, that I had entered at this stage.

"Come on in," my father coaxed. He sounded so inviting, so happy to see me. All three of these characters, for they no longer resembled my father, or the real Mildred and Sonny, smiled at me with their various utensils in hand. I trembled before them. Sonny smirked at my obvious display of terror, pleased that I was rendered speechless.

Laid out precisely on a rolling cart were a big needle with a curved end like Captain Hook's arm, with a long piece of nylon thread hanging from it, and something called a needle gun, and other hook-tipped devices and metal tubes of several varieties.

The room was the size of a single bedroom, which was exactly what it had once been, long ago. Faded wallpaper covered the walls. Bright, clean linoleum in a speckled pattern buckled a bit on the floor. A shade was on the window in the back of the room, but in addition a sheet had been nailed to the wood over it, giving the window an abandoned, ghostly look. I surmised that such apparently careless treatment was a haphazard precaution against spying neighbors.

A naked bulb hung from a long cord suspended from the tall ceiling. The only other light was an accordion lamp that stretched to capacity over the embalming table. Below the table, directly underneath, was the drain for the unmentionable fluids that ran down and out of our house.

And the smell. I glanced at the metal cabinet, the control tower of my father's craft, its doors spread open to display a variety of colorful bottles. Deep orange, pink, purple, and green embalming fluid cast a neon glow in the dark patches of the room. Arterial fluid with names like Frigid Jr. and Champion neatly arranged on the shelves in every shade of pink hinted at the color the deceased's skin would mimic. The pungent odor of formaldehyde mixed with that of cosmetics, hairspray, and the strong iron smell of water hung in the room like a veil, from which there was no escape, ever. I would never be capable of forgetting that smell.

I felt I had caught these people in the first act of a macabre fantasy.

I finally managed to squeak out my given task. "I'm supposed to ask you when you'll be ready for dinner." I thought I sounded quite brave, untouched, even remote, although now I'm sure I didn't.

"Oh, I think in about half an hour."

I managed to nod furiously and then retreated, horrified.

It's true to say that I was lily-livered. I wanted to be blasé about the whole thing, but I never developed a taste for hanging out in the embalming room. From that day forward my stomach somersaulted before I even knocked on the door. It amused my father to rub it in a little bit. Whenever he asked me to deliver an item to the room, he knew I would be skittish. "Go on, there's no one in there," he would say. Right. I could never be absolutely certain that the room was free of some corpulent corpse. Sure enough, when I cracked open the door and peeped inside, a bumpy mound lay under the white sheet, minding its own business. He really got a kick out of that.

After the delayed supper when the dishes had been washed and dried, I skidded back into the kitchen, where I found my mother and father locked in an embrace. It was embarrassing. My mother was not the affectionate type and it looked unnatural to see her body so close to his. Then he kissed her. Good grief. I could count on one hand how many times I'd seen them doing *that*.

In their rooms, Thomas pored over a book and Evelyn talked on the phone for ages. I joined my parents in the living room while they watched television.

My father teased my mother while they sat on opposite ends of the sofa. He reached over and poked her with his foot, playing with her during *Gunsmoke.* The thing was, I couldn't tell if she enjoyed the attention. She pretended to be annoyed, but I'm not sure she was.

"Where are your wedding pictures?" I once asked her.

"We don't have any."

"Why not?"

"Because we got married on the army base. I took the Greyhound bus down to Alabama where you father was in an infantry training camp."

"How old were you?"

"Eighteen. He'd just turned eighteen. They didn't even let him graduate. They whipped him out of school so fast."

"What did you wear?"

"A navy-blue suit."

"What did he wear?"

"His army uniform."

"Did anyone else go with you? Your mother, or sisters?"

"No. We got a couple of soldiers to stand

up for us."

"No white dress then?"

"No white dress."

They'd been dating for only a year. Simple, innocent stuff, dates were little more than a bite to eat after Frank's basketball games, or else he invited her to the farm for his mother's famous Sunday dinners. Photos of Frank before he was whisked away show a slightly chubby young man in a suit standing next to his brother, who was in uniform. In her high school photo my mother's hair was brushed back and swept high off her forehead, her red lips were closed solidly, with only a hint of a smile, and her brown eyes glistened just a bit, but gave nothing away.

I asked her where they went on their honeymoon and she cocked her head and stared at me. "There was a war on, you know. We stayed at an apartment on the base for two weeks, then I came back to Kentucky and they sent him overseas . . . to England first, then to the front line. That was 1944. I didn't see him again for two years."

When he stepped out of the taxi in 1946, she didn't recognize him. "Is that him?" she asked his sister. The two women had sat by the window all afternoon waiting for his arrival.

"No, I don't think so, it doesn't look like Frank. That looks like an old man."

But the "old man" who stepped out of the taxi was Lily Tate's husband. No trace remained of the chubby-faced boy she'd married. This man was gaunt and frail from a near-fatal stomach wound. His grayish skin and the black circles under his eyes frightened her. In a small, fuzzy photograph taken soon after his return from Germany, the black slits that were his eyes were lowered, as if he were cowering away from the camera lens.

When they were finally alone, Frank told his young wife that he wasn't sure he wanted to be married anymore. Stunned, she knew he'd been through something that she couldn't understand and perhaps never would, but surely he didn't mean it? She'd waited so long to see him again. So many men never returned.

She didn't respond. She didn't react, didn't talk about it at all. Her tactic was to focus on his health. His statement simmered quietly between them until it was clear to Lily Tate that he wouldn't repeat it. Then the moment came when he asked her if she would mind being an undertaker's wife.

"I didn't bat an eye," she told me many years later. "It's the live ones you have to look out for, not the dead."

IN MEMORIAM:
LETTICIA OAKLEY

One day while the hearse received a well-deserved bath and oil change and the station wagon was full to the brim with graveyard tents, my father drove Sonny and me to the Spring Farms coffee counter in the ambulance. Our ambulance looked exactly like our hearse and not at all like the square, box-type ambulance that later came into vogue. The only difference was the round light that sat on the roof and the mechanics that created the siren's call.

On this summer's morning the skies threatened a storm and the air was thick with heat that drenched us in sweat. I was anxious to get to a seat at the counter and feel cold lemonade burn down my throat.

We arrived to discover that it was chocolate-meringue-pie day. There was no need to ask Paulette for an order; she placed a big piece in front of me with a wink that was heavy on the mascara. My father and Sonny nursed their first cup of coffee, an act I questioned immediately.

"How do you drink that stuff when it's so hot

outside?"

"It's nice and cool in here, ain't it?" asked Sonny.

"Daddy, how do you drink that stuff in this heat?"

"Don't ignore Sonny. What's the matter with you?"

The first bite of the creamy, rich chocolate sent me twirling on the seat. Whoosh! I spun around and around until I was dizzy. Then, Paulette ran over to my father and whispered that he had a phone call. He disappeared behind the counter to take it. I sat still, all my senses alerted. Hell's bells, it could only mean one thing.

My father raced back to the counter and threw a few dollar bills down in front of his coffee cup. A couple of men a few stools down looked up, saw that it was my father who was in a rush, and returned to their newspapers. I, on the other hand, was paralyzed.

He spoke to Sonny, then literally lifted me from the stool while Sonny held the door open.

My father put me down on the pavement and held my shoulders square. "Now listen to me. We have to go get Mrs. Oakley. I don't have time to take you back to the funeral home because she lives out in the country and we have to get on the road. You're to do exactly as I say, do you hear me?"

I nodded. I'd never been on an ambulance call.

We ran to the ambulance and I scrambled into the front seat, squashed between the two of them.

My father explained to Sonny that Mrs. Oakley had called the funeral home and wouldn't speak to anyone but him. She was told she could reach him at Spring Farms.

"Frank, this is Mrs. Oakley calling. I'm flat out on the kitchen floor."

"I'll be right there, Mrs. Oakley. Don't you worry. What's the matter with you, can you tell me?"

"I've just tripped over the damn cat, pardon my language, Frank, and I think I've broken my leg . . . or maybe my arm. Then I jerked the phone off the table. Saved my life, I reckon."

"Mrs. Oakley —"

"So, I'm just gonna lie here and wait for you, Frank. I'm sure you remember where I live. Do you remember that time —"

"Mrs. Oakley —"

"Hurry though, Frank. I reckon I'm in enough pain to faint clean away."

"I have to hang up the phone now, Mrs. Oakley, I can't get to you until I do."

"Well, all right then, I'll be here, not going anywhere."

As we drove down the country road that was barely wide enough for a car, much less an ambulance, my father set out the rules of engagement. "You know you really shouldn't be coming with us, but I don't have a choice. It just worked out that way. Now, you listen up and you listen good. When we get there, I want you to stay right here in this seat. Don't you move a muscle. Don't say a word." He shook his head. "I really shouldn't be doing this."

I didn't know if it was against the law, or if he just thought it was wrong and unprofessional, but for whatever reason, he was clearly uncomfortable.

"Are you going to put the siren on? Let's crank it up."

"No, not unless I need to later. That's exactly what I mean. Don't ask things like that. I have a job to do and I need you to mind me."

"Will there be blood? 'Cause if there is, I'm going to have to hide my eyes."

"No. You can't do that. I don't know if there will be, but if there is, just look straight ahead like nothing's happened."

"Well, what if her bones are sticking out of her skin? Daddy, I would just die."

"Just look away."

Sonny could hardly conceal his annoyance. The thing was, Mrs. Oakley had been one of my teachers a couple of years back and I couldn't imagine her sprawled out on her kitchen floor. I sat in silence for the rest of the journey and worried about her bones.

On this unplanned race through the town's streets I gained firsthand experience of the version of my father the people of Jubilee encountered not only when their family members died, but also when things were bad in other ways. He arrived on the scenes of broken bones, heart attacks, and car wrecks and became the emergency suction cup of our town.

The ambulance rolled along the gravel driveway to a little brick house where Mrs. Oakley lived alone with her cat. Sonny alighted while my father maneuvered the back of the ambulance near her front door. What a relief. This placed me with a view of the driveway, away from all the action. Before my father jumped out, he warned me again, "Not a word, not a muscle."

I sat still waiting for something to happen. I didn't even play with the air-conditioning vents, though I sorely wished to, and was not the least bit tempted to turn around. Except I did. I heard her front door open and some sort of automatic reflex kicked in. There was Mrs. Oakley stretched out on the gurney, and to my horror she waved at me, her skinny, long

111

arms flailing about, obviously not broken. Her wig, and I never knew she wore a wig, was askew, and she wore a bright pink terry-cloth bathrobe. God, what a frightful sight, I thought. I quickly turned away when I heard her gabbing away to my father while she took a short ride on the gurney.

"Is that your middle girl? Well, Lord in heaven, what a surprise. Hello there, little missy."

Oh, what to do? What to do? I remained silent and didn't turn to her. Not a word, not a muscle, he had said. I doubt if I breathed.

When they rolled Mrs. Oakley into the back of the ambulance, she immediately rose up from the gurney and opened the sliding glass partition between us.

"Hon, have you improved your math yet?"

What? I thought. At a time like this?

It was a strange thing indeed to witness my teacher in such a vulnerable position. I was far more embarrassed than she. Didn't she realize we were sharing an intimate moment? When I next walked through the halls at school and came upon Mrs. Oakley wearing her A-line skirt, crisp blouse, and pearls, would I ever be able to forget her pink bathrobe?

The rest of the journey was uneventful. While the doctor at the hospital x-rayed Mrs. Oakley's leg, my father took me home.

"That can't ever happen again," he said. "I will never, ever do that again."

I was proud that his first reaction that day was not to leave me in the care of Paulette, or to ask my mother to collect me from Spring Farms, but instead he allowed me to go along with them. I felt I had earned some sort of stamp of approval, like I had passed the etiquette test in emergency procedures. A few years later when Mrs. Oakley suffered a fatal stroke and collapsed in her tomato garden, I remembered her broken leg and marveled that it had been instrumental in bringing me closer to my father. I've held a soft spot for her ever since.

CHAPTER 3
THE BURIAL-VAULT BATTLES

If there was one thing the men who controlled Jubilee didn't like, it was outsiders. They especially couldn't abide an outsider who made a splash. Not everyone in Jubilee thought the arrival of Frank Mayfield in town was a breath of fresh air. My father's indoctrination into the world of Jubilee's hierarchy began with a visit from two representatives of a group of men who were known as the Old Clan. In the 1960s they were still as territorial as children in a sandbox. Their families had ruled Jubilee since before the Civil War and they saw no good reason to surrender the reins. Most members of the Old Clan were educated men who knew a bit more about how the world worked than did the simple farmers and other less glorified laborers of Jubilee. Not to be confused with the Klan, the masks they wore were invisible and there could be no doubt as to their identity. Self-

114

assured and at ease in public, they cut a wide swath. Henry Whitehall liked to fondle the gold pocket watch displayed in the vest of his white linen suit. His daddy did the same when he was alive. Rusty Welch darted his head around the town square like a pigeon looking for food, afraid he would miss something important. Long ago they had claimed special seating privileges around the local coffee counters and could be heard noisily arguing with each other. They proudly labeled themselves grumpy, tenacious, and sly old devils, and no one would disagree. They dictated the way things worked around here.

When two of these old lions strolled up Main Street and stopped in front of the funeral home, my father slowly rose from his leather swivel chair. He stood behind his desk with his hands in his trouser pockets, with a clear view through the oblong window directly in front of him.

"Go on upstairs now," he said to me. "It looks like I have unexpected visitors."

I scrambled onto one of the folding wooden chairs and peeked out the window. The men were deep in conversation and looked in no hurry to climb the steps to our front door. "Who are those men?"

My father made his way over to the window and adjusted the venetian blind. "You see that one on the right?" He nodded toward the men. "The one who looks a little cocky? That's Fletcher Hamilton," he said in a chilly tone. "He's a lawyer and a businessman. And that ole boy with him is Chuck Harley, Fletcher's partner in the concrete business."

Perspiration beaded Fletcher Hamilton's forehead and his shock of burnt-red hair, usually swept back with pomade, now fell over his eyes. He pushed his browline-framed glasses up toward his nose.

"That sounds boring. What are they doing here?"

"That's a good question. That's a very good question." My father's eyes were fixed on them as they drew closer. "I guess I'm about to find out."

"Here they come. Run along now." My father gave me a little shove toward the stairs.

He held the door open for his visitors. He was awfully polite.

I ran upstairs to my mother with a full report on a man named Fletcher, who'd come to visit without an invitation.

"Be quiet. Sit down and eat your lunch."

My father's funeral home and the Jubilee Concrete Company wouldn't have had a thing in common except for one product — concrete burial vaults. Burial vaults served an undeniably important function, as the cemetery's caretaker once explained to me. He occupied the former sexton's house on the edge of the graveyard. The poor guy had to live with a forty-year-old ghost story of a young girl who supposedly haunted the square tower of his house. He was dogged by out-of-towners who constantly drove by gawking. Young men on a mission to prove their bravery prowled the cemetery at night. My mother said the caretaker was a nice man, and my father told me not to ask him about the ghost in his house, so I didn't.

One day I watched the lowering of a vault into the ground and didn't understand its purpose.

"It's a pretty graveyard, isn't it?" The caretaker had come by to watch the ground being disturbed.

"It sure is, Mr. Shelton. Nice and peaceful."

"You asked me about the vaults the other day. Your daddy didn't tell you about them?"

"He told me to ask you."

"See how nice and orderly everything is? See how smooth those rows of gravestones sit, and how level the ground is?"

"Sure. I see what you mean, I guess.

They're kind of scraggly in places, though."

He ignored my observation. "Well, without vaults, if one single thunderstorm rolled into town, the ground would get so heavy from the wet soil that it would just cave in. That heavy old mud would crush the coffins. Vaults prevent something bad like that from happening and help keep that even appearance all the way across this cemetery." He gave a sweeping gesture of his hand. "And you have to have something secure enough to protect those caskets from the critters that come out at night."

"Aw. That's creepy, Mr. Shelton."

"Yesum, I know, I know. But it's just part of it."

The meeting between Fletcher Hamilton and my father was doomed before it began. Rumor had it that Frank Mayfield was causing havoc at the vault company because his funeral home wasn't placing enough orders to please the Old Clan.

Like my father, Fletcher Hamilton always wore a suit, though Fletcher's were just a tad more understated than my father's. Their quality and the cost snuck up on you. He may have been wearing a plain white shirt, but upon careful scrutiny it was a damn fine one. A quiet sophistication dwelled within him, the kind that was cultivated just as carefully as my father's meticulous presentation. In a desire to be noticed for what he said rather than what he wore, Fletcher's deep Southern voice was as polished as his shoes. Someone would say he was a class act — with the emphasis on *act.*

It was well-known that if Fletcher Hamilton was on your side, it was a grand state of affairs. If not, you'd better make sure the ground beneath your feet was solid. At different times in life, a man or a woman might well experience both the good and the bad side of Fletcher Hamilton and his excellent legal mind.

It was a little crowded with both my father and Fletcher in the same room. They were never going to see eye to eye on anything. A man of long-winded eloquence when it was called for, Fletcher chose on this occasion to get right to the point, which was just as well because the men weren't offered any refreshment.

"Now, Frank, we sure would appreciate it if you would tell the families you attend about our Jubilee vaults," Fletcher began.

"Those concrete vaults leak and you know it. I don't care for the Jubilee vaults. I don't like any vault made solely from concrete. I've seen them crack, Fletcher. The water from the soil gets in there and then you've got a waste of money. Vaults with some metal in them are more expensive, but they last."

"Well, you think about it, Frank. Alfred sure sells a hell of a lot of our vaults. They're good enough for him," put in Chuck Harley.

"I'm sure they are, Chuck, I'm sure they are," my father said levelly.

It was true. My father's sole competitor, Alfred Deboe, owner of the Deboe Funeral Home, was only too pleased to recommend the concrete vaults. He and Fletcher Hamilton were good friends, and Alfred would sell rats' tails if Fletcher told him to. Alfred Deboe had enjoyed easy business until my father's arrival. Embedded within the good-ole-boy society, he sailed along year after year without any serious competition. When my father bought the funeral home on Main Street, it had been deteriorating for years and its business was almost nonexistent. The only other funeral home in town was for the black community, which was no competition at all. But Deboe resented my father's incursion.

"Well now, Frank, maybe you're . . . well . . . unfamiliar with the residents of our town. Maybe you're too new to Jubilee to understand that not everyone can afford metal vaults. We're a community of hard-working farmers." Fletcher, who'd never farmed a day in his life, shifted from one expensively clad foot to the other.

"My policy has always been to let the families decide for themselves. When it's time to talk burial vaults, I present the choices. And only when and if my opinion is required do I give it," my father said, making a gallant effort to remain calm. "I'll tell you what, Fletcher. I'm not going to push those concrete vaults, but I won't bad-mouth them either. That's fair enough."

As soon as Fletcher and his partner had disappeared down Main Street, my father climbed the stairs two at a time, putting on the brakes only when he reached the kitchen. Jemma was sitting in her yellow high chair. I sat at the kitchen table, waiting to hear why my father's eyes looked like storm clouds. He reached for the Alka-Seltzer.

"I can hardly believe it," he erupted in front of us. "Damn that Fletcher Hamilton! Can you believe he would come in here and try to tell me how to run my business? I know what he thought. He thought I'd just go along to get along. Wasn't it enough that I offered to stay quiet about the damn vaults?"

Oh, boy. My father acted as if he'd been dealt a nasty old poker hand. My mother's silence taught me something she already knew: these were rhetorical questions that invited no answers.

He made a point with his finger in the air. "No, that wasn't enough. It's never enough for those men. Well, he can take his cracking, leaking vaults and —"

"Frank. The girls."

"I shook his hand. And I'm sorry I did." His Alka-Seltzer fizzed away furiously.

What a temper! I'd never seen him so angry. His jaw was so tightly clenched I thought his teeth would crack and my heart raced as I maneuvered to stay clear of his path. His anger was sharp and fixed and I hoped that it would never be pointed at me. I saw then that he was a man who would never be coerced. I would certainly never attempt it. All this uproar because of burial vaults and a man named Fletcher Hamilton. I would hear this man's name in the years to come, always accompanied by some dissatisfaction or annoyance.

"Frank, calm down."

"I am not going to have a man like that, or any other —"

The phone rang. My father rallied his funeral home voice when he answered it.

"Mayfield and Son Funeral Home."

I watched, awed by his transformation; he had to be calm because there was no choice. Even the Alka-Seltzer stopped fizzing. And that was it — we had to be quiet again. We were getting a body.

Shortly after this formal request from the Old Clansmen, an odd thing began to happen at the Jubilee hospital. Normally, when a person called upon a funeral home to drive them to the hospital, if that person died, the family requested the same funeral home to handle the funeral. It was the natural and expected outcome. But for a noticeable number of people whom my father had taken to the hospital, their families did not call him at the time of death. They called Alfred Deboe instead. My father couldn't figure it out, and it was driving him crazy. He was working hard to develop relationships, people were beginning to call him for favors instead of Deboe, and it just didn't make sense that they wouldn't follow through when it was time to make that all-important call. He set out to get to the bottom of it.

A blond, blue-eyed nurse at the hospital was always happy to have a friendly chat with Frank when she found the time. Our hospital was drab and murky, and her presence brightened the corridors. Barbara Jean was so pretty in her starched white uniform and crisp nurse's hat that just looking at her made me want to be a nurse — for two seconds, until thoughts rushed in of corpses on the embalming table and the astonishing amount of blood that flows through the human body. I decided against it.

My father bought insurance from her husband and had a hunch that she would be willing to help. He caught her in the hall on a break, and they stood outside the hospital's snack bar sipping coffee.

"Barbara Jean, you know that woman Mrs. Bellows who died the other day . . . do you remember when I brought her in?"

"Yes, of course I do."

"Well, Alfred Deboe is burying her, and that just doesn't make sense to me."

Barbara Jean sighed. "Now, Frank, I don't think we should be having this conversation."

"Come on, Barbara Jean. I know something's going on. I'll find out sooner or later. I'd rather hear it from you."

She hesitated. "All right. But don't you let on who told you. I really shouldn't tell you this, but . . ." She leaned forward and lowered her voice to a whisper. "Someone's swinging the families. Someone's sending them to Alfred Deboe."

"Who?"

"We've been told, well . . ." She hesitated.

"Barbara Jean, I won't get you in any trouble."

"If a family member's relative has died in the hospital, and they haven't already requested a funeral home, the nurse on duty is directed to suggest Alfred's funeral home."

"You've been told to do that yourself?"

"Oh, yeah, many times."

"Well, where's it coming from, Barbara Jean?"

"Percy Foley. They're his orders."

Straight from the top. The hospital administrator, Percy Foley, a great heap of a man who wore the sweaty pallor of too many Southern breakfasts, had given orders to suggest the Deboe Funeral Home to family members of dying patients. It shouldn't have been a surprise. Percy Foley was a distant relative of Fletcher Hamilton's and a member of the Old Clan.

"Frank, what you need to do is get yourself down to one of those Hospital Board meetings and plead your case," Jim Dawson, one of the town leaders who held a less myopic view of Jubilee's place in the world, advised my father. Most people called him Mr. Jim due to his great height, but he was also great in purpose and strength of heart. When Jubilee needed a diplomat, they most often called upon Mr. Jim.

While my father fumed, he planned to take action to protect his business. Other men in town welcomed new businesses and those who worked hard to establish them. They supported the new funeral director, and they, too, encouraged him to go before the Beacon County Hospital Board.

When Frank Mayfield pleaded his case before the board, he asked that an unfair practice be abolished. He then put all of his cards on the table and suggested that the members of the board seriously consider relieving Percy Foley of his duties as the hospital's administrator. Foley was not fired; he was not even reprimanded. Even with the support of several established men in Jubilee, Frank's actions backfired on him. This was Jubilee and the message was clear: This system has been arranged. Don't try to change things and certainly do not try to run things.

When Foley heard about my father's attempt to have him dismissed, he became vindictive. Now the employees were instructed to become more aggressive at the deathbeds of their patients. Right at the exact moment of death, when families stood in the darkened rooms whispering and weeping, there was no better moment for hospital staff to say, "Why don't you let us call Alfred for you?"

It wasn't always a successful maneuver; some were loyal to my father even when cajoled. But in most cases, it was difficult for a family to back out of their first request. They simply felt too vulnerable. If a family had chosen Deboe in the first miserable moment of death, even if they had second thoughts later, a strong voice within a family was needed to change funeral directors midstream. The damage was done. The Old Clan thought Frank was a fool, too big for his fancy britches and ignorant of how speaking out against a perceived wrong was a privilege afforded only to those whose granddaddies were born in Jubilee. What he needed was an ally in this town, someone who knew how things worked, someone who was established and whose roots ran deep. While he waited for that person to appear, the strain of his endeavors began to show. Mornings began with two white tablets of Alka-Seltzer instead of one, his perfect quiff was thinning, and he was even more short-tempered with my mother than usual. It began to show in other ways, too.

One evening not long after these events, before bedtime I walked through the kitchen, where my father and my mother spoke in heated whispers. I passed by my father and suddenly he grabbed me by my arm and spanked me. It didn't hurt, but it scared me silly because it came from nowhere. My mother was free with her hand — a slap, a spanking, she made good on her threats to "get the yardstick," but not him. Usually he never touched me in anger or as punishment. I knew I'd done nothing to deserve it, but couldn't manage to say one single word in my defense.

"Go to bed," my mother said hurriedly.

I hiked up my blue flannel pajama bottoms and fled.

The next morning my mother asked me to come into the kitchen. My father stood at the counter while waiting for his Alka-Seltzer to calm down. I watched the white tablets dissolve furiously in the glass of water, to which he added several ice cubes. I usually asked him for a sip because I liked the taste and the cold shock it gave my throat. I usually laughed as the bubbles showered my face. Alka-Seltzer was one of those things that immediately connected me to my father. *Plop, plop, fizz, fizz, oh, what a relief it is.* But not this morning. I didn't want a sip; I didn't even want to laugh.

"Your father has something he wants to say to you." My mother stood with her arms folded.

He leaned back against the counter, as if for support. He looked straight ahead, with not even a glance my way. "Your mother wanted me to tell you —"

"Frank," she interrupted with a warning in her voice.

"Well, I wanted to say that I'm sorry about last night. I had a little too much to drink. Things have been a bit stressful and . . . well, I won't do it again."

I felt sick to my stomach. He'd never before had to apologize to me for anything. And I'd never seen my mother give him a direct order. She didn't apologize to me when she spanked me unjustly, so why would she make him do it? Everything was topsy-turvy. Suddenly I found the linoleum on the kitchen floor extremely interesting. I thought about how many times I'd seen Belle's bucket and mop on this floor. I didn't understand what he was saying to me, but I nodded as if I did. The tone of his voice, uncomfortable and shamed, was foreign to me. Embarrassed for him, I didn't look at him directly.

I didn't know one soul who drank alcohol, except for Bobby, and he went to jail because of it. Did this mean my mother was going to have to get my father out of jail, too? She would never allow alcohol in the house, and both my mother's and father's families back in Lanesboro were teetotalers. Beacon County was dry. There were no liquor stores for miles. Did he go to a bootlegger?

I waited for more of an explanation. I waited for the fun, wise-cracking father I loved to show his face. But he stood there, his head bowed, as if he found the floor as interesting as I did.

There was no easy way to learn that my father was not who I thought he was. Or rather, was much more than I had ever imagined.

I wondered where this drinking took place. Being an undertaker in a small town, someone at the funeral home, at least one person, always had to know my father's whereabouts. God forbid anyone should die and Frank Mayfield not be found.

My mother always had two words on the tip of her tongue: "Where's Frank?" I'd often hear her quiz Sonny, or whoever was on duty. The answers varied. Sometimes they stumbled a bit. "Err . . . I guess he's at the hospital." Her face would often cloud over and her whole body would stiffen as she waited for an answer. Lately, one of the most frequent answers was "He's gone to see Miss Agnes." Her face would relax then, and she'd nod and seem relieved.

I'd heard the names of many of Jubilee's citizens as they cropped up in funeral-home conversation, but recently none was tossed into the air as frequently as this one. Miss Agnes Davis, currently just a name to me, would soon prove to be the very definition of a friend and ally.

Mysteries were brewing at the funeral home. I could feel them in the air.

IN MEMORIAM:
THE VISITOR

We knew nothing about him other than he was wholly fascinated with the dead. He was the Mr. Average sort, average in height and weight, and was middle-aged. He never wore a suit or a tie as a pretension, nor tried to pass himself off as a relative or a friend of the deceased's.

My father opened up shop at seven thirty each morning. When we had a body, the townspeople who couldn't call in at any other time dropped by before work to pay their respects. Sometimes they spent a moment in the chapel, but often they just signed the register and rushed out. As was customary, the deceased's family didn't arrive until after lunch.

By midmorning there was usually a lull in traffic. Like clockwork — and I wondered if he lurked around the corner waiting for people to leave — The Visitor appeared. He cast a long shadow on the sidewalk, and his lone figure seemed to creep up the front steps. After he nodded to my father, he proceeded to the chapel, walked straight to the casket, and stood before it, enthralled.

The rows of chairs set out for the family and friends were of no interest to him; he never sat down. If other people who actually knew the deceased strolled in while he was there, he stepped to one side whenever they approached the casket. The Visitor was careful not to be accused of dominating the view. He spoke to no one.

He wasn't a professional mourner, for his demeanor lacked any sign that he was emotionally affected by his visits. When he was alone in the chapel with the body, an air of steady coolness surrounded him, and held by his fascination, it seemed he did not breathe. He appeared absolutely rooted to the spot.

One day after the first few visits, my father opened the door to him and held out his hand.

"Good morning, Mr. . . ."

"Arnold, Mr. Arnold."

"How are you today, Mr. Arnold?"

"Fine, thank you." He walked on past my father.

When he crossed the threshold of the chapel, he strode over the invisible line where any small talk ended. The Visitor was safe, for he knew that out of respect for the dead, the undertaker would not pursue him with questions while he was in the chapel.

This then was the dance between the two men. One, who coveted anonymity, to be left alone with his obsession, and the other, who felt a little used and wanted to know more about the man who wished to remain anonymous. His name meant nothing to my father, and after a feeble investigation, no one seemed to know who he was or where he called home.

There was never any sound reason to ban the man from visiting. He timed his arrivals perfectly and was careful not to overstay his welcome. He never attempted to touch anything — or anyone. My father kept an eye on him, of course. I wondered if one day he might crack and try to climb on top of a closed casket or kiss a corpse or run out with a wreath of flowers in his arms, REST IN PEACE emblazoned across his chest. Sometimes, when the funeral home was busy like a train station with hats and coats flowing in and out, his mysterious bearing faded and he seemed entirely normal, just a regular visitor caught in the morning rush.

The Visitor and my father never became friends, never shared even the smallest of conversations. That's what made his presence so unsettling, and that for thirteen years he never missed a visitation until, one day, he disappeared.

We pondered what had happened to him and years later spoke of his probable death. I imagined his own portrait of repose: his face restored with cosmetics to appear alive, his closed eyes, his hands folded upon his chest. I wondered, too, if someone fixed a stare upon his corpse as he had upon so many others.

CHAPTER 4
THE WOMAN IN RED

On a raw January night in 1960, Miss Agnes Davis turned out the light in her office and locked the door of the business she'd owned and operated for over thirty years. Adjacent to her office, the massive doors to her warehouses filled with fertilizer were already bolted for the evening. She climbed into her odd-job man's farm truck and scarcely five minutes later thanked him for the ride and disappeared through the tall, white columns of her home.

She rattled around the spacious rooms of her antebellum mansion and turned on the lamps, fired up the furnace, and secured the doors. When all of this was completed, she reached for the decanter of fine Kentucky bourbon and poured herself a generous amount into a crystal glass. She thought of happier times, days unlike today, the first anniversary of the death of her only sibling, her much-loved brother, Urey. There were still a few things her wealth could not buy.

She stepped onto a red satin footstool and climbed into her imposing half-tester bed. The half canopy, covered in the same magnificently faded red satin fabric, was neatly ruched to create a swirling effect above her head.

Miss Agnes woke in the middle of the night feeling not quite right. The thought occurred to her that she might not have taken her medication correctly, or maybe she'd had a little too much bourbon. Perhaps the best thing to do was to go to the hospital. For the first time in a long time, she had a choice of whom to call. She could either call Alfred Deboe, whom she despised, or she could call that new young man in town.

My father, at this point only recently arrived in Jubilee, drove to Winter Street and pulled up to a beautiful, old Southern home. Not knowing his way around the place, he chose the front entrance. Quickly, he passed between the tall, white columns of the long porch and rang the bell. A short, rotund lady answered the door and introduced herself as Miss Agnes Davis. She was ready to go. She stood a little unsteadily, dressed as if she were going out for the day in a red coat, which was carelessly buttoned, carrying a bottomless red bag. Her hair was leaning toward one side. He'd seen this middle-of-the-night, disheveled look upon many occasions, but never had he seen it quite so vividly.

"Ma'am, I'm Frank Mayfield, and I'd be happy to take the cot out of the ambulance for you."

"Speak up, boy. I can't hear a word you're saying."

"Do you want the gurney, Miss Davis?" he yelled into the night.

"I can walk. Call me Miss Agnes."

"Well, Miss Agnes, let me take your bag for you then. Here, hold on to my arm. We'll take this real slow."

During Miss Agnes's lengthy hospital stay my father lost several death calls to Alfred Deboe. He discovered that not only had Deboe reaped the benefits of the hospital administrator's vendetta, he had also begun a campaign sending flowers, a dozen long-stemmed roses no less, to the patients my father had driven to the hospital. When the patients died, their families, who appreciated Deboe's thoughtful touch, chose him as their undertaker.

Deboe's steely grasp on the community alarmed my father, and it woke him from some idea he'd had of friendly, small-town competition. He felt compelled to do something, anything really, to create a neutralizing effect.

"You know, I've been thinking about that woman I picked up the other night, Miss Agnes Davis. I've been thinking about her lying in that hospital," my father told my mother one day. "We don't charge for ambulance calls — sometimes we get a little money for gas — and that's okay, we can't really charge if Deboe doesn't. But I'm tired of hauling patients around and not burying them. And I'm afraid she's going to die on me. I can't afford to send her long-stemmed roses, but I'm thinking I could send her some carnations. I heard she likes red — I could send her a dozen red carnations."

"Well, who is she?" my mother asked.

"I don't really know anything about her. But she's old enough to die."

Miss Agnes didn't die on him. She called him from her hospital bed and thanked him for the flowers. And wouldn't you know it? Carnations were her favorite; she didn't even like roses.

"When I get out of here," she roared through the phone, "I want you to take me home. It's got to be you and not someone who works for you. I don't want anyone else to take me."

A few days later my father was at the hospital and thought he would drop by to see Miss Agnes. The nurses told him she'd not received many visitors during her stay. She was an intensely private woman, and most people knew they would be unwelcome at her bedside. The farmers, her customers, would never dream of visiting her when she was indisposed.

But she wanted to see my father. He sat in the chair next to her bed and they spoke briefly. He told her where he was from, about his family, the brother who had died, and that his father had been a farmer.

"You are welcome in my home. I'd like you to come and see me when I'm feeling better," she told him.

Later he discovered that this was a most unusual invitation. Miss Agnes was not in the habit of inviting anyone to her home. She opened her kitchen to her customers' children one night a year on Halloween, when she felt like it, but few people were ever allowed past the kitchen into the main house.

In small increments of time my father and the lady who wore red came to know each other well. As every coin has two sides, so did Miss Agnes. One side, bright and shiny, spoke of her worth, although her exact worth was known to but a few. This side of the coin liked publicity, thrived on it even. She gave interviews to the fertilizer trade magazines at the drop of one of her favorite red hats. The town's newspaper was welcome to photograph her in her office surrounded by her unique collections of farming implements, toys, and antiques. Her door was open to the farmers from early morning to evening, six days a week, and during the planting season she bought pies and cakes and delivered them to the farmers' wives.

Turn that coin over and the markings weren't as clear. When she switched off the light to her office, stepped down the steps onto Main Street, and made her way home, which, until the time she met my father, was in the seat of a farm truck driven by her single employee, she shut the door against the town of Jubilee. Outside working hours she was a recluse, a loner, whose inner circle had dwindled to a handful of professionals: her doctor, lawyer, and banker were the remnants of a formerly active social life.

Over the years I overheard snippets of my parents' conversation about Miss Agnes. Around town, a rumor here, a remark there, filtered through to me. In this piecemeal way I came to understand the woman who became my friend and benefactor. Of all the gifts she gave me, the one I treasured most was a box of letters.

I imagined her, dwarfed behind her massive desk, an antique lamp sharing space with her manual typewriter, her hands stained from the carbon paper she used to make copies of the personal letters she typed to her sister-in-law. In the letters I subsequently read she wrote of her past; her fears and worries and her generosity toward her brother shone through.

I found a dusty, old scrapbook among the box of letters. In it were clippings, notes, poems, and memorabilia carefully glued onto the pages by Miss Agnes's mother, Laura. The mid to late nineteenth century was displayed and preserved in vibrant colors. The scrapbook contained mourning cards, vivid clippings of fashions of the times, obituaries of young children, and the announcement of their arrival in Jubilee.

I learned that in 1889, when she was four years old, Agnes, her younger brother, Urey, and her parents boarded the Princeton, Kentucky, train to Jubilee. For the next fifteen years the Davis family made their home among hundreds of boys. Agnes's father, Richard, had taken the position of superintendent of the Boarding Hall of Jubilee's Beacon College for Men. Agnes's mother faithfully kept a clipping of the announcement of their arrival.

Agnes did not sit on the sidelines while her brother reaped the benefits of living at the prestigious college. As a young girl she took lessons from a German boxing master, learned to shoot a pistol and race across the football field. If the boys ever got a little rough with her, she picked herself up and refused to shed a tear.

Her father eventually passed the bar exams and set up a law practice in Jubilee. As the Davis family's fortunes rose, they moved into a proper house, where Agnes became a young lady in Jubilee town society, joining the literature, music, and card clubs.

With every good and honorable intention she married a man from her mother's hometown and moved to Princeton to begin her new life. In a little over two weeks' time, Agnes took the train back to Jubilee — alone. She told friends she came home expressly to learn how to make biscuits. Agnes never returned to Princeton, and her husband never joined her in Jubilee. She was either divorced or the marriage was annulled, and the reason for the change of heart will never now be known. If she confided in my father about her short stint with matrimony, he never betrayed her confidence. She would never again marry; neither for the rest of her life would she attempt to cook a meal.

Not only did Miss Agnes forgo cooking, my father learned that she didn't find it necessary to learn to drive the big, black Buick that dominated her driveway. Her odd-job man drove her to and from work, but he was getting on in years and so was she. She was tired of climbing in and out of his farm truck, so she asked my father if he would mind taking her to work. No one walked in Jubilee unless they were poor.

Every morning after breakfast, except on Sundays, my father drove two blocks to Winter Street to pick up Miss Agnes and drove her all of seven blocks to her office on North Main Street. She sat in the front seat of whatever vehicle he was driving that day. At the end of the day, before he climbed the stairs to have supper with us, he drove back to her office and delivered her home. He checked on her house, made sure the locks were secure, then sat with her for a while and caught up on the day's news. In all, he spent thirteen years toing and froing, and hundreds of nights sitting in the grand old house that harbored no television or radio, listening to Miss Agnes's reflections and advice. I think he trusted her business acumen above that of all others and knew that it must have taken a brilliant mind and steely determination to become such an accomplished woman in an era that tolerated few like her. He was learning.

After her failed marriage, World War I broke out, and suddenly hundreds of young men made their exodus from Jubilee. Fiercely loyal and devoted to her brother, Urey, she dreaded hearing of where he would be posted. To her relief, he served as a first lieutenant in the Medical Corps and never left the States. As a psychiatrist, he treated the men who returned from Europe with shattered minds. Soon after Urey left Kentucky to serve in various hospitals around the States, their mother became ill and required constant nursing. Agnes cared for her mother for five years until her death.

At a time when Agnes naturally expected support and consolation from her brother, his letters became increasingly disturbing. Urey was shipped out to Alcatraz, the army prison that received the military's bad men. He worked with the men in the Pit, the nickname for the punishment cell. A flu epidemic suddenly raged through the prison and he watched men die like flies. The conditions in which they lived and the death of so many weakened his own mind and constitution while he administered to those who had already lost theirs.

Agnes and her father continued to live together in the house in Jubilee. She noticed his new and strange behavior, but thought it had something to do with the grief they both felt for Urey. She wasn't aware they were living on the precipice of scandal.

It might have been secret card games in a back room somewhere. It might have been the horses in this horse-worshipping state. Whatever his poison, Agnes discovered that her father, respected lawyer and former treasurer and secretary of Beacon College, had a terrible gambling problem.

It got as bad as it could get. He lost everything, practically the shirts off their backs. When he became ill, Agnes stood by him and cared for him as she had her mother. When he died, she was left alone to deal with the fallout.

It wasn't the selling of the family house, though that was as hard as anything else she'd ever done. It wasn't even the public auction, though seeing her piano and other furnishings being sold off was a humiliation she would never forget. What really got under her skin was the scandal it caused.

The eyes that shifted away from her, the whispers that were spoken just loud enough for her to hear, the friends who no longer came calling; slowly Jubilee began to feel claustrophobic and foreign. Certainly some still spoke to her, even remained friends with her, but mostly Agnes experienced rejection. Oh, how Jubilee loved its scandals! Quietly, the social avenues closed to her, backs were turned. To her further dismay, Urey never returned to her, or to Kentucky. He met a woman from New England who made conditions before accepting his proposal of marriage; she could just about stomach Florida, but would never follow him to Kentucky.

Agnes rented a room in a house on Ninth Street, a busy thoroughfare that ran from one side of Jubilee to the other. Her small, furnished room faced onto the street. She was hungry for the first time in her life and went without meals to pay her rent. Emptiness burned in her belly along with her desire to one day better her circumstances.

She paid her rent by taking a job as a stenographer for an old Southern judge. In the evenings Agnes used the time to become the first female reporter in Kentucky for The Mercantile Agency, which later became Dun & Bradstreet. Not content, and hungry for more, while working in the judge's office she began experimenting with another little side business.

Sensing a gaping hole in the agricultural-supplies market and determined to fill it, she began a study program. "Honey, I didn't know fertilizer from talcum powder," she once told a reporter.

She devoured every bit of available literature about fertilizer. She memorized it and practiced quoting long passages in her little room. A close friend advised her to get to know the farmers in the community. He told her the best way to recognize a farmer was by the mud on his heels. So she got out on the street and spent a lot of time looking for mud. When she saw a man who looked like a farmer, she stopped him and asked him for his business.

"Mud, sweat, and tears, that's how I built my business," she was fond of saying.

She strongly believed in advertising and marketing. While walking the sidewalks of Main Street, she thought of adopting the color red. Sure, she loved red; it was cheerful, rich, and aggressive, but more important, it was always terrifically noticeable. It soon became clear that Agnes had stealthily encroached upon the consciousness of the town; no one would ever again see her dressed in any color but red.

The farmers of Jubilee began to spread the word that Miss Agnes had a knack for recommending fertilizers that achieved results. She talked a blue streak about the benefits of Harvest King or "Prolific — the fertilizer with extra producing power!" She reeled off the alchemy of the marriage of fertilizer to soil.

"At first," she said, "only a few listened. But then, as the results began to show, boy, honey, didn't I start to sell it!"

During the planting season she sold fertilizer to farmers on credit until their crops came in, and she carried their account without charging interest. She was better than a walking, talking Visa card.

Miss Agnes's business grew to such an extent that she waved good-bye to stenography and eventually to Dun & Bradstreet. She became the first female fertilizer dealer in the state and one of the first women in the country to own and operate her own dealership. Her reputation spread past the borders of Jubilee into the county and throughout Kentucky and Tennessee. She moved offices three times, outgrowing each one until she settled into an office and two warehouses on North Main Street. She acquired enough space from which to sell well over five thousand tons of fertilizer a year, which she did easily.

Business was good, but she still lived in the room in the house on Ninth Street. Elvis Perry filled her thermos full of coffee each night and gave her scraps of bread with which to feed the birds. She saved every penny she earned, for she was driven by one purpose, one notion that occupied her every waking hour. From her window she could see the corner of Winter Street and the side lawn of the antebellum mansion that she coveted.

Miss Agnes was resolved that one day she would own the most beautiful home in Jubilee and regain the status her family had held before her father's downfall. She would not have just any home, but a home that was unique to Jubilee, a house with a story built into its foundations and a historical past. She continued to work late into the evening, six days a week, and on many Sundays she heard the church bells ringing from her office desk. Comforts that she could easily afford were not a part of her life, and she scrimped and saved as if she remained the pauper she had been.

Some in Jubilee, old friends, couldn't quite give her the credit she was due — not yet. Her reputation was not restored; in fact, they thought the Agnes Davis they once knew was verging on eccentric: the red clothes, behaving like a man with all this fertilizer business, riding around in that farm truck. No, Miss Agnes was failing miserably in the eyes of Jubilee's social elite.

In the early 1950s, in a splendid moment of synchronicity, the man who owned the mansion was ready to sell and Miss Agnes was at last ready to buy. She wrote a check for $40,000 — then slipped another forty grand in cash under the table. This scandalous sum would remain a secret.

Miss Agnes had purchased not only a house, but also a piece of Jubilee's history, and indeed the country's.

Major Richard Bibb, a Revolutionary War officer, was one of the wealthiest men in western Kentucky and was said to be of unimpeachable character. Also a Methodist preacher, he owned a vast amount of land and almost one hundred slaves. In 1821, a year after he built a new town home for his wife, Major Bibb drew up a list of his slaves and the value of each, from $600 to $50.

One frosty day eight years later, Major Bibb, an old man, stood in the wood-yard with his hands uplifted and a Bible and a hymnal placed on an upturned barrel beside him and asked a blessing upon his slaves who were gathered around him. He read a chapter from the Bible and led them in a hymn. The old man had congregated his slaves so that he could publicly say good-bye to the twenty-nine of them who were going to be set free. They were to be transported in wagons to Clarksville, Tennessee, where they would board a steamboat to New Orleans and then a sailing ship to Liberia.

He wanted to send all of his slaves to Africa, but didn't want to send any away who had family members who belonged to other masters. This act of conscience occurred thirty-two years before the nation fought its first battle in the Civil War.

Richard Jr., the eldest of the Bibb sons, became a merchant. The youngest son, George, became a U.S. senator and secretary of the treasurer under President Tyler. Unlike his brothers, John — or Jack, as he liked to be called — was not ambitious. He moved to Frankfort, Kentucky, became a member of the bar, and practiced law for two years before retiring. Jack was past eighty years old when he began giving his lettuce to his friends. How long he worked on his lettuce or how he perfected it is not known, but everyone agreed that Mr. Bibb's lettuce was the finest they had ever eaten. People simply called it Bibb lettuce because Jack gave it to them.

Excluding the twenty-nine slaves who were shipped to Liberia, many of Major Bibb's remaining slaves settled on the two plots of land bequeathed to them, located farther north in the county, and called both Bibbtown. One afternoon one of the descendants of Bibb's slaves walked into Miss Agnes's office to buy a bag of fertilizer. As was her custom, she began a conversation, and she soon learned his history. He became a loyal customer and one day presented her with a black cauldron that had hung from the hearth of Major Bibb's cookhouse. Miss Agnes took the pot home and hung it in the hearth in her kitchen, the same hearth that had been its home for well over a hundred years.

Now that she finally owned a big, fine house, Miss Agnes set about indulging in her passion for collecting antiques with which to fill it. Diligently she planned the remodeling and decorating of her new home in much the same way that she began her business. She researched, quizzed people about, and breathed antiques. She became the kind of creature who found more solace in objects than in people. Then, here they came, seeping out of the woodwork, knocking on the door, stopping her in the street. The people who had ostracized her suddenly swarmed to her like annoying little bees. Now that she lived in the most beautiful house in Jubilee, now that she was a connoisseur in antique furniture, everyone wanted to be her friend again. Completely transparent in their intentions and not at all concerned by that, they smiled at her, flattered her, and even stepped aside for her squat, red-clothed figure as she walked around the town square.

But Miss Agnes had settled scores inside her, where it mattered. The people who'd turned their backs, the people who controlled the social hierarchy and moral views of Jubilee, were like the dead to her.

When my father first met Miss Agnes, her brother had been dead for only a year. His death followed a long illness and was difficult. Urey's wife and Miss Agnes exchanged letters in which thanks were expressed for Miss Agnes's generous gifts of money, presents, convalescent equipment . . . anything he or his wife required. I wondered afterward, had Urey still been alive, if she would have been as taken with my father. Whenever the three of us were together, I felt she treated him like a son, although I think he also reminded her of her brother when he was young and healthy.

No matter how busy my father was at the funeral home, he made sure she was safely home each evening. This unlikely pair, the handsome new funeral director and Jubilee's most eccentric established character, formed a strong alliance. A day came when they realized a closer relationship existed and a pact was made. My father had not only found his ally, he had found a friend in the deepest sense of the word. The unspoken agreement in our family was that when my father was with Miss Agnes, he was all hers.

Now there were five of us — five females who claimed ownership of the man who spent equal time with the dead and the living. My mother appeared to tolerate this arrangement, with no resistance to sharing her husband. I never heard her complain to my father or anyone else regarding the demands that the woman in red made upon him. My mother's acceptance set an example to us, the children. Miss Agnes was now a curiously remote part of our family.

CHAPTER 5
MY MISS HAVISHAM

I first met Miss Agnes on Halloween when I was six. I'd badgered my father to paint my face green with his mortuary cosmetics. I wanted to be the Wicked Witch of the West.

I stood in the kitchen in my underwear and undershirt. I often got dressed in the kitchen as it somehow came to be the room in which either Belle or my mother caught me as I walked through on my way somewhere else.

My father answered, staring out the window well clear of the kitchen traffic, "You can't have a painted face. You're going to have to wear the mask that came with the costume."

"But I can't breathe in it! It makes my face sweat!"

"I'm taking you somewhere tonight before you go trick-or-treating and you can't go with me with a painted face."

"Oh! Where're we going?"

"First, we're going to take Belle home, then we're going to meet a special friend of mine." He looked at his watch.

Belle stood by, holding one of my Sunday dresses.

"Come on now. I gots your best dress ready." Belle held it up at arm's length.

"Gosh, Belle, there's such a lot of starch in this dress. You could kill somebody with the hem on this thing." She raised a sea of crinolines over my head and shimmied it down my body. "It itches like crazy."

"Hush up. You's goin' to meet a fine lady."

"What lady? And what makes her fine?"

"I don't know, she jest fine." Clap. Clap. "Put these here shoes on. Your mama cleaned them today. Look how they shines." Clap. Clap.

"Are Thomas and Evelyn going with us?" I held on to Belle's arms and stepped into the patent leather shoes.

"No," my father said impatiently. He was ready to go. Being overly punctual we always left fifteen minutes earlier than the time he originally appointed.

Thomas would take me trick-or-treating later. He had his driver's license now, though how he lived through our father's driving lessons, I did not know. One day my father insisted that Thomas learn how to back the hearse into the garage. Thomas had a headache and told him he didn't feel like it. But my father wouldn't hear of it, so, bang, Thomas hit the wooden post inside the garage and peeled the chrome strip off the hearse. My father hit the roof, but Thomas just looked at him and said, "I told you I didn't feel like doing it."

My brother didn't mind taking me places and doing things like making Chef Boyardee pizzas on Saturdays. I was impressed with the things Thomas could do. He studied all the time and read books about history and things I couldn't pronounce. I was sorry he wasn't coming with us. I knew that if he were to meet this important lady, he would know exactly what to say to her — he was a born diplomat — and when we arrived home, some keen observation would spill effortlessly from him.

But I was relieved that Evelyn wasn't coming. I'd never seen Evelyn with a book in her hand. She'd probably throw it at me, anyway. Once I stood at the doorway of her room while she practiced dancing to Motown records. When she saw me, she picked up a stack of 45s and threw them straight at me, then slammed the door in my face. Evelyn never missed a dance at Teen Town, a place that sounded exciting, but disappointingly was nothing more than a large room in a building where dances were held. It was the highlight of the weekend — for those who were allowed to dance. Whether dancing was evil was still debated with intensity in many homes.

My elder sister argued a lot and was never where she was supposed to be. The rule of being quiet seemed to be the only rule Evelyn was made to follow. She had to stop playing her records and dancing whenever we had a body, and I was secretly content that the house rule made her cross at something other than me.

"What about Jemma?" I held on to the kitchen counter while Belle tugged at my dress.

No, he said, and my mother wasn't going either. She had just arrived home with a small, red package under her arm, which she quickly handed over to my father.

"You be good tonight and mind your daddy," she said to me. Well, this was indeed strange. My father bit his nails and she straightened the bow on the back of my dress once more. They exchanged glances, and it seemed to me that an awful lot of fuss was being made over meeting this friend. I had no idea why, but I was certain that both my father and my mother wanted the meeting to go well.

Belle sat up front in the station wagon and I sat in the back, where I pretended to be chauffeured. Belle lived in the Bottom, often referred to as Black Bottom. I thought it was an ugly name and I told her so. Well, she said, it's the lowest point of Jubilee and that's a fact. She was speaking geographically, but she also refused to think derogatorily of the Bottom. The Bottom was only a few blocks from Main Street. Everything in Jubilee was close to everything else, but invisible lines separated good neighborhoods from bad ones, black from white, doctors from nurses.

My father drove slowly down Fifth Street. Some of the houses looked like shacks with odd pieces of furniture such as beat-up sofas and chifforobes piled up on the front porches. Big, fancy cars hugged the curbs in front of most of the dilapidated houses. Belle complained about them.

"Humph. They all gots them big cars and big TVs, but they sho don't paint they's houses."

Belle had no car, owned a small TV, and made sure her house always had a respectable coat of white paint.

We pulled up to her small clapboard house, neat and precise in its dimensions.

The front yard smelled of freshly cut grass, and black iron pots of red geraniums flanked her front door. Belle wouldn't let us walk her to the door. She was funny that way.

As she prepared to step out of the car, she asked, "You gettin' up front wit yer daddy?"

"No, Belle, I'm staying in the backseat. He's gonna chauffeur me."

We waited for her to wave and disappear into her home.

We continued our drive through the Bottom and past the Lambert Funeral Home.

Tennessee Lambert was Jubilee's sole funeral director to the black community. He did things his way, and families put their complete trust in him. The mourning period for one death could occupy an entire week at Tennessee's funeral parlor. Three or four days passed before arrangements were made, then visitation lasted for another three or four days. As caring as my father was, I don't think he would ever have had the patience to support such extended mournings.

On the day of a typical funeral in the Bottom, Tennessee drove up to the front door of the bereaved in his big, pink Cadillac. Friends and relatives would gather outside the house and form a procession behind the car; most would be on foot. He drove slowly through the streets of the Bottom to his funeral home, pulling the congregation along with him. Singing, shouting, and arm waving dominated the scene as he paraded the family to their seats in the small parlor. No one was uncomfortable with passionate displays of emotion. The service carried a heightened sense of drama; color splashed from ladies' large hats and men's suave three-piece suits. Many people would pass out before the day was over, overwhelmed as they were with emotion and grief.

People assumed that Tennessee was loaded; the hoi polloi were certain that he lived the high life. After all, he owned the funeral business of the entire black community. People were wrong. Tennessee was always scrambling for money, trying to find a way to keep his business going. His community was poor, full of men and women who cut tobacco and cleaned buildings and homes, and most had no insurance or savings. Money trickled down through the years, but often he would not be paid. Tennessee never refused to bury anyone.

It was a secret to most people that sometimes my father drove over to Tennessee's place and embalmed black people. When Tennessee was low on casket stock or was missing a particular color, he visited our funeral home to select one for his client. Many times when the delivery of a supply of some sort was late, my father would drive down to the Bottom and borrow what he needed from Tennessee. The public did not know of this goodwill and sharing pact because both blacks and whites would have been appalled.

As we emerged from the Bottom, a short drive took us to the opposite realm of the residential spectrum and to the biggest, whitest house I'd ever seen. It made me feel like I didn't know my neighborhood well because this house occupied half a block on Seventh and Winter Streets and I'd never noticed it. My father pulled right up into a small driveway on the side of the house as if he'd been there many times before. A black Batmobile was in the driveway.

"Whose car is that?" I asked.

"It belongs to Miss Agnes."

"You know it looks like the Batmobile, don't you?"

"It's a 1960 Buick Electra 225. The interior is in perfect condition."

"It has wings. It's the Batmobile."

"It's a beauty."

"It's the Bat—"

"Hush."

The blacktopped drive was nestled between immense evergreen trees and a tall, white stone statue of a demure-looking female stood on a lawn enclosed by cast-iron fencing.

"Before we go in, I want you to remember that Miss Agnes is half-deaf. She can't hear thunder, so you've really got to speak up. Don't touch anything unless she asks you to or puts something in your hands. And I've got something for you to give to her," my father told me.

"What is it?"

He showed me the box my mother had brought home wrapped in fine red paper, even though it was Halloween and I thought it should have been orange paper.

"Red handkerchiefs. You're to give them to Miss Agnes. Now we're going inside to her kitchen. On Halloween she decorates her kitchen and invites her farmers' children to come and see it."

"So there'll be other children here?" I was trying to keep up.

"Well, no. Not while you're here. They'll come later and line up outside."

I didn't grasp why I was allowed this private audience with the Queen of Halloween. It made me a sweaty-palms kind of nervous. "Why aren't Thomas and Evelyn

163

with us? Don't they want to see the decorations?"

"She just asked for you. Maybe they're a little too old."

Somewhat uncomfortably I followed my father to the back entrance of the mansion. The autumn light had faded and Halloween was to begin here, in a place unknown to me. There was no moon at all, and only the shrill sound of the katydids serenaded us to the door. The stiff dress and the fussing and perfecting of bows and hair left me feeling like a turkey at Christmas, trussed and ready for the big day.

When my father opened the back door, it jangled with so much racket that I covered my ears. I looked up to see several old bells hanging from the top of the door. They clanged again when my father closed it. I thought of Marley's ghostly chains.

I looked for Miss Agnes. She didn't come immediately.

We walked through a short hallway with white brick walls on either side. Plastic skeletons hung from the low ceiling; we moved through cobwebs as authentic carriage lanterns lit the way forward. Antique ceramic jugs lined both sides of the floor in the hallway like little soldiers guarding the path. Old horse bits and bridles, horseshoes, and blackened iron farming implements jutted out from the white brick walls as we made our way along the passage. We trod upon a worn Oriental runner under which I could feel the hard brick floor. The hallway was frigid. It was a short, endless walk. I sure hoped my father knew what he was doing bringing me here.

She stood in the kitchen doorway in all of her red glory, clashing with the orange glow of the room behind her. My father had told me there was no one in Jubilee who could remember when Miss Agnes began to wear red and only red. I quickly drank her in. Even her stockings were red, and they fell around her skinny ankles like loose nylon bands. Her neck was wrapped in strands of red beads that fell to her ample but fallen bosom. Red bangles hung from her wrists, and her fists were planted firmly on her square hips. The sharp points of her flat leather shoes were aimed straight at me. Her shoes were . . . well, yes, red. She was smiling, but she was scary. I hoped that would change. Deafness was almost upon her now, and as she'd lost more and more of the sound of her own voice, the years seemed to have layered it with coarseness.

"Why, honey child, just look at you! Why, you just come right over here and see Miss

Agnes." She spoke so loudly I felt the vibration resonating in the room. She sounded like she'd been hitting the sauce — her voice was slurred and gravelly.

My father leaned over to me. "This is Miss Agnes Davis. Say hello to her."

"Hello," I said quite meekly. I knew exactly how Dorothy felt upon meeting the great Wizard.

"She can't hear you, speak up."

"Hi, Miss Agnes. Happy Halloween!" I screamed at her.

My father gently nudged me to approach her. As I stepped slowly with one foot in front of the other, she shuffled toward me, leading with her portly belly. How like a man she looked, a man with a penchant for women's clothing. Her face was handsome in its features: dark, arched brows, a strong, straight nose, her lips and cheeks devoid of color. Her manner was supremely confident. She had not a whisper of delicacy about her. Her eyelids drooped a little and turned down at the corners like a bloodhound's, so that even though she smiled, and her eyes sparkled, I thought they looked a little sad. A crown of yellow hair, which some say was washed too infrequently, was piled around her head. She certainly did not join the beauty-parlor set who gossiped under the dryers. That wasn't her style. She attended to her hair herself, and it seemed that she aimed for the top of her head when she fixed and fooled with it, but instead it fell around her ears in a wavy mass. Her hair was similar to the texture of a bird's nest, with stray locks like twigs sticking out here and there.

"You'd think Miss Agnes would have plenty of bathrooms in that big ole house. My God, does she ever take a bath?" whispered the people of Jubilee. From that rumor that took hold easily as rumors usually did, the subject of Miss Agnes's toilette hung in the air. Some people mistook different for dirty.

Miss Agnes was clean. I know this because when she bent down and squeezed me to her and gave me a peck on the cheek, I felt her soft face against mine and she smelled faintly of talc. I had developed a highly acute sense of smell — embalming fluid, refrigerated roses, Old Spice, and lavender water surrounded me daily. I knew what the earth smelled like six feet deep, so I was pretty sure I could pigeonhole an unbathed woman.

All of my preconceived notions vanished. Her face was warm and the saggy skin on her cheek was soft against my own. Her hair, when it brushed against the side of my face, felt cottony. It didn't reek of hairspray and she wore no cheap perfume. The jacquard fabric of her dress, which initially looked coarse and stiff, was actually smooth and comforting when it folded around me in her embrace. She allowed a modicum of femininity to ooze out of her, perhaps carefully doled out for lack of a bigger supply.

Well, I thought. Since I had survived being so close to her, surely I could survive the rest of the evening.

"Come in. Come on in here, child. I want to show you all my things."

I hesitantly followed her into the kitchen. I kept an eye on my father and hoped he would remember to instruct me should I violate some kind of protocol.

In the middle of the kitchen floor stood a harvest table heavily laden with so many items that it looked in danger of buckling from the weight. Windup toys noisily marched across the table while others stood silently waiting to be noticed. A pale-colored monkey wearing a square, red hat played a set of drums that were strapped to its chest. Tap, tap, tap, he drummed as his head moved from side to side. Several jack-o'-lanterns cast their rich, orange light over the room. Miss Agnes's brown-spotted hand picked up a noisemaker from the table, the old tin kind with black cats and witches painted on it, and she twirled its wooden handle. It made a smaller noise than it should have and my father laughed. I laughed because he did and in relief that something horrid didn't come from the strong shake she gave it.

"You can keep that," she said to me.

"Thanks, I'll take it to school and show it to everybody."

"What'd she say, Frank?"

My father said to me softly, "Remember to speak up."

"Thank you, Miss Agnes," I screamed. This was exhausting.

She led me around the table to the hearth, a great stone fireplace where the original black cauldron from the pre–Civil War era hung heavily in the air. The hearth explained the brick walls in the passageway: this room was once separate from the house — it was the cookhouse from where the slaves of this mansion prepared meals for their master.

Tonight, ghosts and goblins, suspended from the chimney, attached to almost invisible strings, danced around the cauldron. Life-size paper witches stood in the hearth. The crones looked as if they were stirring a brew in the kettle. This grand effort was an eerie display of everything I thought Halloween could be.

Miss Agnes and I shouted at each other in short conversation as she thrust unusual objects in my hand and explained their origins; all the while she calculated my attention and interest.

"Are you going trick-or-treating tonight?" she bellowed.

"Yes, ma'am."

"What will you be?"

"A witch."

"A what?"

"A witch," I yelled.

Miss Agnes turned to my father. "What did she say?"

"She's going to dress up like a witch." He was yelling, too.

"Oh, well then, honey, let me show you something."

She moved toward the corner of the hearth and I saw it before she touched it. It was a broom. Not a firm, yellow straw broom like the one Belle used, but a scraggly-looking thing. The handle was crooked and made of a naked piece of wood.

"One of my farmers made it for me." She held it up for me to see.

I was speechless. She looked too witchlike for me to respond.

My father began to laugh. Miss Agnes looked puzzled. He leaned over closer to her ear. "I think she thinks you may hop on it for a ride tonight."

"What? Oh!" She cackled loudly.

I saw a side of my father I hadn't seen since his mother was alive. He held Miss Agnes in such high regard that his personality receded into the mellow light of the kitchen. The respectful stance that he reserved for grieving families was magnified for this lady in red. He seemed to anticipate her movements. She was at ease with his attention, comfortable with his deference to her. I thought of my mother and her nervous fussiness about this evening. The easygoing relationship between Miss Agnes and my father held a light to the wall of tension that sometimes existed between my parents. There were no screaming matches, no slamming doors, but instead, an absence of lightheartedness that ended in silence between them and penetrated a house that already lay under a blanket of quiet. It felt as if there might have been something wrong, some large thing askew, but I couldn't imagine what, which left me confused and wondering.

I turned to look at the rest of the kitchen. From the tall ceiling hung an old shade with a solitary bulb. The walls were clean, but a faded, dull yellow. The kitchen had no oven or stove; only a small, one-burner hot plate rested on the counter next to a porcelain sink from which ancient taps sprouted. The refrigerator was old and hummed in a distressed way. What? No biscuits in the oven? No chicken frying on the stove? No pies set out to cool? What kind of kitchen was this? I imagined it without the drama of goblins and the brightness of the orange pumpkins. I thought that it might be a sad and neglected kitchen, for Miss Agnes never cooked a day in her life and no one ever shared her table. It didn't occur to me that she might prefer the solitude.

My father removed the prettily wrapped gift from his jacket pocket and gave it to me to give to her. So began the tradition.

Miss Agnes and I would exchange gifts whenever we met. My mother stocked a supply of red linen handkerchiefs; my father picked up bits of red jewelry, a pin or a bracelet whenever he came across them. These I would present to her proudly, as if I had thought of them myself. In turn she gave me a collection of gifts over the years, items that I hoarded and placed around me until they were battered and threadbare, or until it was too embarrassing to admit an attachment. A doll, a ruby birthstone ring, a dress, a book; the mementos reminded me of her, as if I needed a single thing more than her image.

When we said our good-byes and spoke of promises to meet again, my father told her he would be back later to help her with the visitors. The rest of the house was closed off tonight, and he would stand guard over the door that led to the treasures in her mansion.

In the safety of the car, for I didn't want my words trailing through the Halloween night air, I asked him what had been worrying me all night. "Good Lord, Daddy. Where did you find her? And does she own some farmers or something?"

"They own each other."

I didn't know what that meant, but I had other questions, too. "Was she drunk?"

He looked at me oddly. "How would you know if she was? Have you ever seen anyone drunk?"

"On TV. Red Skelton plays a drunk."

"No, he doesn't, he plays a bum."

"Lucy got drunk on Vitameatavegamin."

"Miss Agnes was not drunk."

"Is she married?"

"Nope."

"Does she live in that big old house by

herself?"

"Yep."

"Isn't she afraid?"

He laughed. "No, Miss Agnes isn't afraid of much of anything, except maybe getting old. The next time she wants to see you, I'll take you to her office."

Miss Agnes and I held standing dates on our birthdays and holidays, and at other times she regularly called for me whenever it took her fancy. My father always accompanied me, and if there was an explanation as to why she insisted upon my presence to the exclusion of my siblings', I would never hear it. Another unspoken agreement was set: Miss Agnes was to be my Miss Havisham. A formal, yet special relationship between the two of us was formed, and for whatever reason, my father and mother and Miss Agnes all quietly agreed on this.

In an effort to please him, I never complained about the nerve-wracking, shouty meetings. I gave her hours of my best behavior without much fuss, for despite her rather gruff exterior I knew she didn't mean to be intimidating — and eventually I found her infinitely fascinating. Her work encroached upon a man's world in her wildly unique way. Something about observing her was deeply satisfying. I was still at an age where most of my time was spent in the company of adults. Totty, Belle, and the Shroud Lady were to some degree self-sufficient women. But I'd never met anyone like Miss Agnes, someone who despite her hardship had triumphed without sacrificing her individuality. In only a few years I would draw strength from their examples when it was my turn to make difficult decisions.

IN MEMORIAM:
HONEY PRATT

More than anyone else, an undertaker must act as a referee to family feuds. People don't seem to misbehave in front of their pastor, or even their lawyer. They tend to hold it together for their reputations' sake in the company of other professionals. But when it comes to death, all bets are off.

In one corner is the wife of the deceased, who is separated from her husband, and in another corner is the girlfriend, who has been living with the deceased for the last year or two. One of an undertaker's duties is to know the law. The law states the wife is legally entitled to arrange the funeral as she sees fit and even to bar entry to the funeral home to those who are unwanted. But angry, hurt, and grieving people don't care one damn about the law. They come flying out of their corners, fighting, unleashing emotions that have been pent up for years, decorum out the window.

When Honey Pratt died, all hell broke loose. Her daughters had stifled most of their jealousy and dislike for one another to stay in their mother's good graces. But now, the big vat of ill will and emotions that had simmered for years had boiled over. The Pratt sisters were at each other's throats. They sat in the funeral-home office with their father between them. Mr. Pratt, a widower for less than eight hours, made a Herculean effort to prevent a full-blown catfight.

It began in the casket room.

"She'd want the blue one," said Jessie.

"Are you out of your mind? Mama hated that color of blue, and anyway, her favorite color was pink," said Myrna.

"Girls, she told me she wanted white. That's what she's going to get."

"White is boring. We can't put her in a white casket. She's too pale. Unless Mr. Mayfield here is going to give her a tan or something," Jessie snorted.

"How dare you say something like that! I swear, you're as ignorant as the day is long. Don't you have any respect for Daddy's feelings?" Myrna was near tears.

"Well you're a fine one to talk about Daddy's

feelings."

"Jessie, Myrna, that's enough. White, Mr. Mayfield, we'll take the white one, please."

My father escorted them back to his office. He quickly changed the subject to funeral music, hoping that the casket selection was final. These were the type of people who would go back and forth, calling in the middle of the night to say, no, it's the blue one we want. He wanted to avoid moving Honey from casket to casket, tugged back and forth between the whims of the quarreling sisters. He used the most soothing voice he could muster to discuss music and flowers.

Under her breath Jessie broke the sisters' silence. "She meant for me to have them."

"No, she didn't, they're mine," Myrna said.

"Sorry, Mr. Mayfield." Mr. Pratt turned to the women. "This is not the time or place. Stop acting like you're twelve years old."

Both sisters were easily in their thirties.

"Mama told me before you were ever born that all her jewelry would be mine someday," said Jessie.

"Exactly. Before I was born, but not after. You know she meant for us to split it. And I'm taking that cameo, that's mine."

My father let them quibble for a short time, then calmly shuffled a few papers, cleared his throat, and told them that they had just a few more details to attend and then they could go home and rest. Rest seemed to be the magic word, and as if he were Rip van Winkle, he led them through the remaining funeral arrangements.

Later that day while upstairs with his Alka-Seltzer, he relayed these events to my mother.

"Do you think that's the end of it, or do you think there's more to come?" she asked.

"I don't know. Honey didn't leave a will, so I don't know how they're going to sort it all out. I'd be embarrassed if my girls ever behaved like that in public. They'll be back in a couple of hours to bring her clothes. I hope they don't rip them to shreds before I can get my hands on them."

The Pratts came bustling through the door later that afternoon in a wind of fury. Myrna's and Jessie's faces were blotchy red messes, and Mr. Pratt's jaw was set like a stony profile on Mount Rushmore.

"I've made a decision, Mr. Mayfield." He opened a paper bag from the Kroger grocery store and presented a jewelry box to my father. "I want you to put this in Honey's casket. Will you do that for me?"

Myrna's and Jessie's bulging eyes followed the box, and when it left their father's hands, the girls crumbled.

My father, who felt he'd been handed a time

bomb, nevertheless handled the object of contention with firm hands. "Yes, of course," he made a point of saying, "whatever you want. It's your decision." He avoided the sisters' glares.

"You can't do that! That's mine!"

"No, it's mine!"

Mr. Pratt turned on his daughters with the wrath of a man who'd withstood years of bitterness between them. "I am sick to death! Do you hear me? Sick to death of you two and your god-awful quarrels. If your poor mama could see you. Now shut up! Shut up, the both of you!"

The next day they arrived for the private viewing before the doors were open to the public. My father prepared for the worst. He gave the family plenty of time and space, stepped out of the chapel to leave them to it. There were no screams, hardly a whimper.

Mr. Pratt stepped away and found my father in the foyer. "She looks real good, Mr. Mayfield. Thank you. And I apologize. I can't control those girls, never could."

"Well, Mr. Pratt, I've got three girls of my own. It's a terrible time for you, so don't think another thing about it. As long as you're pleased with everything, then forget the rest."

It seemed Myrna and Jessie dressed for the funeral in competition with one another, each in long, flowing skirts, dark navy, frilly blouses, and matching high heels. The funeral service went without a hitch. The Pratt sisters sat dry-eyed and motionless as the preacher spoke of Honey's charity work and her love for her community. As if they had X-ray vision, they directed their searing gaze toward the foot of the casket where the box of jewels lay concealed at Honey's feet.

After the service ended, the family traditionally walked by the casket to say their last good-bye before the casket was closed. The congregation remained seated as my father led the Pratts to the casket, and just as he thought they would make it to the cemetery unscathed, Jessie raised her arm to her forehead and fell to the floor in a badly acted faint. The crowd gasped. Myrna threw her pocketbook down, lifted her floor-length skirt, and straddled her sister. She grabbed Jessie by the collar of her blouse and reared back and slapped her in the face.

"Get up from there, damnit, we don't have time for this!"

As my father moved toward the hellcats, Mr. Pratt reached for Myrna. Jessie rolled over and sat up. The sisters brushed themselves off and the men ushered them out of the chapel as if nothing extraordinary had occurred.

At the cemetery, as Honey Pratt's white casket was lowered into her grave, Myrna and Jessie wept. My father thought they would maybe someday weep for their mother, but he knew that on this afternoon they wept only for the jewelry box that was descending into the red earth forever.

Old hurts, sore souls, and the sneaky destiny of jealousy are difficult to control when death is in the air. They build and build until, in the wake of electrifying air, they either combust or they are buried deeper than the grave. We laughed in disbelief at some of the squabbles, until one unwelcome day, the story of the fighting Pratt sisters would be a painful reminder of a darker time when Evelyn and Jemma and I would have no amusing memories to recall.

CHAPTER 6
NAPPING IN THE CASKET ROOM

Many days the daunting task of waking Evelyn in the morning fell to me. Oh, what a joyous task it was. Even in her sleep my sister looked angry, unsettled. It was the only time I could comfortably watch her without her snapping, "What are you looking at?" Evelyn often made me think she was awake and then went back to sleep when I left the room. But I was under strict orders not to let her fall asleep again, so I stood there, staring. She slept late on Saturdays and woke at the last possible moment on school days. My mother allowed her these long lie-ins but woke the rest of us with a drill sergeant's precision. I wondered if this was a preventive measure, so that we wouldn't get any ideas about following suit. She eventually gave up on any concerted or effective methods of discipline for her eldest daughter.

Evelyn always slept in her bra and in full

makeup. She was too lazy to wash her face before she went to bed, so the pillowcases were soiled with traces of mascara and Pan-Cake makeup that was the texture of putty and came in a white plastic tube. She wore no lipstick, but smeared the Pan-Cake on her lips, a mystery my entire family tried to unravel to no conclusion. Enamored of her tweezers, she plucked her eyebrows. At first she left a quarter of an inch, then she plucked most of that out as well until barely anything was left. She didn't draw them back on, preferring the bare look. She was fiercely loyal to these curious beauty habits, and despite all her efforts, she had an attractive face. Her lips were full and well shaped, which I, with borderline-thin lips, envied. To then see her cover them with the Pan-Cake makeup was bewildering. In spite of her ghost-colored lips she had a pretty smile, almost dazzling, though not often seen.

Evelyn frequently slept with one arm raised above her head. Sprawled across her bed in her white bra and smudged makeup, she looked like the cover of a detective comic. A dark brown mole resided on the underside of her arm near her armpit. She called it her "beauty mark" and made much of it, explaining that only beautiful people have them and that hers was even more special because of where it was placed. I believed her and was devastated that I had no beauty mark and was therefore never destined to be beautiful. I pointed out that I had a spray of freckles across my nose, but she quickly cut me down by telling me that freckles were undesirable and common. Many mornings I stood staring at her beauty mark, willing it to fall off, hoping that she would scratch it off in her sleep.

Waking Evelyn was like disturbing a grizzly in the middle of winter. The arm with the beauty mark came down and brushed the thick, chestnut-brown strands of hair from her face. The mascara smeared around her eyes made her look as if she were peering from two large buckeyes. The first words out of her mouth most mornings were "Go away."

Evelyn had always acted upon her whims without a thought of any consequences. While we watched our home movies on the large screen, Evelyn's young history leaked out. Popcorn, corpses, and Evelyn's angry, little image were our Saturday-evening fare.

"There goes Evelyn again," my father said as we watched an eight-year-old version furiously stomping away from a family gathering.

A deep, guttural sound erupted from Evelyn as she viewed herself — it may have been a laugh.

More moving pictures of Evelyn floated by as she wrestled with her cousins, shoved Thomas, cocked a BB gun, tore through her Christmas presents; there was nothing calm about her. I imagined her bucking like a wild horse in harness, struggling to gain freedom. An impatient or harsh word from my father usually tamed her. She sulked when he was angry with her, whereas she was indifferent to my mother's frustrations.

On this morning I didn't care if she woke. It was the first day back to school for me and I was anxious to get there. Who knew if Evelyn would go to school anyway? Once in high school she'd skipped classes with little or no consequence. Jubilee was too small for truancy to go unnoticed, and she was always found and given a token punishment, but she couldn't have cared less. She wasn't academically motivated and had no particular interests or hobbies. I was usually out the door before Evelyn had a chance to smear her lips with more makeup after breakfast. I felt I'd already lived an entire day by the time I left for school.

I was old enough to walk there on my own now. As usual, Belle put too much starch in my dress and I crinkled and crackled all over the place. When I first attended school and the teacher enforced quiet time, I remember thinking, *oh that's something I know how to do.* I switched off easily while others fidgeted and giggled. I often walked away from the playground covering my ears because the screaming and shouting was too loud for me, feeling isolated and yet buffered. Those first silences I endured as a young child created an organic need. I grew up feeling split down the middle with a partial stake in the robustness of life, and another that needed to retreat to silence and observation, to be alone and undisturbed. It was impossible to claim anonymity in our tightly knit community and as the years passed the more I felt the walls of the town closing in.

The morning was so warm there didn't seem to be enough air for the twenty or so fourth graders in my classroom. Our school had no air-conditioning, and the open windows only invited in a more intense heat though it was still an early hour. I'd felt more air circulate inside a mausoleum than in that classroom.

This year, the doors of our elementary school opened to receive the first black students in its history. This is the moment that cost Paulette tears in the lemon meringue pie; the moment whispered and worried about behind Jubilee's segregated doors. Our teacher asked all four of our new classmates to remain standing by their desks as she introduced them. These girls and boys could not have been more on display if they had entered the classroom naked on the backs of white horses.

When the girl across the aisle shyly introduced herself as Ophelia, I turned to look at her. My stomach flipped over. She was wearing my red plaid dress. I was shocked to see the dress again and had a strange feeling seeing it on her. I had worn it the previous winter and I didn't know it was missing. Whenever my mother gave my clothes away, I had a romantic notion that they were sent across the globe to Siberia, or maybe to the jungles of South America. I did not expect to see my clothes on my new classmate. The dress, made of coarsely woven, thick wool twill, had been one of my winter jumpers, designed to be worn with a blouse underneath. This was a sweltering September day in an airless schoolroom, and this frightened young girl was wearing my red plaid wool jumper with nothing underneath, as if it were a cool, breezy summer frock. For one ridiculous moment I chased the thought that someone might recognize her dress as my own. But no one was concentrating on Ophelia's dress when the color of her skin beckoned. I immediately felt ashamed; my face flushed with a moment of private embarrassment. I realized it was stupid of me to be concerned about whether anyone else recognized that the dress had belonged to me.

Ophelia was the last to be called upon, and her three friends were no longer standing in support. The teacher asked her to tell the class her name. "Oh feel ya," she said in a soft, singsongy way. I stared at her when she sat down. The dress was too small for her. It pulled in all the wrong places and looked as if it might cut off the circulation under her armpits; what was left of her baby fat puffed and poked around the armhole of the dress. I thought she must be terribly uncomfortable, her warmth, the itchiness of the wool, and her blackness all glaringly obvious on her first day in the white school. I knew that in that moment she felt completely and utterly alone. As I tried to make eye contact and caught her eye, I smiled, but she turned away. When I returned home from school that day I wanted to tell my mother about Ophelia and the dress. But she was busy with Belle and Jemma.

"Go do your homework."

"I don't have any."

"Well, stay out of my way, I'm busy right now, can't you see that? And have you seen your daddy?"

"No, ma'am."

"Well, where is he?"

"I don't know, I've been in school all day." I ran downstairs to find him before she could slap me for sassing.

The funeral home was all but deserted except for Sonny. I caught him sitting in my father's chair, his legs and feet propped up on the desk like he owned the place.

Sonny had a wily way of appearing civil to me in public, but certainly less so when occasionally we found ourselves alone in the funeral home. Oh, how we glared at each other. I knew he tolerated my siblings and me only because it would be unwise to show his irritation in the presence of my parents.

He cleaned his nails with his pocketknife. "So how was school today?"

"Fine." I held the phone book up to cover my face.

"Y'all had some new students today, didn't you?"

"Yeah."

"How did it go?"

"Huh?"

"No trouble out of those niggers?"

I got up, went to the bottom of the stairs, and yelled up to my mother, "I'm going across the street."

I didn't wait for a reply.

When I walked past Sonny, he said, "Damn right there was no trouble. They know their place."

I guessed I pretty much hated Sonny.

Years later the desegregation of our school system would be recorded as having been "without incident." In his own detestable way, Sonny was right.

The clouds gave coverage from the stinging sun, and a balmy breeze teased by pretending to cool the air. I walked across Main Street to the building on the corner. The elegant two-story brick building was a former bank with a history that screamed Jesse James. Jubilee's historical memory was a convenient one, and for a long time the story was that Jesse James robbed the bank in 1868. One of the gang shot a man and stole the money, and the legend had lived in vibrancy since. The James-Younger Gang definitely robbed the bank, but people debated for years whether Jesse James was present. (Turns out, he wasn't.)

The bank was now our public library, and that its doors were only a few steps away from my own was like a drop of dew on a dry patch of grass. Jubilee didn't have a bookshop, and I didn't even know that bookshops existed. The first time I opened the door to the library and smelled the scent of a multitude of hardcovers, I was entranced. The high-ceilinged library had tall, dark wooden, freestanding bookshelves. Our librarian, Theodocia Graham — Theo to her friends — introduced me to reading for pleasure. This was a lifesaving solution to the long hours of quiet time during the funerals and nights of visitation. The library was quiet, too; so quiet that if you closed a book too loudly, it echoed in the massive room. But I was a partner to quiet and I felt at home. Most of the time I roamed the shelves alone, the only friend to all the books. Finally, I had thoughts to fill my head other than my own. Theo was single-handedly responsible for implanting glorious mind journeys fueled solely by a book. I visited New England and San Francisco, I discovered the ingredients of that Southern confectionery delight Divinity in a Junior League cookbook, and because Theo wasn't prissy, tales of pirates and knights abroad captivated me. I ran my hand over the covers of the books as if I could feel the story underneath. The little thrill of taking the books home to keep even for a few days was comforting, especially on a day like this when the afternoon turned gloomy.

Cranky with the dank air and the crack of thunder, I walked back to our veranda, where the swing awaited. From where I sat, I looked down Main Street and without moving a muscle saw three churches. We had an awful lot of God in our town. Jubilee had more churches than it knew what to do with. They came in every variety imaginable, from a one-room house where the Holy Rollers spoke in tongues and fainted regularly, to the large, money-drenched building of the First Baptist Church, our church, a half a block from the funeral home.

At the turn of the eighteenth century Beacon County opened its arms and welcomed, or perhaps surrendered, to the Great Revival of America; fevered evangelists called it the Second Great Awakening. It was all go, go, go with the spirit, hallelujah, praise the Lord, just a few miles down the road. Then, in 1807 the Shakers brought their unique dancing and design talents a few miles in the other direction to South Union. I fell asleep every summer during the outdoor reenactment play in which the Shakers' founder, Mother Ann, saw the light. Sensing a warm reception, in 1943 the Mennonites anointed the county with their eccentric ways, accessorizing our farmland with small dots of black buggies. My father had not merely dropped us into another spot in the lap of the Bible Belt; this town was ingrained in the original hide before it became dyed, punched, and buckled. And because death doesn't wait for anyone or anything, not even the last prayer of Sunday-morning services, my father and therefore all of us had to sit in the last pew at the back of the church so that whoever was answering the phones at the funeral home could run down the block and tap him on the shoulder. It happened so frequently that I began to wonder if he'd made a pact with his employees to rescue him just when the preacher was warming up. I made a game of catching his attention and pointing to his watch, mouthing the words "Time to go." He didn't think it was funny. I never heard him sing a note and especially not in church; singing hymns was not something he did.

He never did anything unless chances were good that he could learn to do it well. Under the glare of my mother's hawk eyes I managed to sneak a look at him during the long, drawn-out prayers. I noticed that he never closed his eyes during them and wondered if praying was another thing he didn't do well.

Our mother complained about Sundays, even though she wouldn't be caught dead skipping church. "I have to wash your all's hair the night before. Get your clothes ready. Make breakfast Sunday morning, get you all dressed, and then come home and cook Sunday dinner. Sunday's supposed to be a day of rest. Well, it's not a day of rest for me."

"Let's not go then," I suggested.

"Watch your smart mouth!"

Here's what I learned in Sunday school and church: we're all going to hell. That's what the preacher said every time the doors opened. Everyone in Jubilee believed in heaven and hell whether or not they attended church. There was no possible escape route from the doctrine. We all knew of the burning fires of eternal damnation. But I didn't sit in the swing to think about hell. It was too hot. I wondered what it would be like to be at the seashore wrapped in a cool breeze with the Bobbsey Twins. I thought about how hard-pressed I was to find fairies in fairy tales. The heat became unbearable so I retreated to the coolest room in the house.

The showroom was full of caskets. There was no natural light, and when I switched on the fluorescent lighting, the strips of light came to life one at a time quickly, click, click, click, like the flashes of a high-powered camera. The effect was dazzling. The showroom, kept at a frosty temperature, was a reliable place in which to cool off in the sticky summer months. The caskets shone, row upon row of them, quite like an assembly line, suspended on casket trucks that held them in place. My father always had a fine selection of colors available: lavender, pink, blue, wooden, bronze. The most popular were rose and white for those who favored simple or feminine. And they were cheaper.

Teddy, one of my father's war buddies who lived in North Carolina, once came for a visit with Lenore, his wife. When my father led them into the casket room, Lenore ran over to a lavender-colored casket and threw her arms around it, practically draping her body over it.

"Frank! My favorite color in the whole world is purple. This is the one I want, this beautiful pale lavender casket. It's mine. Don't let anyone else have it."

"Well, gracious, Lenore" — he laughed —

"I'm sure you won't be needing it for a long time."

"I am as serious as a heart attack. You better save me a purple casket like this one."

Later I asked, "Isn't North Carolina far away? How is that going to work out? Will you have to deliver the casket to Raleigh?"

"Aw, Lenore was just being dramatic. She'll go home and forget all about it."

I spoke to Lenore many years later. The first thing she said to me was how much she loved that lavender casket.

Knowing which of the caskets were the cheapest was easy. They were made of pressed wood and covered in a dull, gray felt fabric. For about $350 it was a bargain, especially because the person who bought the least expensive casket received most of the same services as the person who bought the $3,000 copper casket: embalming, extra labor, the registry book, memorial folders, all sorts of odds and ends. The service could be held at the funeral home or at a church or graveside — all for the same price. There were no contracts or written financial agreements. My father took notes on a pad of paper, and sometimes he was paid, and sometimes he wasn't.

"Then why," I once asked, "would anyone ever pay more than the cheapest price?"

"Human nature. Some people regard it as a gesture of final respect. That's a strong pull. And then some people like to show off. That's not bad, but you'd be surprised at how it turns out."

He explained that Beacon County was split into two factions on its end-of-life needs. In the northern half of the county, the people were unpretentious and not necessarily poor farmers. The case of the patriarch of the Blunt family, in which the children insisted that he be buried in his bib overalls, was telling. They arrived clutching a paper bag that contained a brand-new pair of the Pointer Brand, stiff as a washboard, and a new white shirt. They chose a midpriced eighteen-gauge, plain, gray metal casket that cost around $1,700.

Mrs. Blunt opened her purse and produced a big wad of cash. "How much do I owe you, Mr. Mayfield?"

"No, ma'am, now you just keep your money and pay after the funeral." He wanted to make sure they were satisfied with everything before he accepted payment.

But she insisted and peeled off the $100 bills.

In south Beacon County the doctors and lawyers of the country-club set had their own ideas about how to go out in style. They might place a special casket order in advance in which they insisted upon brushed-steel handles on an expensive copper casket; they might choose a big, flashy mahogany casket trimmed with silver hardware. And the flowers — Lord the flowers! A south-county lawyer's wife ordered a casket piece so big that it took two men to carry. Cluttering the floor space were separate standing wreaths from every member of the family, each with his or her name scrawled across a wide satin ribbon: FOR DADDY, FROM YOUR LOVING DAUGHTER ELIZABETH. GOD BLESS YOU. REST IN PEACE. WE WILL NEVER FORGET YOU. They might hire their own organist and choose a vocalist from out of town to perform a few hymns. An entire choir was once called upon to sing a doctor to heaven. That was a first. But then, when the bill came due, my father often had to chase after payment from the wealthier families, who tried to put him off.

"Hellfire and damnation. Like water from a stone, I tell you." My father complained that when he pushed the boat out for those who wanted a big-splash send-off, he relied on the smaller funerals to prevent it from sinking. The bills weighed heavily upon him until finally, sometimes years later, he would receive payment from a golf-course-tanned widow.

He felt that an undertaker need not sell a casket. The only thing that mattered to my father was that the family was pleased with their choice. Once the family had chosen him as their undertaker, it was a matter of budget and desire. It wasn't as if they were going to order a casket from Sears, Roebuck. All he had to do was know his product. If quality mattered to the family, he showed them the better gauge; sixteen-gauge was the heaviest and strongest, twenty-gauge was the lightest and less expensive. If flash and beauty mattered, you couldn't beat a solid, hand-polished mahogany, or the most expensive casket that my father carried, the strong and mighty bronze. Said to be the most durable, better able to resist corrosion, it wouldn't decompose like wood or rust like many other metals.

I walked down the neat rows of caskets often enough that they became a mundane piece of funeral furniture. I never climbed in one. I thought about it, but they were like a well-made hotel bed — I didn't like to crumple the sheets until it was time to go to sleep. The caskets were so pristine and perfect that I couldn't bear the thought of damaging them. And anyway, what if the top accidentally closed while I was in it and then it got jammed and no one could get me out and I died of suffocation?

Before the advent of Harley-Davidson and Kentucky Wildcats casket designs and bespoke, biodegradable cocoons, caskets were relatively plain. Rarely did my father make a mistake when he placed an order. He knew the taste of his clientele and he had good judgment. But occasionally he stumbled.

"What the hell is this?" Sonny asked.

The stiff, brown cardboard that encased the casket fell to the floor to reveal the most hideous thing we had ever seen.

The paint job on this two-tone, steel casket was a shocker. A white background offset the garish gold sides and top. Small, white snowflake-looking designs dotted the sides of the casket. It was as if a bizarre fairy-tale casket had been transported to the showroom by mistake. Sleeping Beauty might look appropriate in it, but Mr. Woodall or Mrs. Lipton would not. It took its zany place in the showroom for two years. No one bought it or even considered it, and my father eventually admitted defeat and had it repainted.

I quite liked it. It reminded me of winter and holidays, so on this swampy day, before the fairy-tale casket was whisked away, I crawled underneath it with my book. The next thing I knew my mother shook me awake.

"What are you doing? I couldn't find you. Where've you been? I've been looking all over for you. Didn't you hear me call you?"

"I fell asleep. I went to the —"

"I don't want to hear it. I'm going to wear you out if you don't start doing as you're told. Now go find your daddy and tell him supper's ready."

He wasn't too far away. Outside, in the back of the funeral home, he and a couple of men who occasionally worked for him stood around an old barrel they used to burn trash. As the flames leaped out and lit their faces, they froze as if in a cabal when I opened the door and stepped outside. My father slowly passed a bottle to Lee, the man standing beside him. Lee nonchalantly shoved the bottle in his jacket pocket. Did they think I was blind?

Our county held an occasional vote. Were enough people ready to claim Beacon County a wet county? Did anyone out there want to *legally* drink alcohol in Jubilee? During the run-up to the vote, Jubilee's preachers went wild. One of the brethren placed a ladder near the courthouse, climbed it with his Bible in hand, sat on top, and sang hymns during the vote. The county remained dry that year.

Jubilee had no bars, no restaurants that served drinks. Those who liked their liquor were shoved back indoors to the privacy of their own homes, or to the country club, where law enforcement officials were paid to turn the other way. A few drove to the closest wet county in Tennessee. And one man stood in the back of his funeral home and passed around a bottle of mother's ruin. I hadn't a clue of its provenance.

"Dinner's ready," I said, pretending that I hadn't witnessed this cocktail hour.

"Be right in." My father made eye contact, smiled, and winked.

Oh, I got it. Our secret.

I carefully watched my father at dinner. I wanted to know if sipping from that gin bottle made him different in some way. I saw no sign of it. Remembering the spanking he'd given me before, any attempt at conversation stuck in my throat and I tried to make myself small and invisible. He was a little quiet, but I would never have known he'd been swigging away had I not seen it. It was the first time I'd seen him take a drink, I believed my mother knew, as dinner was thick with silence. Perhaps she'd sent me to find him to embarrass him. Or maybe she really didn't know where he was. Even though he had to be available at every moment, at times no one seemed to know his whereabouts. Muffled arguments erupted in their bedroom upon his return.

"Where've you been?"

"The hospital."

"Sure you were. And what were you doing there at this time of night?"

But I didn't hear his answer.

That night when I went to bed, I thought that it had been a pretty interesting day. My bedroom was right above the casket room, and when I closed my eyes, I knew that I was lying directly above the coffins. This is where I practiced playing dead, not in the caskets, but lying in my bed at night looking up at the ceiling with my hands resting perfectly, one on top of the other, on my stomach. I finally closed my eyes and wondered if I would wake up in the morning.

In Memoriam:
Linda Mayberry

Come the autumn when school began again, we entered our elementary classroom and were assigned seats. At times we were given a choice, but were more often told to sit alphabetically. I always sat behind Linda Mayberry. One wouldn't notice her. In a classroom filled with twenty or so children born of farmers, factory workers, doctors, and teachers, and me, the undertaker's daughter, it was unusual not to know what Linda Mayberry's father did for a living. But no one bothered to ask.

I sat behind her year after year and therefore became intimate with her back. Her hair was coarse and the color of burned wheat. It fell in tight, fuzzy curls just above her shoulders. Her hand-me-down cotton dress washed to a faded tiredness hung loosely below her knees. In the winter when all the other girls switched to wool, Linda Mayberry dealt with the cold by adding a cardigan to the same thin dresses. She sat with a slight stoop and walked like a boy — a tomboy in a dress — but she was small, petite even, and still and quiet.

When she turned to pass a book or a test paper, she never made eye contact, never said a word. There was no opportunity to study her face until she, like the rest of us, was called to the front of the room to read aloud. She knew the words and read slowly, methodically, plodding along softly in a monotone.

Her skin was flawless, smooth as anything,

and swarthy, as if she spent a great deal of time in the sun. Her eyes were the saddest I'd ever seen, as if they were lonely for a friend. Her thin-lipped mouth was either a straight line across her face or slightly turned down. She never smiled. She had something of a moth about her, as if she would disintegrate into powder after a certain age.

Finally released for the summer, we escaped school by running out through its doors and directly into the public swimming pool. Fed from a freshwater spring, the temperature of the water was always take-your-breath-away icy, even on blistering, late-summer days.

At the end of this particular summer, I was surprised to see Linda Mayberry at the pool, located on the outskirts of town. Someone would have had to drive her there and then pay the fee to enter. I imagined it would have been a special treat for her. I'd never before seen her there, but there she was, alone and quiet in a bathing-suit version of her dresses, faded, out-of-date.

The pool rules included a ten-minute break each hour. She sat on a rough-looking, old towel, her ringlets heavy with water, her eyes squinting into the bright sun. Songs on the jukebox, snacks, and other sunbathers soon took our attention away from her and we forgot about Linda. Midway through the afternoon we noticed the lifeguards were acting strangely during the break. We waited for the whistle to blow, the signal that allowed us back into the water. But the whistle didn't blow again that day. Linda Mayberry was missing.

They found her at the bottom of the pool, tucked away in a corner in fetal position. She was curled up into such a small, little ball that the lifeguard didn't see her until she dove in for the hourly pool check. The eleven-year-old wasn't a good swimmer and seemed to have wandered off to the deep end of the pool and quite simply sunk down without a ripple.

My father was called and brought Linda Mayberry to our house. As was our custom, I was allowed to see her after he had performed his duties, before her family arrived and before the townspeople came to pay their respects to a girl they barely knew. Someone had donated a bright new dress, probably the first previously unworn dress she'd ever received. Mildred the beautician tamed her hair. This was one of those occasions upon which my father was expected to perform better than his best. And she did indeed resemble herself, the same straight lip line, the long lashes intact, but the quietness that now encompassed her was not her own, and death at her young age made her look artificial. Not since I had touched that first dead body years ago had I any desire to do so again. I recalled that I had placed my hand on the lapel of the deceased man's jacket because I didn't want to feel his skin. Yet now, I had a strong, startling urge to touch her face, to kiss it good-bye. The dead face of Linda Mayberry was already haunting me. Perhaps because I'd gazed at the back of her head for so many years, on the day of her viewing, as I stood before her casket for a few short moments, I could not let her go.

The lifeguard on duty that day crumbled under the stress and suffered a debilitating mental breakdown. She never returned to life-guarding, or even to the pool, and some say she never really recovered from what happened on her watch.

Linda's death was important to all of us in that classroom. We were forced to admit that we were not immortal. Any one of us might be taken by death's hand on any random day; our youth offered no protection. The silent babies that had drifted through my father's funeral home through the years had been upsetting, but this was different. I knew what my father had done to Linda's body to make it presentable so that the adults could view her comfortably and whisper that she was in a better place. *She's here!* I wanted to say. *How can she be in a better place?* I was struck by the absence of children whose parents wouldn't allow them to come to the funeral home, as if death were a disease they might catch.

It was harder now to forget about death, more challenging to walk out of the funeral home's front door and leave death behind for a while. I thought it might be following me, and that if I looked out the corner of my eye, it might be there, waiting. Sometimes I thought I saw Linda again in the hallway at school, and in the window of her father's truck. But of course, she wasn't there.

CHAPTER 7
THE GENTLE ART
OF EMBALMING

Over the next five years the funeral home demanded more of my father and so did Miss Agnes. Her confidence in him grew year by year. She came to rely on him for more than just a friendly face at the beginning and the end of each day. The elderly lady in red and the undertaker packed their bags and set out on a yearly pilgrimage.

He accompanied Miss Agnes on marathon trips to Southern cities where she prowled for antiques. They spent long days in his station wagon coasting along to New Orleans, Williamsburg, Virginia, and to the corners of Tennessee. For hours on end he shouted to be heard, and she shouted to hear herself. They strolled through grand antique warehouses and stopped at small junk shops, until the back of the station wagon was full to the brim. He arranged shipping for items that were too cumbersome and handled the deliveries once they arrived. One year, their eureka moment came when they discovered hundreds of feet of black, wrought-iron fencing that had once graced an old New Orleans mansion. She purchased enough fencing to surround her own mansion. These long journeys left him exhausted, and he arrived home with his tie askew, looking haggard and in need of peace and quiet, but there was no peace and quiet at home. An undertaker is not allowed to be tired or to have a bad day. His voice mustn't carry anything but genuine concern and professionalism, and he must be able to switch on automatically.

Miss Agnes permeated my life, too, in ways seen and unseen. When I was old enough to walk downtown on my own, I often saw her, a round, red dot as she approached from the north end of Main Street and I from the south. We converged in the middle of the sidewalk exchanging greetings while people walked around us. Sometimes, when I wasn't in the mood to talk to her, I hid around the corner and spied on her as she studied the mannequins in Helen's Dress Shop window, or I peeked into the hat shop and watched her try on large, saucer-shaped red hats. One day I followed her into Mr. Benchley's Department Store. Mr. Benchley's was the largest store in Jubilee, so it was easy to find a vacant aisle. Curious about her purchases, I hid behind stacks of bib overalls.

When she shuffled in, Mr. Benchley knew exactly how he would spend the next half hour. Almost any type of clothing item could be found in Mr. Benchley's store except the red underwear that Miss Agnes required. Mr. Benchley stood by, pen in hand, ready to place a special order for her. She requested red undergarments without regard to Mr. Benchley's sensibilities. "Three bras, six pair of underwear, a slip," she thundered as if she were ordering a ham sandwich with mayo and lettuce. From the high ceilings to the floorboards in his barn-like shop, the air held on to her voice.

We were allowed to leave the school grounds during lunch, and I often saw her sitting on a stool at the lunch counter of El-vis Perry's Prescription Drugstore and Café. During mealtimes the odor of bacon and hamburgers overpowered the medicinal smell of the cramped shelves. The door swung open and a dozen of us descended upon Elvis and his grill. In the back of the store, the lunch counter offered only five or six stools, and Elvis always saved Miss Agnes a seat at breakfast and lunch. She dined in the company of the men who drank coffee away from the chattering tongues of their wives, wives who weren't threatened that their husbands began their day with Miss Agnes, for long ago she'd ceased being attractive to the opposite sex. Years of eating in the few greasy dining establishments the town offered had added to her girth considerably. She carried herself as well as a short, round woman possibly could. She looked over at me, so there was no way to avoid a public meeting. While I waited for my hamburger, I hesitantly approached her. I was never sure if I should disturb her lunch, but she was always glad to see me.

"Well, hi-dee, hi-dee, hi-dee." She rested her fork and knife on the green-and-white plate of half-eaten chicken-fried steak. I coveted her gravy-smothered mashed potatoes.

I leaned close to her ear. "Hi, Miss Agnes."

She reached into her cavernous red bag and pulled out a fifty-cent piece. I thought she had hundreds of them because whenever she saw me, she gave me one. It was more than enough to pay for my hamburger and Coke.

"My father said it would be impolite not to take this. So, thank you, ma'am."

She wiped her mouth and cackled.

"Here you go. This is for you." I pulled a

piece of paper out of my book satchel.

She once told me, "Poetry is marvelous," so whenever I thought of it I copied a poem out of *A Child's Garden of Verses*. I considered it an even trade. I tried to write a poem for her once, but it was terrible and I threw it away.

When I left Elvis's, my classmates were on my heels.

"You know she's crazy, don't you?" Lucy Ann was dead serious.

Here we go again. "No, she's not."

"My mama says she is. She's got dead animals in her house and hides all her money under her mattress instead of putting it in the bank."

"No, she doesn't."

"How do you know?"

" 'Cause I've been to her house, and if there was a dead animal in it, I would have smelled it."

"What about the money?"

"What? Do you think I looked under her mattress?"

"You haven't been through her whole house," one of the boys piped up.

"Yes, I have. She has a playroom with a table set for a tea party and everything."

"Tea party? What's that?"

I rolled my eyes. "It's when you sit at a

table and someone serves you Cokes and potato chips and cookies. Or sometimes, you can have iced tea in a teacup. That's what they do in England, where it was invented."

"What crap," he said.

But I knew that when Christmas season arrived, those very children would be lining up on Miss Agnes's office stairs to claim whatever she handed out that year.

When Jubilee's citizens tore November from their calendars, the atmosphere became charged with a month of goodwill. The less fortunate and elderly were attended in a more generous way as boxes of toys and food were distributed to those in need. Women tore through pounds of sugar and flour baking enormous quantities of cakes and cookies. Eggnog floated in thick, creamy pools in crystal punch bowls, and the whole town smelled of cinnamon and evergreen. Jubilee transformed into a picture-post-card twinkling fairyland.

I secretly hoped that no one died during the holidays, but couldn't say it aloud because of the electric bill, the employees' salaries, and a dozen other things of which I was reminded whenever I expressed that wish.

In the days of December the frost on Miss

Agnes's office window was so decorative it looked as if someone had painted it. Northerners misunderstood Kentucky winters; the humidity and heat gave way to icy roads and sharp, cutting winds that whipped through our clothes. Traditionally, during the Christmas season Miss Agnes's farmers hauled a seven-foot tree up the stairs to her office. She collected unique tree ornaments from Germany, Austria, and who knows where else. The same children who filed into her kitchen on Halloween eagerly formed a line in her office to view the biggest tree in the county and to receive a trinket and a Christmas cookie, the cookies faithfully supplied by a farmer's wife.

The streets were deserted tonight, and my father and I rushed from the car to escape the cold. Miss Agnes sat at her typewriter holding a worn, stuffed Santa doll. She never crossed her legs like a lady when she sat; her dress fell in between her slightly parted legs. Enveloped in red clothing that did little to hide her paunch, all she needed was a beard and a Santa cap.

When we entered, she cranked the winder on the back of the doll. "Listen to this!" Her eyes danced.

The track on the old doll was a little off, so instead of "Ho, ho, ho," we heard a strange and garbled "Ha, ha, ha."

Of all of her toys, the Santa was my father's favorite, and like two children they laughed and laughed when she wound it. I was a little too old now for her toys and the strange noises they made, but I smiled and told her how nice they were.

The plump, multicolored bulbs on her Christmas tree glowed in the darkening room, and the small light on her desk gave off a red aura as its glare hit her scarlet dress. Bracelets of red rubber bands clenched her wrists, and I wondered what task they performed. Christmas cards and red pencils surrounded her. I liked her office. I liked the way my shoes sounded on her wide-planked wood floors. I enjoyed sitting by her rolltop desk and felt at ease with the sweet and musty scent of papers that protruded from the cubbyholes.

I walked over to the front-window ledge and admired the long row of photographs. Over twenty individually framed school pictures of girls and boys stared back at me.

"Those are my farmers' children," she bellowed.

I didn't recognize any of them; they were from agricultural families in the county. She asked for my photo every year, but it wasn't on display with the others. My father told me later that when the farmers entered the office to conduct business, the first thing they saw were their children's photographs. Their hearts were subliminally softened. She was a relentless and rabid business-woman.

"I see you wore your Christmas red dress for me?"

I stood close to her so that she could hear me better. "Yes, ma'am, do you like it?"

"Why, yes, honey. It's just beautiful. Do you like ghost stories?" she asked as she held me next to her.

"Oh, yes, ma'am! I love them."

"Did you know that my favorite story is a ghost story?"

"Really? Me, too!"

"You tell me about yours first, honey, then I'll tell you the name of mine."

"It's called *A Candle in Her Room,* and it's about these three sisters who live in Wales . . . have you heard of Wales? . . . And one of them is wicked and then . . . oh, well, it's complicated. There's this doll and she's evil. And one of the sisters has an accident and she can't walk, and then the book changes and you read someone else's story, the daughter of the wicked sister, and . . ."

But in my passion to tell the story of what I thought was the best book I'd ever read in my whole entire life, I'd made a mess of it, and I could see I was losing Miss Agnes. She nodded, but I'm not sure how much she heard.

"Anyway, it has a happy ending," I said as loudly as I could.

She moved her ever-present VC Fertilizer writing pad closer to her and picked up a red pencil. "Go to the library and see if you can find this book." She wrote neatly across the pad *The Complete Tales of Edgar Allan Poe.* Then she wrote, "The Fall of the House of Usher," and underlined it three times.

"Read that story and tell me what you think."

"Yes, ma'am, I will."

Then we both remembered that my father was sitting in the corner.

"Merry Christmas, Miss Agnes." I wrapped my arms around her soft frame and gave her a present covered in shiny red paper.

"Merry Christmas, honey." She handed me a cloth-covered diary. It was red, of course.

"She's a character, isn't she?" I asked my father on the way home.

"She's been a good friend to me." I could tell by the tone of his voice that her friendship was something he greatly valued.

Miss Agnes continued to introduce my father to people who were not in the Old Clan's camp. Perhaps this was her Christmas gift to him, a word to her business colleagues that Frank Mayfield was a good friend and a reliable, caring undertaker. Despite the predations of Alfred Deboe, my father's business was thriving with her help.

Before the library closed for Christmas vacation, I approached Theo with the piece of paper Miss Agnes had given me. "Can you help me with this?"

Theo wore her glasses on a chain around her neck and placed them now on her delicate, pale nose. The snow had begun and we both turned toward the windows, which trembled from a swift wind. Theo clutched at the cardigan she wore on her shoulders. It was four o'clock and the room was dark and quiet.

"Hmm," she said peering down at me. "This is a ghost story that you may not be ready for." Theo's voice sounded as if she didn't talk much, as if her vocal cords had turned into pillows of dust.

"But you gave me that other book to read — the one with the doll in it, you know, the girl used witchcraft with it."

Indeed, she had. She'd told me I looked

like a girl who might enjoy a ghost story. I don't know why she said that. She moved slowly to the *P* shelf in her granny shoes.

"This is a different kind of ghost story. But if you want it," she said slowly, "I'll stamp it. I just hope it doesn't give you nightmares."

"I live in a funeral home, Theo. I'm bound to have nightmares."

Theo was right. Although, the story didn't give me nightmares, Poe's colorful language and my difficulty in reading it almost did. I could scarcely understand the thing. Our next meeting would probably be on Valentine's Day and I didn't want to disappoint Miss Agnes, so I hightailed it back to the library.

"Theo, I need a summary, please, ma'am. I need to know if this story is worth spending the whole Christmas vacation trying to understand it."

Theo never reacted to anything or showed an ounce of emotion. If she ever had a sense of humor, I never came across it. My father snapped stems off flower arrangements in the chapel and sent me to school with them to give to my teachers. They looked at me with amusement when I presented them because they were sure to know their origin. Theo wasn't moved by the flowers I brought her, or the conversation I attempted, but she always came through for me and I depended on her.

"The narrator tells us of a brother and sister who live in a large, crumbling mansion. Both are ill in different ways. Both are crazy as loons, but they're very close to one another. Lord Usher buries his sister alive in the house. She breaks out of her entombment and falls upon him as he collapses and dies from terror and despair. The narrator escapes and bears witness as the house crumbles into the lake."

"Why did he bury her alive?"

"She had a disease that left her paralyzed at times and he thought she was dead."

"My daddy said that if a person wasn't dead before they were embalmed, they sure would be after."

"Child, I'm sure that the Lady Madeline was not embalmed. And you must remember, it's not a true story."

Well, whoever heard of anyone not being embalmed? I certainly had not.

If death was the last taboo, then embalming was the last, last taboo. People wanted the service performed, it was inherent to the Southern way of death, but, boy, they sure didn't want to know anything about it.

Though I roamed the rooms of the funeral

home from the beginning of my life, mine was a gradual awakening to the fact my father was not only a funeral director, but also an embalmer. I'd traipsed in and out of the embalming room hundreds of times before I summoned the courage to ask my father exactly what he did in that room that took so many hours. Why did he do it immediately after he collected a body, sometimes at four o'clock in the morning, or on a Sunday when the rest of our family clung to our hymnals and sang "Blessed Redeemer"?

He never blustered about embalming's being an art. He never relayed how many people held back tears as they said, "It looks just like him." Or, "Frank, she's just how I remember her before the illness set in." But I knew, I knew by the number of people who told me so.

Many people of Jubilee remembered stories their grandparents told them about what it had been like when they lived in remote areas in Kentucky, such as Appalachia, where undertakers were few in number, and where, even if the undertaker happened to pass through, they couldn't afford to embalm Uncle Jed. The family placed Uncle Jed's coffin in their parlor and did the best they could. They laid coins on his eyes, not only to prevent them from popping open, but also to stop the devil from entering his body. A cloth tied around his jaw and head made him look as if he suffered from a toothache, but was necessary to prevent a gaping mouth. With difficulty, they folded his arms and stuffed a towel that had been soaked in a soda solution around his body to prevent discoloration. Finally, strong-smelling spices, fresh cedar chips, or eucalyptus leaves were placed in the coffin, especially on humid summer days.

On porch-sitting evenings friends spun tales about "the rigger mortis" and relayed disturbing experiences their families encountered back in the day. Ida Mae Clark's great-grandmother told her that right in the middle of Ida Mae's great-grandfather's funeral service, the old man sprang up from the coffin. The preacher stopped the service while the men pressed the corpse back down. But when the poor man finally lay supine again, his legs rose. The men rushed back to the coffin and held his legs down, but his back rose again. With the service now completely at a standstill, one of the congregants ran to the nearest barn and arrived back swinging a hammer. The men tucked Ida Mae's great-grandfather back into the coffin and nailed the lid shut. The preacher quickly ended the service.

What a tall tale. Think of the effort used to sit up in bed after a night's sleep. If a body sits up, it's not dead.

No one in Jubilee wanted to be laid down into the earth by way of their ancestors. There was never any question or suggestion that my father forced embalming on any family. They not only wanted their deceased embalmed — they felt they needed it for themselves as much as anything else. No one was told it was necessary, or a health hazard or illegal not to embalm. People wanted their loved ones to look good and smell nice. It was as simple as that.

When I first asked my father what embalming meant, what it entailed, I had no expectations. I thought it was best to know and get it over with.

"What's the first thing you do?" I asked him one day when he was in the chapel. He was fooling around with the floor lamps and rearranging baskets of flowers.

"We check to make sure the person's dead."

"Oh, no. You don't. Do you mean that sometimes when you collect them, they're still alive?"

"Of course not," he said as if I should know better, "it's a good habit, that's all."

"How do you do that?"

"Check for a pulse and a heartbeat. Maybe even rub the breastbone, because that really hurts."

"Daddy!"

"Well, you asked."

"Then what?"

"Do you know what rigor mortis is?"

"Umm, not really."

My father described the condition that is the link to all the jokes about "stiffs."

"It's only a temporary thing, but basically, the muscles stiffen. It begins in the eyelids, neck, and jaw, and in an hour or two it spreads. That's why the next step usually involves massaging the hands and limbs, to work it out. And that's why I don't wait to embalm. I set the facial features pretty quickly. I close the eyelids. You might hear people say they're sewn shut, but that's not true. I glue them with a special glue. I sew the jaw together. Set the mouth. That takes time to get right. You don't want a smile, or a frown, just something peaceful. After the embalming, there's no going back, the features, the body, the way it lies, they're all set."

"How?" I couldn't quite take it in. I was still thinking about the massaging-the-limbs bit. "How do you sew the jaw together?"

"It's complicated. I've got special needles that are hook shaped on the end."

"Oh. So that's what they're for." I quickly changed direction. "Are those stories true about bodies sitting up in the casket?"

"What do you think?"

"I don't know. You hear all sorts of stuff, you know."

"No. Don't be silly. But sometimes, because of a temperature reaction the muscles of the arms, hands, and upper legs might twitch a bit. And when I place the hands on the torso, sometimes the hands will close into a fist."

As that image sank in quite quickly, I remembered how cold a dead man's hands felt. "Why are they so cold?"

"You know when your mother takes your temperature and how we always want it to be 98.6 degrees? That's a healthy, normal temperature. But when you die, the body cools to room temperature. It's usually about seventy-two degrees, maybe even a little less, that's more than twenty degrees cooler than normal. It feels cold by comparison."

"I guess that makes sense, Daddy, but still, they feel awfully cold. What do you do next?"

"Then I wash the body."

"Hm. Like a bath."

"Sort of. Like a sponge bath, and with a hose."

"You mean you hose it down? Like washing a car?"

"Aw, hell. No, not like that, exactly. It's very respectful. And no one is allowed in the embalming room except the staff and your mother. No one. Ever."

"Okay, that's enough for now."

I pieced it together over time, short conversations punctuated with questions. It was a great deal easier to understand after I'd studied a little science and biology. Those tall, complicated charts of the human body took on a new meaning.

"Is it true that your hair and nails keep growing after you die?"

"Absolutely not."

"Someone at school had a book with pictures of dead people with really long hair."

"The skin, well, it kind of shrinks. It makes the hair and nails look longer, especially if the nails haven't been cut after death."

"Do you . . ."

"Yes, I trim the nails and clean them."

There were all sorts of myths about what happens in an embalming room. The most bizarre of these was that someone in Jubilee believed that the blood that was drained from the body was stored in jars, then removed from our funeral home to be buried elsewhere. Others thought he sent the blood of the dead to the Red Cross. My father said some people are just plain stupid.

"After the body's washed, I make an incision."

"Where?"

"Different places, sometimes on the chest, sometimes the groin; there's an artery under the armpit, too."

Without going through too much detail he explained that *in* went the embalming fluid, two gallons or so; *out* went a portion of the blood. *In* went the cavity fluid to treat the organs where gas and bacteria would build up; *out* went the bile and urine. Treating the organs, he explained, prevents unpleasant odors and seepage.

"It sounds messy, but I never come in contact with the fluids. It's all very clean. And my embalming room may be small, but it's tidy. And it's not true that all the blood is drained out — you can't really drain it all and it's not necessary, anyway."

The blood and fluids flow from the tubing directly into a drain underneath the embalming table and into the sewers, where, my father said, a lot worse than that goes down every day. But at that moment, I swore I couldn't think what.

"But what does the embalming fluid do?"

"Well, it's hard to imagine if you haven't seen it. You can watch sometime if you want."

"No, thanks."

"It's kind of miraculous in a way. *Deathly pallor.* Have you ever heard that expression?"

"No. But I've seen Dracula movies."

"It's not like that. The dead do not look like Dracula. There's discoloration. They're not alabaster. The fluid puts color back in the body, evens out the color underneath the skin. The skin and tissues, well, they look alive again. A good embalmer knows how to match the color of fluid with the skin tone. The sunken features disappear, the person looks more the way they did before they were ill, or you could say they look good for their age. Death is a natural thing, but it's not very dignified. Embalming hasn't changed much since the Civil War." He paused. "War . . . well, embalming brings dignity to the deceased and to the family. You really want to do your best to please them. That's what it's about.

"Then I wash the body again and wash

their hair. Of course, that's the scene when everything is going well. But a body that's been autopsied is different. A car wreck, or accident or something that's disfigured the body — all those take a lot more time and care."

"How long does the whole thing take?"

"About two hours for the embalming and another couple of hours for grooming, dressing, cosmetics, and placing the body in the casket."

"Does anyone ever tell you they don't want to be embalmed, or does their family ask you not to do it?"

"Hardly ever. It's unusual."

"Well, what do you do?"

"It's up to them. I suggest that the funeral should be the next day. The casket should be closed. It depends."

"On what?"

"On what kind of shape the decedent is in."

"What if the family wants the casket left open?"

"I try to explain that it will upset them — without upsetting them."

"I don't understand."

"It's very upsetting for a family to witness decomposition. They don't understand what happens to the skin color, the seepage, other things that you don't want to know about."

I didn't want to sound ungrateful for all the "interesting" information, but he was right, I'd heard enough for the moment.

So, this idea of Lady Madeline of the House of Usher and her awful plight was quite horrific. I picked up the book again and tried to read the story, one word at a time. It was still difficult to grasp. I remembered hearing my parents say that Miss Agnes had a brother who was only a year younger than she and they had been close. He lost his mind. She'd sent him a ton of money so that he could have the best of care. And now he was dead. And Miss Agnes lived in a big house like the siblings in Poe's story. Was that why she liked it so much? Was this story her favorite because of her own history? I would never know, for Miss Agnes never asked me if I'd read the story and we never spoke of it again.

On Christmas Day, after we had our dinner, my mother piled food on a plate and wrapped it in tin foil. As my father pulled on his coat and prepared to leave us, I felt conflicted. I loved Miss Agnes, but Daddy left a hole when he walked out the door, especially on holidays. My mother was suddenly in a bad mood, Evelyn would slam her door, and even Thomas would sometimes leave the funeral home to visit friends. Things kind of fell apart a little.

"Why won't she ever come over here and have Christmas dinner with us?" I asked my father.

"She doesn't want to intrude."

"Well, she's intruding anyway. You always have to leave us on Christmas Day and Thanksgiving and —"

"That's enough. That's just the way she is. I don't mind."

He took her the plate of food and stayed with her so that she wouldn't have to eat Christmas dinner alone. She was glad to see him, and grateful for the food, and when he was gone, she was content to be alone again.

I imagined her wandering through her rooms on Christmas night. The decorative lights from other homes on her street glimmered through her front windows. She probably saved the thick piece of jam cake my mother had sent over for a late-night snack. I imagined her reading Poe in her decorative red house, while I read Poe in the funeral home.

In Memoriam: The Sheridans

"The raccoons ate Miss Alice Larkin's tomatoes. What a tragedy!"

"Well, it's just a tragedy that Morris Simpkin left the Baptists for those heathen Methodists."

"Have you heard the tragic story of how Mrs. Pennyrile's gooseberry pies fell off the windowsill? That blind old bird dog of hers . . ."

Tragedy was all around us in its small and inconsequential way. Tales of tragedy floated from house to house, from the grocery store to the pharmacy, usually accompanied by laughter and surprise. Everything, it seemed, was a tragedy, until our provincial lives were forced to redefine its meaning.

When I viewed the bodies of the Sheridan family, I struggled to make them speak to me. I searched their faces for some kind of explanation. How silly I felt, but I could not stop hoping I would learn something about what had happened to them. They were arranged in a semicircle in the chapel — four caskets, three adult-size and one smaller, junior-size casket, built and used for that awful occasion. Gunshot wounds were concealed beneath their clothing, or, in Mr. Sheridan's case, his temple was covered with makeup, his hair combed to cover a lump.

I was about twelve years old when Mr. Sheridan loaded his shotgun and shot his wife and two children. The boy was a teenager and the girl, younger than me. Then he turned the gun on himself. His wife didn't die immediately and was taken to the hospital, where she died soon after, but not soon enough, for she fully comprehended what had happened, a catastrophe in itself, a bitter horror of a truth to swallow before her death.

We remained troubled by the Sheridans long after they were buried.

I had already peered into the faces of many dead bodies by that time, though not as long and as hard as I did the morning my father created that sad semicircle. I looked for meanness, for insanity, for some tormented explanation from the dead man's face. Of course, I found nothing but a shell of a man, a shell of a family. My father worked particularly hard to form Mr. Sheridan's expression. There could be no slight upturn of his mouth, nor could there be even a hint of a grimace. His face was blank, his mouth a straight line, his expression without tension, but also without humanity, because no matter how he actually looked lying in the casket, his deed determined how he would be perceived.

Dead children never look natural. The Sheridan children did not look angelic or as if they were merely sleeping. They looked dead and too young to be so. But it didn't matter what they looked like; the particular features that made them unique individuals could have been those of any of us. The shock lay in that.

When Jemma came downstairs to see them, she approached the caskets already visibly shaken. "Why?" she asked. "How could something like this happen? I don't understand."

Our parents didn't try to hide death of any kind, but on this occasion, my father sent her away. "Some people . . . they're just crazy," he told her. "Go on back upstairs to Belle. She'll make you some peanut butter and crackers."

I'm sure there must have been other murders in the previous history of Beacon County, but no one could remember a single one, it had been so long ago. The event impacted our community in such a way that the visitation period for the family was like a huge car wreck. People lined up to see the Sheridans because they were curious to look calamity in the eye. Tragedy, always a magnet for the creation of celebrity, drew them in by the hundreds.

Though we were mobbed during the visitation period, the funeral service was lacking, one of the least attended.

"What did the preacher say in the service?" I asked.

"It was short. He just made some very general sort of remarks. About how sad things happen. He said it was a tragedy."

We never learned why Mr. Sheridan murdered his family. He was poor and sometimes hit the bootleg whiskey, but many in our vicinity were like that, too. It was an unsatisfying and general conclusion. The preacher told me privately that Mr. Sheridan would be punished in hell. But I said nothing to that, because I saw no God in the scene before me, no heaven, no hell. Prayers would not have prevented this tragedy. When the Sheridans were finally buried, for it seemed their short time under our roof was elongated somehow, I no longer prayed for bad things not to happen. I knew they would.

CHAPTER 8
FUNERAL-PARLOR POKER

Within a few years of our arrival, my father managed to encroach upon Alfred Deboe's domination of the funeral business in Jubilee. Half of the business now went to us, in spite of the Old Clan's continued efforts to thwart it. My father was more energetic and outgoing than Deboe. People liked him, even when they didn't want to. The pace of death picked up at our funeral home through his efforts and the connections he made through Sonny and Miss Agnes. Often two, even three, funerals needed his attention at once. Visitation hours were extended so that a constant flow of people passed through the doors from early in the morning until late at night. Cars peppered Main Street and snaked around the block; men and women streamed out of them and spilled into our home. An abundance of flowers, delivered like clockwork, permeated the air with their fragrance. My father and

237

his employees rushed around quietly with purpose as they attended to the needs of the mourners of Jubilee. A shuffle of gurneys and caskets in and out of the embalming room occurred out of view of the public. I wondered if the elderly population of our town was in danger of becoming extinct, such was the succession of deaths from old age. This was quite a lot for our little funeral home to handle. Something had to be done.

The calamity that marked the end of my childhood came when my father decided to remodel the funeral home. I watched with great distress as the veranda fell to the blows of the demolition team. Mr. Riley, the painter, tried to console me by letting me help him paint the new white brick facade. My homey seat now destroyed, the funeral home looked even more like a business than a home. The loss of the veranda was my father's gain, for now there was room for more of Jubilee's dead, and that was the point of it all. Somehow I felt as if I might lose something of my father, too. On the swing I could hang around without being in the way. I could monitor the events on Main Street. I was often the first person to see a visitor approaching and run inside with the announcement. How was I to make myself useful without the veranda and swing?

My father and I stood on the sidewalk and watched Mr. Riley paint MAYFIELD & SON FUNERAL HOME with broad, black strokes across the white bricks.

"So, do you think Thomas is going to be an undertaker?"

"No, I very seriously doubt that."

"Then why does it say 'Mayfield and Son'?"

"It's just an expression."

"Well, I think I might be an undertaker. Are girls allowed to be undertakers?"

"You have a long time to think about that. I don't know any women undertakers, though."

"Maybe I can be the first woman undertaker then."

"I have a feeling someone will beat you to it. Anyway, you still haven't watched me embalm yet."

"Nah, I don't really want to."

"Didn't think so."

I didn't have the heart to tell him that the thought of watching him embalm made me downright queasy. I wanted to stand beside him while he performed the job he was clearly meant to do. I wanted him to think I was courageous when I was not. I wanted to create a camaraderie in this special area of his life, but I couldn't. I wasn't ready and was unsure if I would ever be. Thomas had stood in that small, dark room once and told me he never wanted to watch again. Though he said it was clinical, like a surgery, he thought it was creepy.

I found things to do downstairs so that I wouldn't be told to go away. I de-smudged the caskets — he was a stickler about fingerprints. I made sure the folding chairs in the chapel were perfectly in line, the way he liked them. In the summer I carefully placed a paper fan on each seat with the image of Jesus facing up. I wondered if anyone ever turned the fan over to read the advertisement on the back: "Mayfield & Son Funeral Home — our service is guided by the Golden Rule. Your confidence is our sacred obligation."

As my father began to make a name for himself in Jubilee, the funeral home became a social club during downtime, a place to stop by for a cold soda on a summer scorcher, or a cup of coffee in the dark winter afternoons after the men about town had exhausted the coffee counters. He made friends easily and loved nothing better than to host afternoon games.

It was a bridge-party day, and having been scolded and sent to my room, I employed Operation Sneak Downstairs. I'd stolen a few biscuits filled with slices of country ham that Belle had left unmonitored and stuffed them into my pocket.

"What are you all doing, Daddy? Can I stay down here a while? I'm in trouble. Dropped a plate of ambrosia on the kitchen floor. Belle's dizzy from it, she said —"

I stopped midsentence. Edgar held a gun.

"We're being entertained by Edgar's rifle skills," my father said.

Edgar had recently spent time in a military situation about which he was pretty sparing of the details. He knew how to handle a rifle, though. Edgar marched for us and spun his rifle around and barked out orders until my father told him to knock it off so as not to disturb the ladies upstairs.

"What's the temperature like up there?" my father asked me.

"They're serious now. Mrs. Appleton has her glasses on, she's going on about the Civil War again, and Miss Becky Lou took her shoes off — you know how she likes to stretch her feet."

"Okay then, boys, let's get a game going. Edgar, you're on guard duty."

To relieve the boredom during downtime, the fellows played checkers in the back section of the chapel. This growing group of men favored a more inclusive game, so my father bought a big folding table to play Crazy Eights. Just as I began to get the hang of Crazy Eights, they moved on to poker. Poker stuck. At first they bet with matchsticks, but then quickly emptied their pockets of nickels and dimes and played for money. Gambling made them feel guilty and they were afraid of gossip, so each time they played, one of the men was the designated guard. The guard's duty was to sit in the front office, keep an eye on the window, and warn the men if anyone who wasn't in the loop approached the funeral home.

Even my mother joined in the poker games at times. She had a cardplayer's mind and the demeanor of a professional. Lily Tate was quiet when she played, quiet and deadly. She seemed to recede into the wallpaper while she silently watched the men's cards as they yapped on about the perfect kind of weather for growing crops, or a business deal. Then she would wipe the floor with all of them. When she leaned over the table and swept up the whole pot, my father would jump from his chair and throw his cards down in disgust.

Poker has a certain rhythm, and nothing jarred it like having to answer the phone, so the guard fielded the calls and left the men undisturbed unless it was an ambulance or death call. Everyone gave Edgar a pat on the back as we left him sitting forlornly at the desk.

Usually four or five men were around the table. They were the kind of men who made their own schedule — Eugene, an insurance salesman; J.W., a farmer; and Brother Sam, who was associated with one of the churches. I wasn't surprised that one of God's servants gambled. Due to my father's profession I knew just about all the preachers and church officials in the county.

When I entered the room, Brother Sam smiled at me as if some part of him ached. He motioned me over to him. While the rest of the men were settling in with the first hand of the day, he leaned toward me like he wanted to whisper something. I lent him my ear.

"I'd appreciate it, young lady, if you wouldn't tell anyone that I sit at this table once in a while."

I looked at him like he was an idiot. I felt I could afford to be haughty; no one else was paying attention to me at that moment. "Don't you think I know that? I'm not a snitch. You just need to concentrate on your cards and not worry about me, because you've got a pretty sorry hand," I whispered back.

While the women ate gussied-up chicken salad upstairs, I passed out peanuts and cold drinks to the men at the poker table. I ran back and forth into the hospitality room, where next to the snack machine a ginormous red Coca-Cola machine hummed away like a refrigerator. It was supposed to take money, but didn't. My father had rigged it somehow so that his guests enjoyed a free-flowing supply of bottles of Coke, Sprite, Dr Pepper, and Nehi. And a pot of coffee was always going, aided by plenty of milk and sugar.

These men were easy with each other, even in the uncomfortable area of emotions. I could see they enjoyed the undertaker's company. When they talked about other men, they referred to them as boys. "That ole boy Ralph, he's never gonna give you a damn nickel off of anything." But they would never refer to each other as boys; these were men.

The funeral home was their haven. They created a jovial atmosphere in spite of all the mourning and death the place had witnessed. Tucked back in the rear of the chapel, they joked with me and didn't seem to mind having me around. I knew how to disappear into the woodwork, practiced as I was at sitting silently, but I often circled the men and learned to play poker by standing at the shoulders of a few good players. The atmosphere always had a slight edge when a game was on. The men threw their cards on the table at the end of a hand, snapped them when they were proud, and sent their nickels spinning with a bet. Whenever I tried to spin a nickel, it fell on the floor.

They spoke in shorthand, like men who've lived closely with each other for a long time.

"Trip Harrison got a . . ."

"Yep, heard about that."

"Not like last time."

"Nope. But that wife of his . . ."

"Yeah, got that right."

Then Edgar came running into the room. "J.W., your wife's on the phone, she's lookin' for you."

"Tell her I'm not here."

Edgar left, but ran back in again immediately.

In unison, without looking up from their hands, the men chimed, "Goddamnit, he's not here!"

They settled down again, picked up their cards as a new hand was dealt.

Just as Brother Sam's eyes bulged, a sure sign he had finally received good cards, Edgar ran into the room yelling his head off.

"Old lady Peabody's coming up the walk!"

Silence. My father stood immediately. He turned from the men, adjusted his face for the widow, and strode purposefully through the foyer to his office. It suddenly felt dangerous, as if we were hiding from a murderer rather than the elderly and frail Mrs. Peabody. The poker boys and I sat motionless. Suddenly these grown men looked like schoolboys again, sitting perfectly silent, knowing that if they made a sound my father would hit the roof.

As soon as my father stepped out of the room, the men shook in silent laughter. They could only remain quiet by not making eye contact, for each time Eugene looked over at J.W., Eugene's face turned red and his shoulders trembled.

"Afternoon, Mrs. Peabody," we heard the undertaker say in his most dignified and respectful voice.

Everyone in the neighborhood, and certainly the men in the back of the chapel hidden from view, knew Mrs. Peabody. Two years previously she had made her way slowly up the steps to the funeral home. A small, round hat sat atop her gray head, a simple handbag dangled from her wrinkled wrist, and she more or less attempted a bright-colored lipstick. Mrs. Peabody had made an effort to look respectable even though her husband had died that day. She had no other family and not much money; she was worried about paying her husband's funeral bill. My father noticed she twisted a thin, worn-out flowered handkerchief in her hands. He remembered such things. Please, could her husband have the least expensive casket and a no-frills service, she asked. She couldn't afford flowers, not even the casket piece. It pained her to ask for long-term credit.

The next day my father waited for a flower delivery for Mr. Peabody's funeral, flowers that never arrived. He thought maybe a friend or the widow's church would provide at least a simple wreath. So he called the florist and ordered a spray of carnations and placed it on the man's casket. Every week after her husband was buried, Mrs. Peabody returned to the funeral home. She sat down in the chair opposite my father, opened her small, black purse, and handed him one dollar. She was a regular visitor to our funeral home for years, until at long last she'd paid her husband's heavily discounted funeral bill in full.

If she had visited on the same day each week, it might have been easier for the poker games to proceed without the niggling thought that Mrs. Peabody might just be on her way. The last thing my father needed was to shock a respectful widow with swirling cards and mounds of nickels and dimes, the evidence of gambling, before her very eyes. He sat behind his desk during the transaction. Mrs. Peabody took her time, unfolded the bill, and told him once again how grateful she was for his patience. As a matter of friendliness and ritual, they had a short discourse about the weather and Mrs. Peabody's health.

After he helped her down the front steps and she was safely away, my father returned to the game, where a new hand had already been dealt. The hilarity of the moment was calmer, but they all shook their heads and giggled like girls.

The poker boys became a bit obsessive. They showed up during nights of visitation, paid their respects, then one by one slipped out back. They set up a gurney and dealt a few hands. Even on frigid nights their stiff fingers placed the cards on the blanket that protected the white sheet, while they exhaled a combination of tobacco smoke and their natural breath.

I was glad my mother was playing bridge and not poker today, because if anything was worse for my father than losing, it was losing to my mother.

Sometimes in the afternoon games the playing became so intense that no one would move from his seat and the men lost all track of time. Today's game was fervid and my father's cards were stinkers — never a good thing. They'd been cutting cards all afternoon, except for the ten-minute break brought to them by Mrs. Peabody and a phone call for Eugene. I'd never seen so many nickels and dimes piled high in the middle of the table. One of the men reached into his pocket and pulled out a roll of quarters. This was serious. My father wanted that pot badly. He was betting on two pair, queens high. I had pulled up a chair beside him, near enough to keep an eye on his cards, though now I stood and canvassed each of the men's hands. Oh, Lord, I could see what was going to happen. I peeked over J.W.'s shoulder; he held trip aces. I could scarcely keep my expression blank. I moved back from the vortex and waited. Here it came. J.W. laid down his cards. A manly gasp of admiration followed. My father threw his cards down, stood up quickly and angrily, and the table swelled into the air as his chair went flying across the room behind him. To the sound of a chorus of "Look out!" and "Oh, no!" coins rose up and spilled over the men's chests, dropping into their laps.

Edgar came running in again, obviously not cut out for guard duty, his face the color of a strawberry, and a thick mass of yellow hair stood straight up on his head as if he'd just tried to pull it out.

"Eugene, your wife is here! She's just parked her car out front."

I have never seen grown men move so quickly. Suddenly the cards disappeared, the coins were snatched up, and the poker boys ducked out the back door headfirst. My father looked at me as he grabbed his suit jacket. "Upstairs," he directed me, and slipped into his jacket as he walked calmly to the front door. I ran along behind him and veered off up the steps. But not before I heard, "Afternoon, Fern."

I never tired of the company of adults and thirsted to know what it was like to be one. They behaved in the most extraordinary ways!

The rivalry between Alfred Deboe and my father kept him on his toes. One day he came home with a suit bag from his favorite men's clothing store. Unzipping it, he revealed a white, double-breasted suit.

"What are you doing with that?" I asked him.

"Come and see."

Outside, parked in front of the garage, was a gleaming white Cadillac hearse. He'd traded in the black Packard for this big, white monster. Next to the hearse was a smaller monster, a white ambulance built in the same elongated shape as the hearse, both like white, winged omnibuses.

"Isn't that a pretty sight? We're going to have white funerals."

"Is that why you bought that suit? You're going to wear a white suit at the funerals?" I asked, stunned.

"Not many of them, just the high-profile, bigger funerals."

His white funerals were a first in Jubilee. Everyone in Jubilee was seeped in the culture of dark, somber mourning, and that image remained, except for my father's figure. Slowly the funeral procession made its way through town, the white hearse leading the way. Folks pulled over to let the cortege pass, and when it reached the cemetery, my father stepped out and moved through the green shade trees, his white suit glaring.

It didn't stop there. The flashing lights on Deboe's ambulance were red, so my father switched his red lights for blue ones. But the police force, all of two cars, used blue lights, so, much to his chagrin, they insisted that he return to his red lights.

Every autumn Deboe drove his ambulance onto the sidelines of the high school football field during the games in case of an emergency. He'd held that prominent advertising position for years. Undaunted, my father muscled his way onto the field for the games played away from Jubilee. He drove for hours to other towns so the fans could see him at the games. I rode along, stretched out on the gurney, and emerged from the ambulance onto the football field, refreshed and ready for the game. Eventually he won the right to service half the home games as well.

I wondered if Miss Agnes had given him a little shove to promote himself in these ways. I'm certain they at the very least discussed his ideas.

Percy Foley, the hospital administrator, continued to do everything in his power to give Deboe an edge. Foley secured free hospital beds and wheelchairs and gave them to Deboe, who loaned them out to people free of charge, securing future business when the time came. It made my father furious. Not to be outdone, he bought hospital beds, wheelchairs, crutches, and extra folding chairs and loaned them to anyone who wanted them, also free of charge. And no need to worry about coming by to pick them up; he delivered them, too. I overheard Sonny tell someone that Percy Foley hated Frank Mayfield and his whole damn family. Whenever my father's name came up in conversation, Percy could only bring himself to refer to him as "that son of a bitch."

He may have been a son of a bitch to some people, but others thought he was close to being a hero. A family, the Nelsons, lived on a small, ratty old piece of land outside of Jubilee. My father would describe the family as hard up, and when the couple walked into his office, he knew he would never see a penny for the service he was about to perform. The Nelsons had several children, maybe nine, maybe ten. Now they had one less. Their two-year-old had died and they asked my father to bury the child. They struggled to say they would pay "when things got better." He put them at ease, buried their child, and never sent a bill.

At times a hero was the last thing he wanted to be, when duty called and he would have given anything not to answer. On a morning when the sky was dark as granite and the roads, dusty from a dry spell, had become slick and dangerous from a light rain that fell the previous evening, Miles Parker's car slid off the road and hit a tree. He died instantly. Miles had often come by the funeral home and had long conversations with my father. The tone of their voices was always smooth and calm, and I discovered it was all about insurance, families, and the state of the world. I remembered the day Miles walked by me on his way up the steps to the funeral home. A patch of earth stuck out of the concrete where the tree trunks plowed into the ground.

"What are you doin' there?" he asked.

I dug slowly and patiently with a white plastic spoon. "I'm digging a tunnel."

"That so? Where to?"

"China."

"How long do you think that will take you?"

"Not sure."

"What will you do when it's finished?"

"Why, go there, of course."

"I'll tell you what. Here's a quarter. When you get there, let me know and I'll make a full investment in your tunnel."

"Miles was too young to die," I said to my mother. She told me to stay out of the way so my father could work on him.

"Your daddy's all torn apart. When he

brings Miles out, don't go into the chapel until he's finished." I noticed her voice was softer, more patient than normal.

Miles made a larger-than-life impression when he walked into a room, although he was basically shy and it pained him to be noticed. He was tall, with jet-black hair held in place with plenty of pomade, and dark, exotic looks. My father said his friend was a well-dressed sophisticate. My mother sometimes played bridge with his wife, and Jemma was good friends with one of their children.

My father had to put Miles's face back together. There wasn't much to work with. He would have preferred a closed-casket service, but Miles's wife wanted to see him. So the undertaker pulled himself together and worked on his friend for hours with the few reconstructive tools that existed. I stood beside the casket before Miles's family came in to see him. My stomach tightened, but I made myself look. Miles had a swarthy complexion, now unrecognizable under thick, orange-tinted makeup. One of his temples was swollen and a little purple, the other was dented. My father carefully dabbed the side of Miles's face with powder, as if it might still hurt. He was silent while he worked. It was a bitter thing to witness and I wanted to make my father feel better. It was the first time I felt that the undertaker needed consoling.

"He still looks like Miles, Daddy. I bet his family's really going to appreciate it."

He remained silent, nodded, and bit his lip.

As distressed and weighed down with grief as they were, Miles's family was indeed appreciative. They had to see him, no matter what, even if they no longer recognized him. They were grateful that my father gave them that opportunity and were visibly relieved when they did recognize him. They would never know the hours my father spent working on him, or the depth of his own anguish.

Sometimes when illness had ravaged a body, the family couldn't understand why their undertaker couldn't perform miracles. He tried to prepare them for their first viewing, to explain that after long hours in the embalming room, he worked for the best result, which might still not suffice. "I've done all I could. I know he might not look exactly as you'd like."

But most of the time, he was surprised to hear how relieved, how satisfied, the family was with the results of a difficult case. At times under challenging circumstances, he couldn't stop fiddling with the decedent, and I would come upon him while he stood over the casket, the flowers already delivered and in place, moments before the family was due. He would rather not charge for the embalming than have a family unsatisfied.

Bad weather brought another act of heroism. One winter night an unexpected and furious snowstorm fell upon Beacon County. The roads were quickly coated with ice, and several feet of snow fell during the evening. A woman called the funeral home in dire straits. Screaming in pain, she could barely speak. After a few nerve-wracking minutes my father managed to extract the story from her. Her husband was out of town and she was in labor. Her house was tucked away on one of the back roads in the county and she was stranded. She'd already phoned the police, the fire department, and friends with trucks. No one would venture out to get her. They claimed it was impossible to drive safely on the narrow country lane that led to her house.

The white ambulance, with only snow chains for protection, crept along the country roads. My father made it to the house, but it took him so long to get there that by the time he carried her to the ambulance and began making his way to the hospital, it was too late. She was having that baby there and then and he had to help. He had no choice but to stop along the side of the road. My father knew a lot of things, but his knowledge of midwifery was nonexistent. The ambulance was equipped with a tank of oxygen, a mask, a blanket, and a less than impressive first-aid kit. He picked up the handheld two-way radio and contacted the hospital. The doctor on duty that night guided him through the birth, step by step. In the ambulance, with the snow piling up around the windows, under the small indoor roof light, the undertaker delivered a baby.

One of the drawbacks of the funeral business was the sense of confinement, of always being on call. He offered himself to the people of Jubilee twenty-four hours a day, seven days a week. Even when he tried to leave things to his employees, a shocked and grieving family member only wanted to speak to the owner, to the person who had spent a great deal of time, even years, building a relationship with the person.

Every summer we tried valiantly to get away. We couldn't make plans until my father was sure that no one looked in obvious danger of dying. Arrangements were made for Miss Agnes to be cared for until our return, and someone had to spend nights at the funeral home while we were away. We tried to behave like normal people. We packed up and headed for Florida. We scrambled, sleepy eyed, into the station wagon at the crack of an ungodly hour; it felt like we were sneaking out of town. Jubilee had no bakery and we worshipped Krispy Kremes, so our first stop was the nearest town where we could find the sugary doughnuts, warm from the conveyor belt. Thomas told us that Krispy Kremes were first sold in Kentucky and that not a lot of people knew that.

Thomas would leave for college soon, and this might be his last trip with us for a while. We went to the school auditorium to see him perform in the senior play. I'd never seen a play before and was astonished that he was transformed into someone I didn't recognize. Bewitched, I didn't move a muscle for two hours. He wore a doctor's coat and his hair was completely gray. He showed me later how they used special silver spray paint. When I saw him walk across the stage, I sat on the edge of my seat and said to myself, *That's what I want to do. I have just got to be in a play someday.*

When I heard "Pomp and Circumstance" and saw Thomas walk down the aisle at his graduation, a surprising lump developed in my throat and I was useless at holding back the tears. Who would tell me things I needed to know? Thomas told me once why he thought Miss Agnes wore red all the time.

"Miss Agnes is really smart. She knows exactly what she's doing. She wears red as part of her public relations and marketing plan. It's her way of advertising. Think how well it worked. Everyone knows who she is."

That was the kind of thing I needed to know. My father said that Miss Agnes just liked red a lot, but Thomas provided me with details. He was going to be a journalism major. Evelyn, on the other hand, slept almost all the way to Florida and woke up cranky when it was time to eat or go to the bathroom. I doubt if I would cry when she graduated — if she ever graduated.

On this trip, we left Jemma at the funeral home with Belle, for which Jemma never forgave us. She and Belle were the best of friends, but even so, I'll never forget the image of Jemma sitting in Belle's lap forlornly waving good-bye, her big eyes filled with tears.

With the open road in front of us, we never knew what was going to happen. My father possessed a radar that honed in on the unusual or hidden gem in a sea of mediocrity. He found an A-framed pancake house off the main road where we stopped for breakfast when the doughnuts wore off. He'd never stop in a generic burger joint, but would find the best damn truck stop with the best damn hot plate in the middle of nowhere or stumble upon an elegant steak house in a city.

He suddenly pulled the car over to the side of a busy highway, straddled a fence, and unashamedly stole juicy, ripe oranges from an unknowing grower's trees. He performed this mild act of vandalism without mussing up his clothes or bringing any of the grove's dust back with him. We rode deeper into the South and he pulled over again and bagged the moss that hung from heavy-laden trees.

"Here, smell this. Feel what this is like. This is Spanish moss."

"They stuff mattresses and furniture with this stuff," Thomas said. There was that detail again.

As we sped along farther and farther away from Jubilee, I began to sense the great expanse of America. *How small our little town is,* I thought. Not for the first time, I held the notion that I might not always live in Jubilee. Perhaps, when I grew up, I would move far away.

After hours and hours on the road the salty ocean's perfume finally drifted in through the open windows. We waited in the car at a hotel praying for a thumbs-up. My father always conducted a room inspection. If he didn't like it or if the hotel didn't meet his standards, onward he drove until the search for the right room, on the right stretch of the beach, was completed.

He became a free man in the ocean. He dove in, swam, rode a raft, and sunbathed all day, every day. It seemed he craved time to be alone. The waves rocked him, he walked silently on the beach looking for seashells, and stretched out on a lounge chair by the pool, his eyes closed. He didn't ignore us, but he relished his stolen moments of solitude. I sensed this, and though I would have liked nothing more than to build sand castles with him, I made no demands.

We arrived back at the hotel room each day sandy and salty, hoping that the light wouldn't be flashing on the phone — usually a harbinger of death.

When we changed for dinner, I waited for the fashion show. Out came clothes that my father never wore in Jubilee. Knee-length, white cotton shorts were perfectly pressed and showed off his tan. He wore short-sleeve, knit shirts and dark sunglasses. He strolled around in spiffy canvas shoes, never sandals. My mother wore dressy shorts, too, and brightly colored Hawaiian-print blouses, or cotton sundresses that she wouldn't be caught dead in at the Jubilee Kroger's. We went to a different restaurant every night and ordered exotic foods such as lobster and broccoli and fruit drinks with paper umbrellas. We played miniature golf and went to amusement parks and became incredibly sleepy by eight o'clock.

My parents always got into at least one fight on vacation.

My mother tried to follow a map. "You're supposed to turn here to get back to the hotel."

"No, we turn at the next junction."

"No, Frank. It says here —"

"I don't care what it says, I'm turning here."

We were lost. This made him angry and he took it out on her. He swerved over to the side of the road and slammed on the brakes.

"You drive then, goddamnit! You think you know so much." He stepped out of the car.

"Frank, get back in the car."

"No. You drive. Let's see how long it takes

you to get back."

My mother was always right when it came to directions. She had a head for it. It didn't take her long to get us back, and no one breathed until we pulled into the hotel's parking lot.

"I told you." She couldn't leave it alone; her voice held a tinge of smugness that she didn't bother to hide.

He left their hotel room while we were getting ready for bed. A worried look fell upon my mother's angry face.

"Where's he going?" I asked.

"I don't know. To cool off, I guess." But she sounded unsure.

She sat in their room and waited for him to return. I don't know what time my father eventually came back.

His sharp tongue and the shard of stubbornness in my mother that wouldn't be silenced throbbed in the confined spaces of the hotel room and car. They couldn't hide their disagreements here as they did behind their bedroom door at home.

The next morning both were quiet and barely spoke to each other, but his mood was back to joking around with us, the children. It took a couple of days for my mother to come round and appear normal.

Eventually, a few days into the vacation,

the call would come from Jubilee. Someone always died. We packed our suitcases be-grudgingly. Seldom would my father leave the funeral arrangements and embalming completely in the hands of staff. More often than not, my father felt he owed it to the family members with whom he'd cultivated relationships over the years to be present. He'd experienced their displeasure, anger, and even their despair when he was not.

Days after we returned home, Jemma and I climbed up on the sofa beside our father and played with him. While he tried to watch television, we peeled the skin off his head after his sunburn healed. The rest of his body tanned to a deep bronze, but the top of his head where his hair was thinning was all ours. Sometimes we asked about his scar. He often wore pajama bottoms without the top as if he were reclaiming the freedom he found on vacation. He was a tall, well-built man except for his slightly swollen belly, and the scar on his stomach begged our attention. I ran my fingers down his torso from the top of his ribs to his navel, tracing the thick scar usually hidden by his beautiful shirts.

"Show us the trick, Daddy." Jemma grabbed his lighter and handed it to him.

"Leave your father alone." Mother was in

no mood for tricks.

"Come on, Daddy. Do the trick."

He opened the lighter and snapped the wheel until the flame grew long. Carefully, he directed the flame to the scar and did not flinch when it made contact. We squealed with delight and marveled that our father could have such a thing on his body that felt no pain.

"Go get the pins, Jemma."

"No, now you all leave him alone." My mother looked up angrily from her *Reader's Digest*.

We giggled and Jemma ran off to find a straight pin.

I slowly stuck the pin in the scar while I kept my eye on him to gauge his reaction. He felt no pain. We thought his whole stomach area was a numb, vast receptacle for anything to which it might be subjected.

"Stop poking him!" my mother insisted. "Your father was in the hospital for weeks because of that wound! Why else do you think he drinks Alka-Seltzer all day long? He was very, very sick! He was in the hospital for weeks and weeks. . . . He only has half a stomach!"

"Stop. You'll scare them to death," he said to her. Then, to us: "Your mother's getting upset. Better put that away. Here, give me back my lighter."

I took the pin out and waited for our mother to resume reading.

"Now tell us about the war. Tell us about how you got shot," Jemma whispered to him.

He put the lighter away and stared at the television. "I was in a jeep driving a German prisoner to another location, and he grabbed my gun and shot me in the stomach."

"That's it," our mother said. "Go to bed. Both of you."

Jemma and I were so caught up in our play that we didn't notice the change in him, the dark expression, how he clammed up in seconds. To us, my father's war was just a story covered by a scar, nothing more.

CHAPTER 9
MAUSOLEUM OF DESIRE

"Come on, I've got something to show you."

"Where're we going?"

"Just get in the car."

My father was a purveyor of surprises. He drove down South Main Street, our end of the street, to Miss Agnes's office at the end of North Main Street.

"I know we're not going to visit Miss Agnes," I said, possibly overconfidently.

"How do you know that?"

" 'Cause I'm wearing these shorts and Keds. You'd never take me to see her looking like this."

"That's right, I never would."

He parked the car and led me into one of Miss Agnes's warehouses, a massive barn-like building. He pushed the tall doors open and we entered a gray darkness that only gradually welcomed the natural light. Then my eyes fell on the bags and bags of fertilizer stacked up, skirting the high ceiling as if Miss Agnes anticipated a flood. I sniffed for a scent from the hundreds of bags, but there was none. The air was cool and the bare concrete floor felt cold beneath my feet. In this building Miss Agnes let my father garage his beloved 1937 Buick Roadmaster. It sat majestically in the corner like a dark knight. Beside the car was a damsel of the water world, a vanilla-colored boat, out of place among the VC Fertilizer bags, but gleaming in the darkness. When I moved closer, I saw that the boat was trimmed with a striking red stripe.

"Are we rich?" I asked.

He laughed. "Hardly."

He'd bought a speedboat and became a man newly unburdened while at its helm. Lake Herndon was only a short drive from Jubilee, thereby making it a little easier for him to get away for a few hours. He liked to stand while driving it, surveying the lakeside around him, waving to other boaters, nodding his head as if to say, "Good afternoon, fellow boaters." I have no idea where he found them, but he always wore the most magnificent bathing trunks. The colors were bold and rich and the fabric flapped in the breeze like a flag. When the suits and ties came off, he did casual ridiculously well.

He had a palpable sense of freedom about

him when he was on the lake. No one could summon him to an accident, no one could call him to report a death; nothing was in front of him but miles of water, the surrounding trees, and lakeside cabins speckling the hilly shore. My mother drove the boat while he skied. She seemed anxious to achieve the right speed and understand his hand signals. We cheered him on and waited for him to give a signal, or worse, we saw him lose his groove and fall. "He's going down! He's going down!" we shouted. It made my mother nervous. She didn't enjoy being on the lake. Something about the wind destroying her hair and a worry that she wasn't pleasing him, and she was always concerned for our safety.

The summer I learned to water-ski, I was graceless. Evelyn pointed and laughed at me as I choked on mouthfuls of lake water. She stewed with boredom each time I fell, a frown of irritation darkening her face when the wooden planks on my feet became entangled and my legs splayed from another failed attempt. I was attracting too much attention for her liking. But my father was patient with me as I struggled to defy the water and rise like the Lady of the Lake to a standing position. The day I finally conquered the feat it gave my confidence such

a boost that I considered becoming a professional skier. Why not? I thought. If someone
beat me to the title of first female undertaker in Kentucky, then perhaps I would
move to Florida and work in the Cypress
Gardens waterskiing shows. It was the nearest I had ever come to performing a sport.
Here was a solid thing we all had in common; I could now include myself in a family
of water-skiers. Oh, happy day. But why
didn't I feel oh, happy day? Something,
some gray thought, nagged at me as I
floated in the black, opaque water.

It was a muggy August afternoon. The
heat had warmed the lake all summer and it
felt like bathwater. After a brilliant ride on
the smooth surface, my skis hit a patch of
rough water and I went down suddenly in a
harsh sprawling splash. I treaded water,
waiting for the boat to swerve back my way.
Evelyn was the human equivalent of the
choppy water; her bad moods rose unex-
pectedly. The sun was hot on my head, but
underneath the warm water a sudden cold
current shocked my legs. She was like that;
at certain moments she appeared warm and
sunny on the outside . . . but I knew she
was as cold as ice on the inside.

Evelyn became a different person around
her friends. Her sullen expressions dis-

appeared and I heard her laughing in her bedroom when they came to visit. They thought she was a lot of fun, a real life of the party. While she listened to them chatter, her eyes grew wide, her mouth opened into a perfect circle as if she were enraptured; so different from her bored, frowning silences. She was doing that now, laughing in the boat with a friend she had invited along. Two conspirators looking my way.

When I was younger, I attempted to wangle my way into her room to see what she and her friends were doing, but she promptly slammed the door in my face and I heard a subsequent squeal of delight that I had been shut out. I no longer made an effort to be included.

She had a new hairstyle, a kind of semi-shaggy bubble cut. Grabbing hold of a tuft of hair, she furiously teased it with her special teasing comb that if I touched I died. Then she used her fingers to create a curl, which she plastered to the side of her face with Dippity-do and a piece of tape. I always hoped that she'd forget the tape was there and walk out of the funeral home looking ridiculous, but she never did. She combed her hair now as it dried in the lake's breeze.

Evelyn ignored me in public. Once, I sat

at the counter in the drugstore and saw Evelyn sitting in the back with her friends. When I waved, she turned her back on me. I busied myself by watching life pass by the long picture window that ran across the front of the store, until she stomped over to chase me away. My face reddened at her disregard for me, painfully on display for everyone in the store.

Mr. Swann placed a Cherry Coke in front of me. "There you go." He winked. "That's on the house, little lady." Mr. Swann leaned in and explained, "Your daddy, now, he did such a good job on my aunt Myrtle, I just don't see you ever paying for another soda in here."

I wondered if that was true. Mr. Swann's nonchalant way of wiping the counter was deceiving. I observed him observing us. Perhaps his offer of a free drink was a salve to soothe the sting of Evelyn's brusque treatment of me, which he was sure to have noticed.

It took an extraordinarily long time for me to get the message that we weren't going to be friends. Whenever I walked into her bedroom, for whatever reason, she shouted at me for trespassing, then held me with one hand and beat my arm with the other. She knew exactly how to hit with her fists to achieve the most pain by making consecutive punches in the same spot until I cried out.

It was hard to understand. Thomas never struck us. Jemma and I never hit each other. We weren't the kind to go looking for a fight. There was no fighting back with Evelyn; there was only a search for protection, which never arrived. I sometimes felt my mother was completely deflated by Evelyn's behavior, although she defended her in the wildest circumstances. Evelyn was a storm to be weathered, and her blows and smacks went unpunished. What little my mother meted out to her was not enough to deter her. And as Evelyn grew older, my mother's attempts lost all potency. Frustration churned in my stomach and I wanted to scream, *"Why can't you control her?!"*

For whatever reason, perhaps after endless private attempts to address them, Evelyn was allowed her mood swings. They were like the wakes behind the speedboats on the lake; it was necessary to cross carefully to get to the other side.

Floating in the water, I gathered my strength for one more ride. I flew across the lake until my stamina was zapped and an unbelievable tiredness set in. My arms and legs ached until they trembled and it was time to stop. I gave my father the thumbs-down and he pulled back on the speed. When the rope could no longer hold me up, I let go and slowly sank into the water. In those few minutes that I waited for the boat, I remembered the snakes. Lake Herndon was home to water moccasins; we often saw them slithering, their heads stretching up from their underwater home. My eyes followed the boat while I waited for safety and tried not to think about the snakes, or the emptiness in the pit of my stomach that came from being alone in what could easily become unfriendly territory. That's what it was like to live with Evelyn.

I didn't know what, if anything, was wrong with her. Though my parents may have thought nothing in Evelyn's behavior was pernicious, that it was just a case of kids will be kids, it was bewitching to think that deep down they knew that, of course, something was wrong, something that would not be discovered for decades.

No one in Jubilee was mentally ill. The words were foreign to us. There were *retarded people,* the unfortunate label used at the time, and people who weren't *right in the head,* who were ostracized and suffered ridicule. A psychiatrist was defined as a quack who experimented on the insane who roamed the halls of Gothic mental hospitals. We knew the term *manic depression* only vaguely in the form of domestic-suspense novels, soap operas, and B movies. But those had nothing to do with *our* lives. Certainly this condition called depression did not include children, and even if it did, no one would ever admit it. If Evelyn's behavior had an underlying diagnosis, it remained buried in an area as dark and murky as the waters of Lake Herndon.

Jemma and I never realized what a buffer Thomas's presence had served us against Evelyn's wild world and we missed him terribly. She chose her battles more carefully when he was around, except on the occasions when one of her stormy moods came upon her. One weekend when Thomas came home from college, he and a friend sat around the kitchen table talking, a rare sort of thing. It dawned on me that Thomas hardly ever had friends over. Now I knew why. Evelyn walked in and, as if possessed, began babbling on and on, interrupting them and laughing at them. It began as annoying banter, then escalated. When Thomas asked her to leave, she became more hateful and vulgar. Embarrassed and too polite to wring her neck, he waited until his friend left and then scolded her with the sharpest tongue anyone had ever dared. Evelyn ran to our mother and made up some blatant lie about how Thomas had attacked her. This, I was to learn, would be her lifelong tactic to preempt anyone's effort to bring her to task. When my mother defended Evelyn and grew red-faced and angry at Thomas, he had clearly had enough. He set the record straight. My mother backed down, but it did nothing to change the pattern that had been set for years.

On the few occasions when it seemed that Evelyn had turned a new leaf and decided to be nicer to me, it always turned out badly. I didn't realize that I was being used as a ploy to hurt Jemma's feelings. One day Evelyn allowed one of her friends to show me a few cheerleading moves, but when Jemma came to the door to watch, Evelyn shut her out. I didn't come to Jemma's rescue and it left me feeling wretched.

When she wasn't taunting Jemma, Evelyn ignored her entirely. The ten years between them left a gap with no common ground. In one blindingly clear moment, my mother once said, "For the longest time Evelyn was the only girl in our family, including our extended family. When you and Jemma came along, it was hard on her."

Hard on *her*? Not half as hard as it would prove to be on Jemma and me.

My younger sister and I were thrown together in our family's hierarchy and it was a good fit. We shared a kindred fascination for Jubilee in mourning. Risking a smack from our mother, she often joined me on the steps to spy on the people in the funeral home. From our elevated position, time was lost to the soft chatter of the visitors. We poked each other and pointed when a person attracted our interest. Our curious streaks mingled as we scooted our nightgown-clad bottoms to a better view. When something odd happened, such as the time a whole row of men fell asleep at the same time, we clasped our hands over our mouths to keep from laughing out loud. Tears in our eyes and bent over one another trembling with silent laughter, we bonded over Jubilee's dead.

I figured it took an independent spirit and taste for oddities to come up with some of the things that pleased Jemma and amused me. At the tender age of nine, she decided she absolutely must have a wig. Our mother preferred our hair short, but Jemma de-spised wearing hers that way. She roved the floors of department stores in other towns on the hunt for her dream wig. She tried on a thick, black headband to which a long wad of dark hair was attached. The hair curled into a flip at the end. The ladies in the wig department called it a fall, not quite a full wig, and Jemma talked my mother into buying it for her. It was supposed to be a dressing-up toy, but once she owned it, she wore it everywhere. It was a lot of hair for a short, skinny little girl to pull off, but she wore it with audacious confidence.

After school, I usually found her sitting on the floor in front of the TV if we didn't have a funeral going. She looked like a dark-haired Barbie doll that had rumbled with the Salvation Army's shoe department. Her favorite pair of Buster Browns looked like bricks at the end of her thin, bare legs.

She camped out on the floor in her wig and Buster Browns with a plate of her favorite foods in front of her. She adored peanut butter on soda crackers and was addicted to bean-with-bacon soup. The soup needed diluting and a minute or two on the stove, but if Belle was busy, Jemma ate it straight from the can with a huge spoon. I liked variety and thought it astonishing that the mainstay of her diet consisted of three foods.

A small, white plastic bottle sat next to

her on the floor. She carried it around with her like a talisman, the contents of which relieved her itching skin. Wool carpets, grass, just about anything, gave Jemma a nasty red skin rash. She won an unlimited prescription from the doctor.

At times I made an effort to protect Jemma when Evelyn emerged, determined to ruin a perfectly pleasant day. Not until we were adults did I tell Jemma about the bitter day Evelyn chose to blurt out the story that laid waste to my perception of my father.

On an ungodly hot day I sat atop my bed with the air conditioner cranked up as high as it could go, wrapped up in my favorite blue-and-white quilt that Belle had washed so many times it was as soft as a baby blanket. Though I was deep into a Nancy Drew detective story, I sensed Evelyn standing in the doorway.

"Do you want a Popsicle?"

Something was up — Evelyn never asked if I wanted anything. "No." I turned back to my book.

"You wanted one last night."

"No, I didn't."

"You don't remember because you were sleepwalking."

"What? No, I wasn't."

"Yes, you were. You came into the kitchen last night after you'd been asleep and I asked you what you wanted, and you said you wanted a Popsicle for breakfast. Then you turned around and went back to bed."

I was alarmed. I'd heard about a woman who was often seen sleepwalking in her nightgown. One night she walked right out in front of a car and was killed. Was I a crazy sleepwalker? I couldn't tell if Evelyn was lying or not.

"I'll ask Daddy about it. He'll know if I'm a sleepwalker."

"Daddy doesn't know everything."

I'd learned to ignore Evelyn by burying my head in a book, but sometimes she just wouldn't be ignored.

"Yeah, Daddy isn't perfect, you know." She waited for a response, and when there was none, her tone grew conspiring. "Do you know Viv Salloway?"

"No."

"Sure you do. She used to work at the church. That skinny little thing."

Evelyn described people in the way of a caricaturist. Now I would be subjected to an exaggeration of all of Viv's shortcomings.

"She wore those ugly glasses and had that funny mouth. You know, her teeth stuck out."

"I kind of remember her. What about her?"

"Don't you know? There was a huge scandal. Daddy got caught with her."

"What do you mean 'got caught'?"

"He had an affair with her." Her eyes, shiny with delight, grew in size. There! She had plopped it in my lap and shocked me just as she'd wanted.

"How do you know?" I managed.

"Everybody in Jubilee knew all about it. It happened years ago. You were real young. She must have been in her twenties. Daddy was in his thirties, maybe even his forties. I don't know. Oh, yeah, it was a big thing. He used to be a deacon at the church, but they kicked him out of the deacons after that. So, you see, he's not perfect." Evelyn turned around and left with a little laugh that unsettled me.

I didn't know whether to believe Evelyn and there was not a soul I could ask. I pulled the quilt over my head and waited for the anger that I thought should be aimed at my father, but it wasn't there. I was intrigued. Where did he find the time? I pictured him standing at the door to the funeral home shaking hands, offering an elderly lady his arm, leading family members to their last moments with their loved one. I had trouble reconciling the other image, the one in which I imagined him sneaking into a motel room and into the arms of any woman other than my mother.

Yet, I did not think of my mother. Evelyn had forced me to imagine my father as a sexual being, a point I had not yet reached when I thought of my parents; their intimacy was quiet and private. This was something entirely different. Something wild and clandestine had been painting the landscape of my father's life. Something passionate, with which, in a strange way, I identified.

But why did he choose Viv? Evelyn was right about one thing: Viv wasn't half as pretty as our mother. Nor, as my mother would one day tell me, was Viv half the fighter my mother was.

I later learned that it wasn't the first time; my mother had fought for him before, in Lanesboro. She changed Evelyn's diapers, saw young Thomas off to school, and courageously battled it out with Patsy, a preacher's wife with whom Frank was having a passionate affair. Lily Tate went to great lengths to break it up by following him from rendezvous to rendezvous, even reaching out to Patsy's husband for help, to no avail. It was, strictly speaking, a mess. When Frank and Patsy ran away together, Lily Tate finally admitted defeat and hired a lawyer, who drew up a separation agreement. At the dawn of the 1950s she felt she was entering a strange and frightening world. They were swiftly on their way to a divorce when Frank grew tired of Patsy. He missed his two young children and his job in the Lanesboro funeral home, all of which he had abandoned. When she agreed to take him back, Lily Tate decided that never again would she let him go. "There will never be another Mrs. Frank Mayfield while I'm alive," she told herself.

My mother couldn't have guessed where that statement would lead or how solidly she would have to stand behind it. Relocated to Jubilee with her children, my mother didn't have time to pick up the faint clues to her husband's whereabouts. When she learned that he often wasn't where he said he would be, her heart sank. For a while she sought rational explanations, to no avail, for he soon burst on the bad-boy scene with an unprecedented flourish. Nor could she guess that the seed of this fracas had been sown in, of all places, our church.

The First Baptist Church in Jubilee meant many things to many people. For some, it served as a place to realign their moral compass. For my father, the church offered an opportunity to return to his passion for adulterous romance.

The new magnet to his groin worked in one of the church's offices. They became careless in their passion, and in the heat of a less than sacred moment, he was caught, some say literally, with his pants down, in the choir loft of the First Baptist Church. Viv was a slip of a woman, angular and sharp-featured, unlike my mother, who was soft and curved. Viv, birdlike in her movements, lacked the good looks most often associated with mistress material. But one never knows what kind of transformation occurs under the sheets, or indeed in the alcoves of a church.

Once, years later, in a few candid moments on the telephone, my mother spoke to me for the first time about that painful episode.

"What happened when it all began again in Jubilee?" I asked. I heard her sigh, but she reached back in her memory, and the decades that had passed since the scandal seemed to evaporate after my question.

"I'd already made up my mind that I was not going to give him a divorce. I went to see Viv's mother. I told her she was going to have to do something about her daughter. I'll tell you, what happened next that made me so mad I don't have any use for that man to this day. All that going on, and the preacher, it was Brother Norris at the time, came to *me* and said, "If you want to move back to Lanesboro, I'll see that you get help to move and we'll get you back over there."

"Why was the preacher even discussing this with you?"

"I don't know. But do you know what I told him? I told him I'm not going anywhere . . . if anybody leaves, Frank will. And I've never had any use for that preacher since."

"Was Daddy planning to run off with Viv?"

"No. Not that I know of. I guess he could have after she moved to Louisville, if he'd wanted to. But he didn't, so I don't think he planned to. She might have thought he was going to."

That is exactly what Viv thought, until her mother disillusioned her.

Viv's mother knew that Jubilee was not big enough to carry the weight of Lily Tate's wrath and the profusion of gossip that erupted. Nor could she save her daughter's reputation, except by encouraging her to leave town.

"Was it strange and uncomfortable for you when Viv eventually moved back to Jubilee?" I asked my mother.

"Yes, it was for a long time. I didn't see her that much though."

"Did Daddy ever say anything about her being back in Jubilee?"

"No. I've often wondered how she feels when she sees me. I've often wondered that."

"When you run into each other in the grocery store, do you speak?"

"Oh, yeah, she just acts like nothing ever happened. I want to say something ugly to her, but I don't."

"What did your friends say about it?"

"No one ever mentioned it or said anything to me about it. Not until after it was all over, and the only person that I can think of who ever mentioned it was Mary Alice Timmons. She said she didn't see *how in the world* I did what I did."

"Meaning . . . what?"

"Well, just, you know. I guess she thought I stayed calm and, you know, worked through it all, I guess."

"Did you stay calm?"

"Oh, gosh, I don't know. I imagine I blew up a time or two all right."

"What did you say to Mary Alice?"

"I told her I just did what I thought I had to do." My mother paused. "You can do a lot of things when you have to. I heard people say, right in front of me, and I don't know whether they just weren't thinking or whether they didn't know about it, but they would talk about someone running around on someone and say, 'If that was my husband, I couldn't put up with that. One of us would have to leave.' And I wanted to tell them that they don't know what they would do. You don't know what you'd do in any situation until you go through it yourself."

After I put the phone down, for the first time in the years and the distance that had passed between my mother and me, the penny dropped. How selfish my father had been, how hurtful, how careless . . . the deceit and embarrassment he foisted upon my mother would have been crushing. Yet, the scandal had already been buried, if not forgotten, and Jubilee had once again moved on. I don't know why it took me so long to imagine her misery.

The caring, hardworking undertaker of my childhood was still there, but he existed alongside the new stranger that he had become to me. My first instinct was not to blame him or judge him, perhaps because I was on the verge of becoming like him. As I first began to leave my childhood behind, though my life with the dead would remain a constant, I slowly ventured toward the forbidden. I would soon take risks to that end, just as he had.

CHAPTER 10
BURY ME WITH MY BUD

The tastes of the people of Jubilee had changed. In the late 1960s the final image of their mothers and wives lying in pastel negligees didn't sit well anymore. The Shroud Lady caught on quickly and designed backless, matronly dresses with Peter Pan collars in staid colors. But this new look was a flash in the pan — what severed the relationship between the Shroud Lady and my father was an act of patent disloyalty that he couldn't forgive. Alfred Deboe buried one of her relatives. My father hit the roof. She told him that she wasn't to blame; it was a family decision. Unsympathetic, it was simple to him: Why should he give his business to her if she took hers to the competition? But in the end, it was an elderly widow who drove the Shroud Lady out of business when she told my father she wanted to be buried in her own clothes.

Now, for the first time, family members

came to make arrangements carrying the deceased's clothing for use in burial. My father never knew what kind of garment crisis would be thrust upon him. He turned to my mother for help. He thought she knew more about how female clothing should fit and welcomed her feminine touch.

When my mother entered the embalming room, my father had already washed the body a second time and dressed the deceased woman in her underwear. Usually the family brought underclothes: a bra, a slip, underwear, and stockings. But sometimes they couldn't afford a new set and were embarrassed to bring in the old, frayed, and stained pieces. My father discreetly told them not to worry, that he would take care of it, then sent my mother out to purchase whatever was needed.

The first time my mother helped my father dress a female corpse, she seriously thought that the poor woman's bones might snap in two. The stiffness was breathtaking and startled her. And the body was much heavier than she'd imagined. It was all queer and awkward. She was unprepared for how cold the corpse felt. It was one thing to touch a dead hand as I had, another to handle the entire body as she did. My father was always there to help; it took at least two people to dress a body. He positioned and then held up the woman's torso while my mother pulled the dress or blouse over her head. Buttons and zips were fiddly and time-consuming, and my mother had to maneuver carefully around the body and my father.

A surprising number of people stored special clothes before they died to be used for their burial. They harbored suits and dresses and lingerie in their closets and cedar chests for years. This was hugely problematic for an undertaker. The clothes represented the deceased when they were thinner, when the clothing was in style, when the fabric was new and not faded or delicately disintegrating. The relatives, in their grief, were adamant that their mother be buried in the dress that had been hanging in her closet for ten to twenty years and would not be reasoned with.

The families never knew it, but my father took scissors to the backs of hundreds of dresses and men's suit jackets. My mother then either sewed a few stitches into the back of the garment to make it appear tidy, or more often, she tucked the fabric around the back of the torso.

My father preferred long sleeves on the women, especially on those who'd been ill for a long time. It was hard to explain to a family what dead arms looked like, how they took the attention away from the face and the overall image. They stood out like separate entities, even after they'd been made up to match the color of the face and hands.

If ill-fitting dresses and blouses weren't difficult enough, the shoe issue would raise its ugly head. There was absolutely no reason to be buried in shoes, but many people requested it. My father tried to explain — delicately — that the shoes would probably no longer fit. No matter how sensitive and subtle he was, sometimes an irate and hysterical person would complain, "I'm paying almost five thousand dollars for this funeral, and that means I'm paying for the right for my husband to wear shoes. So put the damn shoes on his feet, and if they don't fit, put the damn shoes at the bottom of the casket right next to his damn feet. All right?"

Hair, hair, and more hair. Lord! Southerners are particular about their hair.

Women became excruciatingly specific about how they wanted their hair to look when they were viewed.

Mrs. Dover used to grab me whenever she spotted me downtown. "I told your daddy about my curlicues, will you remind him for me?"

I nodded. "Sure thing, Mrs. Dover. Curlicues. Got it."

When I returned home, I asked my father about Mrs. Dover's spectacular request. He laughed and imitated her: "I want these two curlicues right here, do you see?" She'd pointed to the right and then to the left of her forehead. "I want them in place when people view me. Now, Frank, I don't care how much hairspray your girl has to use. And I think you better make a note of it."

There were others:

"I don't want Janice to do my hair; she never gives it enough lift. If Mildred can't get there, then don't bury me until she can."

"Frank, could you make sure my mother gets her blue rinse?"

And another:

"Mr. Mayfield, I've been thinking about Leonard and his hair for burial."

"Why goodness, Tandy, is Leonard ill?"

"Oh, no, no, Nothing like that. I'm just thinking out loud here. . . . Leonard has a haircut every third Thursday of the month. You'll need to work around that, 'cause if he dies on the Wednesday of his haircut week, you'll have to get Carl to cut his hair. He's quite particular about his haircuts; no one but Carl has cut his hair since he was a young man."

Leonard's wife seemed oblivious to the fact that Carl could barely see anymore to cut anyone's hair and was likely to die before Leonard.

With all the new requests and demands, sometimes it just didn't work out the way people wanted. Mildred or the family's chosen beautician might not be able to attend to the deceased for a dozen reasons. And at times the family's budget was so tight that in lieu of paying Mildred my father called upon my mother. I found this hilarious. The last time my mother actually washed and set her own hair must have been during the war. But she rallied and picked up a few tips from Mildred and rose to the occasion like the Southern beauty-parlor-going professional she was.

"We never do the back of the head," Mildred once told her. "There's no need, 'cause her head is just lying there on that pillow and no one will ever see it. Just a waste of hairspray, really."

"Now, Mildred," my mother said. "You can skip the back of every woman's head in this county, but I want you to do the back of mine when I die. I will not have the back of my hair not done up right."

No one ever complained about my mother's hairstyling talent, or lack of it, and most family members were unaware that she had stepped in and helped. She was always in the background, loyal to my father and his work. She remained aligned with the social mores of the day and resisted any urge to behave otherwise. He was her life.

People continued to demand burial quirks. As I sat in the office one day, a man opened the door, stuck his head in, and with a wide smile said, "Howdy, Frank. Now don't forget, I want you to put a can of beer in my pocket."

"Oh, I won't, Mr. Miller. A Bud, right?"

"That's right, over the state line, my friend, over the state line." Then off he went, whistling down the street.

My father promised Mr. Miller that he would drive over to Tennessee, purchase a beer, bring it back to Kentucky, and place it in Mr. Miller's pocket at the time of his funeral. Not just in the casket, but in his trouser pocket, right next to his body.

Then, as if the whole town were listening in on a party line, other requests poured in. Horace wanted to be buried with his whittling knife. Mrs. Palmer insisted upon lying in her casket with her iron skillet in full view. A farmer would not part with his John

Deere blanket. John Deere was a favorite —
the hat, the toy tractor, almost anything with
the logo on it.

My father viewed the changes in burial
customs and the fulfillment of ever-growing
special requests as a natural evolution of
the business. But he would never admit that
he was taken completely unaware when
Sonny pulled a fast one on him. Sonny
wasn't as thickheaded as he looked.

"Where's Sonny? Is he on vacation?" I
asked.

"No, Sonny's gone."

"Did you fire him?"

"No, I didn't fire him. The son of a bitch
has opened his own funeral home."

"Where?" I couldn't believe it.

"Right around the goddamn corner, that's
where."

Later that afternoon, the men gathered at
the poker table and discussed this sensa-
tional news.

"Well now, Frank, you knew it was bound
to happen. He's a homegrown county boy.
Why, he's got all kinds of connections."
Johnnie Ray dealt the cards.

"Yeah, he's got that relative in the sheriff's
department, and the coroner's a good friend
of his, too," my father said. And these were
most likely the only reasons he'd never fired

Sonny years ago.

"The hometown boy who had nothin', poor as dirt, now he's gonna start up his own business, gonna make good. There'll be some in Jubilee pullin' for him, Frank." Brother Sam stated the obvious.

"They'll forget who taught him everything. He sure has. He wouldn't have his license if it weren't for you." Johnnie Ray threw in his hand.

They played cards silently while the question in everyone's mind was *Why didn't Frank make him a partner?* My father had discussed the possibility with Sonny, but when my father mentioned this to my mother, she went berserk. She'd endured Sonny's bravado on several occasions and early in his employment overheard him bragging to salesmen about how he would one day own the whole business and that he was solely responsible for making the funeral home successful.

She couldn't have been more clear, or more serious, when she threatened my father, "If you make Sonny a partner, I will leave you."

My father always tempered Sonny's eagerness with "We'll see. We'll see." What happened later was something my father would never tell the poker players. An elderly man who hadn't much money was in need of a ride to his doctor, an hour's drive from Jubilee, and was required to keep to a schedule of regular appointments. He was dependent on the funeral home's service to drive him back and forth. Sonny was given this task and my father told him not to charge the man, even if he offered to pay. One day my father ran into the elderly man and discovered Sonny had indeed charged him each time and had pocketed the money. Good riddance.

After Sonny left, a few new employees drifted through the funeral home, until a man named Fount walked through the door. He was the one who stayed. I guess if you were going to work with my father, you had to become accustomed to his children hanging around and running down the stairs when the funerals were over. Sonny always bristled when Jemma and I ransacked the snack machine or lurked around the office and listened to his phone calls. But Fount was different. He was quiet, with feathery, white hair and a barrel of a stomach. Thin, black-framed glasses sat snugly on his temples. He reminded me of Colonel Sanders. Fount looked as if he'd already had a life and anything else was a bonus. I never knew what he was thinking, but whatever it was, it didn't feel bad. He never tired of Jemma and me running in and out the front door when the funeral home was quiet. He stood at the door and opened it for us with his chunky arm about a thousand times a day. Fount didn't mind when I practiced the organ, even if I got carried away and dramatically blasted the "Theme of *Exodus*" over and over. I was eager to prove that my music lessons with Totty were not in vain.

Fount wore the face of contentment when he was working. My father said Fount was happy to fill his hours with our family and the folks of Jubilee rather than stay at home with his difficult wife. She might have been fun to court, but turned sour and demanding when the marriage had aged. His avoidance of her bred loyalty to my father.

One morning Fount and my father were in the showroom, putting the finishing touches on a body while I looked on.

"Totty can't make it to the funeral tomorrow," my father said.

"What are we going to do?" Fount asked.

"Aren't you going to call Mabel? She always fills in for Totty," I said.

"Mabel's out of town. You're going to have to play."

"I can't! I'm not ready."

"Aw, hell, of course you are. It's a small funeral. You only have to play three hymns."

"I'll mess up. Or I'll play at the wrong time."

"Not possible," said Fount. "You can't play at the wrong time. Your daddy controls these things. He'll tell you when to play." Fount spoke the absolute truth.

"I'll pay you," my father offered.

"How much?"

"Exactly what I pay Totty."

"How much is that?"

"Twelve dollars."

I thought about it. School had ruined my home life. The days of traipsing through the cemeteries with my father had dwindled. Spring Farm's coffee counter had closed, and I no longer ate pie with him at ten o'clock in the morning. My mother bought eggs at the grocery now, so the Egg Man was history. I was too old to play in the casket boxes. This might be a way of staying connected, a way of garnering a little more attention from my father.

"Okay. I'll do it."

I practiced all night on three hymns and woke early the next morning and practiced again, still in my pajamas. My rendition of "Washed in the Blood of the Lamb" at eight o'clock that morning brought cries of "Will you stop that racket!" from my mother.

Before the funeral service began, my father took the pallbearers aside and gave them directions on where to stand, how to stand, which way to face, how to hold the casket, when to move forward, when to move backward. He pinned carnations on their lapels with each flower leaning in the same direction.

Jesus, I thought, *this guy is particular.* It dawned on me that I'd never seen my father in action in quite this way, never seen him actually conduct an entire funeral.

Earlier that morning he'd given me instructions. When he looked over at me at the beginning of the service, it was my signal to play two verses of the first hymn. And the next time he looked at me I was to play the next hymn.

"But what if you look at me and you don't mean for me to play, you just happen to look at me?" I was slightly panicked.

"I won't."

And he didn't. At the beginning of the service he stood at the wide, open entrance to the chapel and looked over at me. I played the first few notes of "Amazing Grace" with sweaty fingers. He turned away. Whew! When I began the second hymn, he turned around sharply, frowned, and with his hand tactfully motioned for me to lower the volume. Immediately I let up on the pedal and silently cursed myself.

I sat quietly on the bench during the eulogy, palms still sweating, waiting for the amen. At the end of the service he looked over at me again and I played the last hymn. Then he walked down to the front of the chapel where the preacher stood waiting for him. With a small gesture, just large enough for the congregants to see, he directed everyone to rise. The pallbearers didn't move a muscle until they received his signal, a slight nod, to move the casket.

When my father returned from the cemetery, he presented me with a check for $20.

"But you said twelve!" I was thrilled.

"I didn't want you to do it for the money. I wanted you to do it because you wanted to."

Evelyn cornered me that night. She turned off the television right in the middle of one of Perry Mason's big cases. She'd grown more moody and, when in a bad phase, intolerably hateful.

"So, I guess you think you're pretty important now."

"No, not really." I had no idea what she meant.

"Sitting up there on that organ bench, like

you're Miss Liberace."

I said nothing, sensing a scene that might wind up with her fist on my body.

"Can't you speak up for yourself, or are you just going to sit there like a knot on a log?"

"You could have played for the funeral if you'd just stuck with the lessons. But you quit. That's not my fault."

And there came the fist. I showed the bruise on my arm to my mother the next day.

"You should have kept your mouth shut. You know how she is."

Evelyn's bullying had no effect on my effort to insinuate myself into my father's busy life. I felt compelled to be near him, to watch for signs of this secret, private part of him.

One afternoon after school I pulled on a pair of dungarees, an old sweater, and tennis shoes, then announced that I was ready to go hunting.

My father didn't have any hobbies like most men. Boating didn't count because he didn't fish, and no other men in Jubilee went antiquing for a hobby except for a man who was noticeably unmarried. I put hunting down to the farmboy in him that needed an airing. The other men showed up at the funeral home in their scruffy hunting clothes, but when my father emerged from the back wearing his camouflage regalia, I thought, *Here is a man who really likes to dress up.* The crisp, clean, full camouflage went from head to toe, and the fabric was pressed as perfectly as a uniform. Somehow he made it look as if it were the only way to be, and the other men dimmed in comparison. It felt out of character for both of us, but we loaded up the jeep — oh, yes, he also owned a jeep now — with his friends and gear and we took off to the country, intrepid travelers to the fields and woods.

Our motley crew descended upon a field cast in the autumn twilight. The air was full of the strong smell of the earth, and woods that rose behind us. After we settled in a spot, and at the direction of five men who gave me an assortment of instructions, I readied myself to fire a rifle for the first time.

"Kneel down," my father said.

"No, stand up," Billy ordered.

"No, it'll knock her down," my father said. "Kneel down, put the gun on your shoulder."

He positioned himself behind me on one side, with Billy on the other.

I aimed at nothing. The rifle kicked back and I thought my shoulder would fall off.

Well, hell. It knocked me down anyway. Oh, how they laughed. I scrambled right back up and laughed with them.

I wasn't going to be a hunter; I haven't touched a gun since that day. I suggested that instead I should pick up the kill, but they were hunting doves and wanted the bird dogs to do what bird dogs do, so I just crouched down in the field and watched. During a break we drank black coffee from a thermos and ate pimento-cheese sandwiches, melted from the end of the day's heat. That night my father took the doves down to the Bottom to Miss Rosalie, who cooked the birds in a rich gravy. We brought them back home still warm and ate dozens of them on toast and washed them down with iced tea. The tiny little things had soft bones and a faint gamy taste.

I wasn't allowed to go deer hunting with the men because they thought it was too dangerous. My father fell out of a tree once and got banged up pretty badly. But he got his deer in the end, and when he placed it in the back of the jeep and took the deer to school to show Jemma, it nearly traumatized her.

When she was called out of the classroom the morning of the hunt and saw the dead, bleeding deer hanging out the back of the jeep, she screamed bloody murder. She sobbed uncontrollably and scolded him in between gulps. He was surprised by her reaction and that she didn't appreciate that the deer would be on our dinner table later. He never killed anything he wasn't planning to eat.

Jemma was a deeply devoted animal lover. We were sure she would court a career as a zookeeper. It wasn't easy to keep a pet at the funeral home, so my father bought a few exotic, but quiet, animals to keep her happy. Two baby alligators arrived by mail in a square cardboard box perforated with air holes. We took them outside by the garage where my father had filled a small plastic pool with water. He let them loose and we watched wide-eyed as they tumbled from the box and scrambled, their thin tails beating the water, two little exotic creatures swimming behind the funeral home. Jemma visited the pool twice a day to feed them bits of raw ground beef. The ambulance, hearse, and gurneys that carried dead bodies passed by the pool of alligators for a few weeks, until one day a piercing squeal brought us running. Jemma stood by the pool, distressed that it was empty. The alligators had eaten their way out through the plastic. We searched the area, not knowing what we would do if we found them, and we never did. I fantasized that they had made their way through Jubilee's sewers and would one day pop up in someone's toilet.

Pastel-dyed chicks at Easter lasted a few weeks. A descented skunk slept in a special cage. These strange animals either died a natural death or suddenly disappeared when they became a nuisance to keep. My father mysteriously disposed of them; no area surrounded the funeral home in which to bury them, so we had no plots of animal graves, or funerals for the creatures.

Though my hunting days were well over, I continued to rely on the company of adults as a young teenager. The men at the funeral home and Belle, Totty, and Theo were my friends because they were near, but also because I found it hard to make friends, especially when I was younger. Girls didn't appreciate my chirpy tours of the funeral home, even when I tried to emulate Jackie Kennedy's tour of the White House. I walked slowly and strived to be gracious and informative.

"Now over here we have the embalming room, which I'm afraid is closed to the public today. But just next door, the casket room is available for viewing — we call this room the showroom." Not a hit with girls whose dolls waited for them at home, and I confess that an invitation to join me in the cemetery for a little monument reading was hardly tempting. I could easily spend hours in the cemetery. I read the tombstones and wondered why so many people who lived in the nineteenth century died at alarmingly young ages. I searched for the oldest grave, delighted that an even older one could be found on my next visit. I marveled at the names; Eliza, Obadiah, Marston, and Bridie, names foreign to our town now.

Then Jo moved to Jubilee. She and her family arrived with a huge moving truck, and I stood on the sidewalk and watched as the moving men made umpteen trips into a house just two doors down from the funeral home. Jo was the same age as me and I didn't see how we could not be friends. That summer our first and foremost pastime was to run to the library, where we checked out two or three books, then raced home to see who could read them quickest. Her reading skills were phenomenal and she always won.

Jo wasn't afraid to come to the funeral home and was brave enough to sleep over. I think her lack of fear had something to do with her intelligence and disinterest in superstition. She had wavy, unruly hair, pasty skin, wore thick glasses, and had a mouth full of metal. Jo knew she wasn't pretty and I guessed she hid behind her big brain. When she laughed, her snobbishness melted away, so my daily goal was to make her laugh at least once. We ate banana splits at the dime store, climbed a mimosa tree in a neighbor's yard, and listened to records. Jo was particularly interested in the lyrics, and I was interested in singing them. She had a stack of spiral notebooks in which she painstakingly recorded every lyric to every record she owned. I never knew what she did with the notebooks. I practiced singing in the funeral home upstairs in the bathroom with the door closed so that no one would hear me. The silence rule demanded that I not sing in full voice so I whispered, my face contorted with the passion of the song and the frustration of not being able to belt it out. Occasionally I tapped out a Motown tune on the organ downstairs but it sounded wrong in every possible way; hymns, possibly Rodgers and Hammerstein, but never Motown on the Hammond.

Jo and I listened to the Beatles and anything on the Motown label. Then one day we made a discovery. We were walking down one of Jubilee's tree-lined streets when we happened upon a yard sale.

"Look at this," she said. "Here's a whole

box of albums."

"Look," I said, "they're only fifty cents."

"I don't know any of these, do you?"

"Never heard of them."

I picked up an album, *Mingus: The Black Saint and the Sinner Lady*. We had never heard of Charles Mingus.

"What do you think this is? I like the title."

"Yes. It's very evocative." Jo tried out new words every day.

"A quarter each?"

"Deal."

Jo's room was upstairs in the back of her house, where we could listen to records and not bother the dead people's relatives who filled my house. She took out her notebook and pen and then put the needle on the record. When the music began, we looked at each other, waiting for someone to begin singing, to no avail.

"Jo, I think this is something different. I don't think you're going to be writing down any lyrics."

"No shit."

We listened for a while, and then I thought I'd had a breakthrough.

"Okay, okay. You just have to think about New York City, or maybe Paris. This is Greenwich Village stuff. You have to close your eyes and put yourself in a smoky room with people wearing strange clothes and berets."

"Actually, I prefer San Francisco." Jo knew her own mind.

We then became silent, arrested by music so completely foreign to us. A great yearning took hold of me. Again I thought that I would perhaps someday visit and maybe even live in a place far from Jubilee, and that perhaps Jo would, too. A place where music like this might be an everyday occurrence and not an accidental discovery.

On Sundays our twosome was torn apart when her parents marched her to the Presbyterian church while I sat in the back pew at First Baptist.

My mother disapproved whenever I asked permission to visit Jo's church. "You need to go to your own church. I don't know what they're teaching over there.

Was she concerned that I would be branded a traitor to the First Baptist tribe? Was there a particular doctrine she was set against? No reason was offered. But I knew in my bones it had something to do with appearances. Because when I was permitted to go and afterward offered to describe the differences in the services, she wasn't interested.

I decided that Jo was the only person in

the world in whom I could confide. I had a terrible, nerve-wracking secret and it was becoming a burden to keep it. I can't say that it began innocently because I knew exactly what I was getting into. Such is the law of attraction. I didn't know of anyone, nor had I heard of anyone, who had crossed over into this forbidden territory. So I approached the boundary line alone.

I was twelve, close to thirteen, when my eye fell upon a boy in my class. Already he was handsome. His skin was the color of coffee with cream. Even though most black boys were beginning to wear Afros, his hair was short, and the style complemented his chiseled features, devoid of any childish plumpness. When he smiled, his face opened up and displayed perfect, sparkling white teeth. He was friendly and funny and seemed to be more accepted by the white boys than any of the other black boys. Not that it would have mattered to me. I was captivated. I wanted to talk to him, alone.

One day I gathered the courage to pass him a note: "Meet me in the coatroom at recess when everyone else is gone." I thought the coatroom would be safe because it had two doors of entry and we could easily slip out. Nevertheless, I stood shaking from the adrenaline as I waited for him. Not only was friendship with our black school-mates not encouraged, if we were caught alone in the coatroom doing absolutely nothing but talking, it would be tantamount to a crime. He was brave, he showed up.

I had a pencil and paper in my hand. "Hi."

"Hi." He didn't look frightened, only curious.

"We don't have much time. What would you think about giving me a call tonight? No, maybe I should call you. Would that be all right? Can I call you tonight?" I blurted out.

"Yeah." He smiled.

"Good, what time is good?" I thought again. "Exactly. What time exactly?"

"How about seven o'clock?" He smiled again.

"Okay. Well, good. Okay, then. Okay."

Now I was really nervous. He was on his way out of the room when I remembered the pencil and paper and realized I hadn't taken his number. Too late. I heard footsteps approaching, so I grabbed my coat and ran out the opposite door. He bumped right into Mrs. Mills.

"Hi, Noah. You better run along, you'll miss the break."

"Yes, ma'am."

Thank God for that second door — she

never saw me slip out.

That night I looked up his family's name in the phone book. There were two listings for his last name and only initials for the first names. Damn, I didn't know his father's name. It was hard enough to make the call at all. The thought of calling two different numbers was almost too much for me. With no small amount of anxiety, I finally dialed a number. A woman answered the phone.

"Hello, is Noah there, please?" I wondered if I sounded white.

"Yes, hold on, please."

For God's sake, his mother had answered! I believe I spent the first five minutes of the conversation explaining to him that it would be better if he could answer the phone when he knew I was calling. Noah was calm and told me that his mother wouldn't mind if I called. Somehow I found that hard to believe. We talked on the phone several times a week. He liked books and movies and had more of a brain in his head than many others I had encountered from our young male pool. Noah was more mature than most of the whiny mama's boys who surrounded me daily. I asked him about his family life and told him I heard his father was a bootlegger. He said he couldn't talk about that, so I took that to mean he was.

Then I read in the paper that the police raided his father's store in the Bottom. "Did your father get into any trouble?"

"Naw, it's just something they have to do ever so often."

"They won't arrest him?"

He laughed. "No, they give the stuff back to him after the newspaper prints the story."

"You're kidding."

"Where do you think the police get their booze?"

One day in my English class, Noah's long, lean legs were stretched out into the aisle close to my desk. Our teacher stood at a podium right in front of my desk reading from "Casey at the Bat." I don't know what possessed me. I tapped Noah's foot with mine right under the teacher's nose. He tapped mine back. It was a terrifically stupid thing to do because of course she saw us. Her eyes glanced from her book to our feet and back to the book again without ever missing a beat as she continued to read about Mudville. When she didn't confront me about the incident, I forgot all about our toe tapping until two days later. As I walked through the hall during a break in classes, I saw my mother enter the school. She walked right by me without saying a word and gave me the most searing stare I had ever received. I couldn't imagine why she looked at me with such venom. I always walked home from school, but when I stepped out in the afternoon's late-autumn air, she was waiting for me in the car.

"Get in this car."

"What? What's the matter?"

"Get in this car and shut up!"

I closed the door and sat in silence until she was ready to speak.

"They called me and told me to come to the school today. I had to go the principal's office."

"What for?"

"Shut up. I've been told that you're being too friendly with the colored kids."

I didn't say anything.

"Well? What *in the hell* do you think you're doing?"

As ordered, I said nothing.

"Answer me!"

"Nothing, I'm not doing anything."

"Don't you know how people talk in this town?"

"I don't really care."

She slapped me in the face with the full force of her anger. Her wedding band made a thudding sound against my cheekbone. "Well, you better care!" she shrieked. "You better care!"

I caught my breath and wondered if she'd marked my face.

"Who do you think puts food on the table? The people of this town, that's who. Do you have any idea what this could do to your daddy's business?"

No, at that point, I didn't. I was stupefied by her words. I didn't see what talking to a black boy had to do with my father's business. But I certainly wasn't going to say so. I'd never seen my mother so angry. She looked straight ahead as she drove and ranted. Never before had I been so acutely aware of her rules: Nothing was discussed. Obey without question. No opinions were allowed.

"You're not going anywhere or doing anything until you straighten up and fly right. You're grounded. You're not talking on the phone or seeing friends. You'll go to school and come straight home. You'll go to church whenever the doors are open. You're going to walk the chalk, young lady. You've had it too easy."

When I faced my father, I waited for the ball of his anger to drop. He had few words for me. "I don't know what you think you're doing, but it's wrong and if you don't stop . . . Maybe you'd be better off in a girls' school somewhere, out in the middle of nowhere. I will send you away faster than you can breathe."

We were already in the middle of nowhere, and in trying to find somewhere, I had embraced the beginning of trouble. I didn't believe that my father would send me away, but it crushed me that he said it and he wanted me to believe it. It took my breath away. I thought when this trouble began the door to redemption was slightly ajar. My mother could possibly have steered me in some other direction, but her threats and punishments only made me dig my heels in. Perhaps if I had been approached with less wrath of judgment, less searing criticism, I might have been receptive to a better understanding of the consequences of my actions. I don't know. I was fighting for something, maybe for an inch of freedom, maybe just a touch of individuality, but she stamped on it with a big and furious foot. I wondered if she had ever been this hateful toward my father. Had she driven him toward a woman with a softer attitude? Or, had he driven her to this angry life?

I was met with a cool breeze from my father, but he was boiling underneath. I felt dismissed. His disappointment — and maybe even fear of what was to become of me — was worn like an undershirt, out of sight, except for a faint shadow.

I didn't want to do anything to hurt my father's business, and I was not strong enough to face ostracism, yet I felt so compelled to continue to explore this irregular path that I did not stop or even slow down. I'd been stupid. If I was sorry for anything, it was that. I should have controlled myself at school in front of the teacher. When I told Jo why I was grounded, she was impressed.

"I have a black boyfriend," I confessed.

"Damn. That's very cool of you. I didn't know you had enough guts to do something like that."

"I don't think anyone else will think it's cool. You have to swear you won't tell a soul."

Jo promised to take my secret to her grave. She checked out extra books at the library and brought them to school so that I could smuggle them home. I wasn't allowed to go to the library or read anything except schoolbooks until the punishment concluded.

It felt like prison, and the seriousness of my crime was not to be underestimated. The mixing of races was a great taboo. Perhaps in some large Northern city one could walk along the street without incident, but not here; Jubilee would not tolerate it. Only in 1967 had antimiscegenation laws, the laws to "protect my white womanhood," been thrown out. Young black men had been lynched for far less serious crimes than whistling at a white woman. And what of me? I could never publicly step over the wrong side of the tracks, for if I did, I'd never be allowed to come back. The 1970s had brought little change.

On a Tuesday afternoon — choir practice was always on a Tuesday — I walked to the church after school in what was left of the day's light. As I entered the hall of one of the church buildings, the preacher suddenly appeared and stopped me.

"I'd like to see you in my office for just a moment."

"Me?" I looked around. Brother Lyle scarcely took time to speak to me in passing; what could he want with me now? *Oh, God,* I thought, *I hope he's not going to ask me to do something embarrassing like pray out loud next Sunday in church.*

"Uh-huh. Yes, you. I just want to speak to you for a moment." He sounded cheerfully false.

He smiled with a crinkled nose and eyes that squinted. I thought I sensed from him a small, electrifying moment of discomfort, but it passed. I became curious. We approached the door to his office, with a brass plaque boldly noting PASTOR'S STUDY. He led the way into his office and closed the door. I'd never been in the preacher's office before. Brother Lyle was not one of the poker-playing brethren, we didn't socialize with him, and as far as anyone knew, he had not succumbed to any of the normal temptations. He reeked of self-righteousness. I thought his office might be a holy place where miracles stood a chance of occurring, but once I was inside, it didn't feel holy, it felt grand and rich. My feet sank into plush carpet and I sat down in a comfortable stuffed leather chair. The bookshelves were lined with appropriate titles, all of which were biblical. The desk was large and wooden, more of a structure, similar to the pulpit that kept his flock at a safe distance. The lighting was quite low, and a desk lamp lit his pad and pen. I sank into the chair, and not for one instant did I expect what was to come. A large Bible lay sprawled across the desk like a fat lady sunbathing, open to the elements. When he picked it up and moved toward me, I could hardly believe it. *What's he going to do, hit me with it? And why? What is this about?* The next thing I knew, he read aloud a passage of scripture.

Then he said, "Did you understand that?"

"Understand it? I didn't hear a word you said."

I thought I might have experienced some kind of auditory blackout. I couldn't believe that one moment I was walking in the hallway and the next I was listening to Brother Lyle, with whom I had no relationship, save a "Good morning" here and there, as he brandished his big, floppy Bible in my face. After all, we were not a hand-raising, knee-buckling congregation, we were a civilized bunch, easily embarrassed by those who spoke in tongues and kept snakes in jars. But Brother Lyle read again, something about the fowl of the air, the fish of the seas, and the beasts of the fields. Then he carefully placed the black silk ribbon in the book to mark the page. He closed the Bible and returned to his desk. I looked at him as if he were crazy.

Then he hit me with it. "You see, God is telling us that the birds don't mix with the fish. The fish don't mix with the beasts of the fields, now do they?"

Who was I to argue this? "No, they sure don't, Brother Lyle."

He cleared his throat.

Then my body became hot, my face red, and I felt like mush in that big, comfy chair. I was thirteen and already up to my neck in awkwardness. The preacher was on the verge of drowning me in awkward because now, finally, I knew what was coming.

"So, God also does not want the races to mix. White and black — they don't mix." He said this matter-of-factly and with great authority. "Do you understand?" The desk lamp illuminated the preacher's kinky, light-brown head. "Do you understand?"

I didn't answer him and I didn't look at him. I tried to find a point in the window-less room upon which to focus.

"The scripture says it plainly right here, right here in front of us." He leaped from his chair, grabbed his Bible, and came toward me again. He placed the Bible in my lap. "Read it for yourself. Read it out loud. Let me hear you read it." His voice verged on the evangelical.

He returned to his chair, sat back, and adjusted his thick, black glasses, then closed his eyes, pressed his fingers together, and waited for the scripture.

I looked at the words, but they seemed to blur before me. I could have been looking at a grocery bill. "I'm not going to read it." These words came not from bravery, but from embarrassment and frustration. I was almost in tears now.

Brother Lyle reached over his desk. "Give it back to me."

I handed over the Bible.

"I think you understand now, don't you? Those aren't my words, they're God's words. Do you understand God's words?"

I'd never been one to offer quick comebacks. I desperately needed a wise retort, a fact that was on my side. But instead I looked down into my lap and nodded my head.

"Okay then. Glad we had the opportunity to speak today. Now you run along and have a good choir practice."

Ten minutes, that's all it took. Ten minutes to get the message — not the message he meant to impart, but the message that I took with me as I left the preacher's study. This preacher had said not one memorable thing in all the years I had known him. Now he had. And I hoped that someday, someone would make him feel as small and flawed as he'd made me feel that Tuesday afternoon.

I walked back to the funeral home after choir practice. I had planned to confront my mother when I arrived, but I didn't. I lost my nerve and then decided that I didn't want her to see any kind of reaction from me at all. I knew by the way my father greeted me that evening that he knew nothing of this. That wasn't a bad thing. It would be my mother's and my unspoken, uncomfortable little secret. I became more careful, more deceitful, and much more determined.

Noah and I planned our first date during the summer of that year. We were meeting at twelve o'clock in broad daylight in a wooded area on the edge of town and were careful to stagger our arrivals so that we wouldn't be seen together in the area. I nursed a panicky sweat during the long walk to our meeting place, and even my feet tingled with fear. The coatroom at school was a walk in the park compared to my journey to the woods. What would happen, I thought, now that we would finally be alone? I heard the twigs snap under his feet as he approached me. The fire whistle blew at that moment and we both jumped. Every day the firehouse cranked up its siren at twelve noon; we called it the twelve o'clock whistle. Although it could be depended upon to sound its long, loud whine without fail, one would just forget about it until it happened. Two normal people would have laughed, but neither of us felt normal that day.

I had never been kissed. A little boy or two had stolen a silly peck on the cheek, but I was never kissed in any way that was memorable until that summer day when the branches of the trees hid the warm sun and the smell of the baked woods hit my nostrils. I thought he was beautiful. I knew that almost everyone else in Jubilee would be sickened by this. Noah put his hands around my waist. I had only recently discovered that I even had a waistline. I caught sight of it in the full-length mirror in my bedroom, and it took me completely by surprise. *A curve! When did you arrive?* Now he had his arms around it as if he knew it better than I. His lips were soft and warm, and when they parted, I felt I was being safely led to a place that would change me. He tasted of sweetness dusted with a light sprinkling of salt.

The kiss was the only physical exploration made that day and was quite enough for both of us. The consequences were daunting enough without any extras. The reality of leaving the woods separately and making sure we weren't seen was sobering. We both knew the seriousness of the situation. The barrel of a gun was not considered an unseemly sight in our town, and it would not have been far-fetched to imagine one at Noah's temple. I feared some angry landowner — we were trespassing — plodding through the wood's growth would greet us with his favorite hunting rifle. My parents would have made me their prisoner, every waking moment monitored, all privileges revoked, until I reached legal age, at which point they would disown me.

At the edge of the woods we parted. I left first, saying, "See ya."

"Yeah, see ya, too."

I stopped downtown at Elvis's for a hamburger, then killed some time in the library. I longed to walk up the steps of the old bank building with the tall shelves and wooden floors. They had never got around to providing chairs or a bench for visitors, but it didn't matter. I recalled a cozy corner where my back fit perfectly against the wall, my legs crossed, a comfortable hideaway on the floor. I wanted to sit there and watch Theo, hoping to see if she noticed anything different about me. Was it somehow written on my face, where I'd been and what I'd done? But that library was just a memory now. Theo had retired and Jubilee had built a new library on another street, a boring, modern building with low ceilings, drab carpets, and punishing lighting. Still, the shelves of books relieved me of the daze in which I found myself and helped to prepare me for my return home.

I approached the back of the funeral home in early evening and adopted a casual stride as I walked past my father. He was out back turning Omaha steaks on the barbecue, his eyes slitted for protection against the smoke. We spoke about nothing as he poked at the filets mignons, one of the treats he ordered for us, along with Florida oranges and massive cheese balls from the East Coast. I assumed I was back in his good graces as he'd not said anything else about the incident at school. The steak was good, and as I ate that night, I slipped back into something closer to normal. No one suspected that I had returned with the traces of a black boy's kiss still on my lips.

That was how my secret life began. That's how I became a liar and a sneak. Amen, Brother Lyle. I had tapped a black boy's foot in school and kissed him in the woods. I knew that I was playing with fire and my parents' disapproval didn't surprise me. But discontent from another source caught me entirely off guard.

Late on a spring afternoon, before the days became long, I strolled home from visiting a teacher who lived near the school. I often walked this route, a shortcut home on a familiar passage that allowed me to free whatever loose thoughts had crowded my mind that day. I didn't hear the footsteps on the grass, but I felt an invisible pressure behind me and looked over my shoulder to find two black girls several feet away. I thought nothing of it, even when I saw several more girls, all black, coming toward me. As they drew closer, I could see that they were familiar to me and each was about the same age as me. One of them, Nanette, seemed to act as their leader, and out of respect for what I gathered was her important position, I spoke to her first.

"Hi, Nanette." I was friendly.

"Humph." She was not.

As if the exchange were a signal, the other girls closed in on me. A feeling in the pit of my stomach told me something was wrong. I tried not to panic and continued to walk slowly. I was now surrounded, but oddly, still walking. In some strange and precarious balletic movement we crossed the schoolyard together.

"So what you doin' with that Noah?" Nanette demanded.

"Nothing. What do you mean?"

"You got no bi'ness with Noah, you hear me? We see you talkin' to him all the time. You leave our boys alone. What you want to go and do that for? Go back to your own kind. Find some white boy to talk to." She didn't draw a breath.

Nanette was the biggest of them, tall and solid. Nothing could hide the pugnacious bully that lived beneath the soft folds of her faded cotton dress. I looked down at her thick, white socks and sturdy, black shoes while she gave me a piece of her mind. In an attempt to remain calm and appear mildly in control, I shifted my focus from her shoes and intended to meet her eyes. But one of Nanette's eyes, the left, was stuck, immovable in its socket, and she looked permanently out of that stationary eye toward her left. I kept thinking of Cyclops. I was afraid she would be even angrier at me for staring at it, so I counted the squares on her head from which coarse, black plaits sprouted in unruly spires. Five were visible from where I was standing.

"I think you crazy. We all," she said with a grand gesture of her arm, "think you crazy. And we don't like it. We don't like it one bit, Miss Mayfield," she spat.

The other girls began to touch me. They pulled on my clothes and poked at me. I searched through the faces of Nanette's coterie for the most sympathetic onlooker. I found her, stared her down until she dropped her eyes in, well, if not shame, then an uncomfortable moment. But she didn't help me.

"Stay away from us. 'Specially the boys. You stay away from our boys."

Nanette became more agitated, and while her anger fizzed, I began to feel sick. I turned from her, again searching for a way out. I looked around for another living soul and there was no one. Not even a car passed us. The drooping, heavily branched trees hid us from view anyway. I thought of breaking through the circle of girls and running for it, but I was a lousy runner.

Nanette slapped me on the back of the head. "Did you hear what I said? You be lookin' all off somewheres for some help or somethin'. There ain't no help here."

The sky began to darken, and I was certain that as soon as the sun lowered and disappeared, I would be beaten.

I'd witnessed boys as they fought on the playground at school, red faced and angry, their clothes a mess and their faces wet from what usually ended in tears. This was not like that. We were junior high students and I thought my playground days were well behind me, buried in the ashes. I don't know what kind of courage possessed the other girls on that evening. They acted with an unfettered disregard for any consequences. Cowed by the withering glare of Nanette's good eye, I dismissed the thought of running and was on the verge of begging when my savior came walking toward us — the school's janitor. He had just begun to lock up the buildings for the evening. He was tall, huge, a wonderful, imposing figure of a man. To me, he represented a crepuscular miracle. He walked deliberately toward us and quickly took in the scene before him.

"You girls go on home now. Leave her alone."

I stood next to him, unable to move until I saw the outline of their dresses disappear toward the Bottom, the opposite direction of the funeral home. The miracle man and I didn't exchange words until then.

I offered him my hand, which was swallowed whole by his big, black hand. "Thank you."

"Run along now. And don't worry, they won't bother you again."

I didn't begin shaking until I continued the walk home. The calm that I'd forced upon myself during the time of fear and panic readily gave way now. During the endless walk of two and a half blocks, I decided not to say anything to anyone. I didn't know how to explain why the young group would risk attacking a white girl. I was unsure how much of this warning of violence I had brought upon myself. I was so obsessed with what white people might do if they found out about me that it never crossed my mind that the vast majority of black people might agree that crossing the color line was wrong and somehow sinful and, evidently, crazy-making. The janitor was right; they never bothered me again. He must have known that the situation was a time bomb and warned the girls. A gang of black schoolgirls had never beaten up a white girl in Jubilee. Nor had a black man ever touched a white man in violence. Sometimes the things that almost happened were more important than the things that did.

Every day I monitored Belle's reaction to me. If the posse of girls who surrounded me talked about me in their homes, then I feared she would hear about it and tell my mother. I anxiously looked for a sign, but found none. She never spoke of it. But Belle, too, was steeped in the only kind of world she'd ever known. Jemma provided proof of that.

I no longer came home during the school lunch break, but Jemma did, and as Belle always had for me, she now prepared lunch for Jemma.

"Please, Belle, I don't want to sit here by

myself. Eat lunch with me."

"Now you knows I can't do that."

"Yes, you can. Did anyone tell you that you couldn't?"

"No. That's just the way it be, though."

This would go on day after day, neither tired of the back-and-forth, the yin and yang of lunchtime. But Jemma persisted and coaxed Belle into sitting at the table with her while she ate, though Belle still ate the sandwich she brought from home on her own after Jemma went back to school. It took years, but finally, one day, Belle made two ham sandwiches. She sat them both on the kitchen table, pulled up a chair, and Jemma and Belle had lunch together.

"Thank you," Jemma said. "You are my family."

An opportunity arose one day when I was at Belle's house. My mother remained in the car while I went in to collect pies she needed for a church social. As I waited for Belle to take the sugary goodness out of the oven, I toyed with the idea of seeking her advice. I sat on Belle's sofa while the aroma of the cooling pecan pies filled the house. Of course she'd baked three extra and brought me a piece of one of them, still warm and oozing. I had just filled my mouth with the first bite when there was a knock on her screen door.

"Miss Belle? Miss Belle? Is you home?" Buttermilk Betty cupped her eyes to fight the glare of the sun behind her and pressed her nose up to the door. Her tight, green cardigan swelled with her ample bosom; the top button was missing and she spilled out. Her hips stretched the bright red fabric of a worn and slightly tatty A-line skirt. But what really caught my eye were her purple, pom-pom house slippers.

"What you want, Buttermilk? I's busy right now. I got comp'ny and I gots baking to do."

Belle slipped the little lock into place on her screen door and was not too subtle about it.

"I won't takes up much of your time. I'm a little short on the rent this month, I gots to get up 'bout fifteen dollars."

"I don't have no fifteen dollars for you. You crazy?"

"But, Miss Belle, you's always got money."

With that Belle clapped as if she were trying to make thunder. "I has no money . . . no money for you." Clap, clap. "Here you go round 'bout spending your welfare check on Lawd knows what" — clap, clap — "comes round here aksing for money." Clap, clap. "You better be gettin' to work like me!

I works for my money. I pays my taxes and my ten percent to Jesus." Clap, clap. "Now get on out of here."

Belle said to me, "There you goes," as she stood at the door and watched Buttermilk Betty shuffle down the street in her purple house slippers. "That right there. That be a prime example of a bad black person. And don't you ever let any black person ever tells you there ain't no bad black people. They is. They is lazy, and some is drunks, jest like white people."

I desperately wanted to ask Belle if she'd heard any rumors about me. But any thought I might have entertained about speaking to her evaporated with her display of temper. Perhaps she would be angry at me as well. I realized how much I cared about what she thought of me. I couldn't risk losing her friendship. This woman had, day by day, been a solid, dependable, and caring person in my life for over ten years. I would have done anything to keep her good opinion of me.

CHAPTER 11
DEM BONES

Thomas was drafted in 1970. The notice
arrived the moment he graduated from college. My mother moved through the house
like a nervous ghost. For once in his life,
when his only son's future was at stake, my
father became proactive. He rushed around
seeking advice about how to keep Thomas
out of Vietnam. My parents held late-night
discussions in somber tones. When we tried
to listen at the door, Jemma and I were
ordered to keep quiet and stay out of the
way. We were nervous, too; the idea seemed
so foreign that we couldn't imagine Thomas
in a uniform, with a gun, killing another
human being — and that led to the terrifying thought that someone in a foreign jungle
might get to him first. Suddenly my father
had a fire under him. His memories of the
war empowered him with a strong conviction that Thomas should be spared a similar

ordeal. He changed visibly, his face pale and drawn.

Adamant that Thomas should not enter military service, my father pressed him to consider the National Guard. The sergeant in charge of enlistments for our local troops gave them the bad news: there were no openings in Jubilee. He directed them to another town, where Thomas, without fanfare or fuss, was able to enlist.

After weeks of his initial basic training we were allowed to visit him. We packed up the station wagon with a huge picnic basket full of Thomas's favorite homemade foods: pimento-cheese sandwiches, fried chicken, potato salad, coleslaw, freshly sliced garden tomatoes, and a couple of thermoses of iced tea.

Emily, his girlfriend, rode with us in a two-hour drive fraught with our inauthentic cheeriness, the air laced with the odors of the picnic basket and the atmosphere charged with apprehension over how Thomas had fared. Evelyn didn't make the journey; I don't recall what excuse she made.

We drove into a dismal, barren area where it seemed only an army-training base could have been built. We parked under shade trees near the base and tried to make

Thomas feel better.

Usually, my brother's idea of a push-up was pushing his tie in place. Thomas looked like a complete stranger in olive-green khakis. He'd always leaned toward my father's sense of style and, like him, was well groomed, never wore denim, and was rather fond of suits. But the figure walking toward us was barely recognizable. His thick-lensed, black glasses had reappeared after his years of wearing contacts, and his hair was so short the white of his scalp shone like an ostrich egg.

He was miserable. We were appalled that he'd cut his arms in a training exercise. He described how he was made to crawl on the ground using his forearms to move forward as he held his rifle up. His arms pressed into broken glass while his drill sergeant barked at him to keep moving.

My mother filled his plate with food over and over, and no one else was allowed to eat until he couldn't stuff another bite into his mouth. She fussed and fiddled and seemed not to know what to do with herself. He remained calm amid all this attention. Meanwhile, I asked questions on behalf of us all. Where did he sleep? How often did he have to cut his hair? What was the food like — didn't they feed him in there? Jemma was clingy and couldn't understand why we couldn't see him whenever we wanted. We had to pry her off Thomas to give him some time alone with Emily. Not very discreetly, we turned our backs and walked away while he and Emily stood alone under a tree holding hands. In high school Emily had been a beauty queen, a drum majorette, Miss Congeniality, an accomplished musician, and all this without an ounce of self-consciousness. She was in college now, a sorority girl studying for her master's in education. Tall, thin, and blond, she possessed the manners and grace of a Tennessee Williams character having a good day, and we loved her. So did Thomas, he adored her. They would be married as soon as he returned from his visit to hell.

My mother was weepy on the way home. I'd never seen her show much emotion, other than anger. My father was hugely relieved. He knew that this discomfort, this five-month interruption of Thomas's plans and the inconvenience of a commitment for a few years on weekends with the guard, was a minor sacrifice. He'd kept his son safe. His family would not have to think about the possibility of his body's never being returned to us, left to decompose in some godforsaken jungle. Nor would the undertaker once again receive a knock on the door to find a serviceman holding a box of bones, as he had received his brother.

One day, when I was still of an age to tag along with my father, we made a run to the cemetery to drop off a flower arrangement at a recently dug grave. On this cloudy autumn day the cool wind blew gritty, red-tinged leaves across the manicured patches of lawn. Brown leaves fallen from the hickory and red-buckeye trees crackled under my shoes as I traipsed around the cemetery, oblivious of my surroundings.

"Don't do that," he said.

"Don't do what?"

"Don't walk on the graves. Step over them or walk around them," he said softly. "Walk behind the tombstones."

I quickly stepped around as if my feet had been planted on hot bricks. "Why?"

"Out of respect."

I stood still, in the middle of the cemetery, which until that moment had been a familiar, pleasant few acres of land, a backdrop, and my father's outdoor office. This place shouted at me with its broken angels, clasped hands, cracked doves of peace, and engraved laurel wreaths. It insisted that I wander from name to name and become aware of its one-hundred-year-old habitants. What shrouds did they wear? What old-fashioned clothing were they buried in? Was there jewelry in their coffins? Who had they been? But now was the time to face another reality, one that I had perhaps subconsciously ignored. I took a deep breath and exhaled the question.

"What happens to them, Daddy? What happens to all the bodies buried under this cemetery?"

He looked out over the graveyard and then down at the ground as if he could see through the green carpet of grass, the dirt, the vaults, and into the caskets. He slipped his hands into his pockets in a settling-down way.

"Embalming doesn't last forever. The chemicals, well, they eventually break down. And even steel vaults, they can't keep the water out forever, and water reverses the effects of embalming. Are you sure you want to hear this?"

"Yes, just try not to make it too gory. Is it like a horror movie? You know, those zombies?"

"I better never hear you, or hear *of* you, talking about the dead like that. You will not be disrespectful. I won't have it."

"Okay, okay. Gosh, I was just asking."

"It's a natural thing. The body will eventually decompose. The flesh breaks down. Do you want to know how?"

"No, I do not."

Here we stood in a whole community of stinking, rotting flesh, which is the only way I perceived it in that moment. "What's left after all that, then? Just the bones?"

"Yes, eventually."

"And how long do those last?"

"Oh, it depends. A long time."

"A hundred years?"

"Well, they could last for hundreds of years, or thousands, depending on the climate and conditions, but not here. Some may not last as long as forty or fifty years."

I looked up at him now, for the first time during this quick education, and asked him something that had bothered me for quite a while: "Then what part of us goes to heaven?"

He laughed. "I guess the soul, isn't that what all the preachers say?"

"Is that what you think?"

"Well, sure, that's what we all think."

"There's no proof, you know."

"Proof of what?"

"That there is a heaven."

He was silent.

I pressed. "I don't understand it. I don't

understand it at all. Some kind of invisible thing called a soul floats sky-high into another invisible thing called heaven? All I understand is that we die and we end up here."

"Well, I guess that's a good start. Come on, it's getting chilly."

He was clearly not interested in talking about souls. An enormous number of prayers had fallen from the lips of Jubilee's preachers in his funeral home. Jesus could have set up residence in the chapel, so many times had his name been invoked in a last effort to usher the deceased to heaven. Yet my father remained tight-lipped about his thoughts on religion and would not philosophize over the existence of a soul. Perhaps his demons demanded constant attention.

I'd seen quite a lot of corpses by then. Now a new image crept into my growing collection and summoned yet another intimacy with the dead. The cemetery's pleasant lawn of greenery and trees was but a carpet that hid bones and varying states of decomposition.

I wondered if the idea of heaven was a sugarcoated fallacy to keep us calm when wrongs were not set right, when inexplicable suffering had no meaning; that the only way we would be good people was by the threat of eternal damnation. And I entertained the most bitter doubt: that the greatest promise of all, that of being reunited with those we'd loved and lost, the largest Band-Aid to grief, was also a beguiling misbelief.

IN MEMORIAM:
TITUS BROMLEY

Titus and Annie lived in a shack. The unpaved road that twisted through an overgrown, neglected bit of land near a wood made it difficult to find them. They lived in poverty. The few people who knew of their existence criticized them for going out of their way to take in any stray dog in the county when they struggled to feed themselves. They had no electricity and no indoor plumbing.

My father never solved the mystery of how they squirreled away a few dollars to make a small down payment on their funeral arrangements. Prearranged funerals were rare at that time, and my father thought it ironic that two people who couldn't afford a pair of Salvation Army shoes could spare the change they brought to the funeral home.

They drove a beat-up, old-model farm truck that they'd borrowed from their cousins. It clanked and rattled down the street at a pace that created a traffic jam in Jubilee — and that was no mean feat. When a glance out the window of the funeral home revealed that Titus and Annie would soon be upon us, the room cleared quicker than in a fire drill. They were the dirtiest, filthiest, smelliest people that ever existed in Jubilee. They were so dirty that my father, who'd handled hundreds of dead people with his bare hands, had to gird his loins to offer his handshake.

Thank the Lord they never sat down and didn't stay for more than a couple of minutes; that was quite long enough for their visit to make an impact. Titus reached into his dirt-rimmed trouser pocket and offered a thread-bare bandanna filled with change.

As the odor of unwashed flesh grew stronger, my father opened the handkerchief, and the quarters, nickels, and dimes came tumbling out onto his desk.

Titus reached out. "I'll have my hankie back, please."

My father was happy to comply.

Annie stood by silently, uncomfortably, as if unaccustomed to a clean, orderly environment.

After the truck jerked down the street with a backfire or two, my father, or the unlucky employee who'd had the misfortune to attend them, ran to get the Lysol and sprayed half a can around the office. Still, the odor lingered, eyes watered, and the environment wasn't normal for hours.

"God in heaven, what is that smell? Did someone die?" I asked the first time I passed through the office after their visit, nearly gagging from the strength of the odor.

"Dead people don't smell like that. At least not here they don't," my father said.

When Titus Bromley was dead and laid out on the embalming table, soap and water was not enough. For the first time in his career, my father bought scouring powder. He and Rex, his new employee, scrubbed away the caked-on dirt and the grime that held stubbornly in the creases of Titus's skin, until they were weary. They shaved his beard because it was so dirty and tangled in knots that it stuck straight up when he was supine. Shaving a dead man's beard is an altogether tricky thing. Dead skin doesn't heal, and nicks are to be avoided at all costs. Three new blades later, the face of Titus Bromley emerged.

They trimmed his eyebrows and nasal hair, cut his nails and dug out the dirt from beneath them, and combed his hair. Fount donated one of his own suits because Titus's clothes were too dirty to wash and he had no others that were befitting. Finally, he was ready for Annie's private viewing before the doors opened to the public visitation.

Annie arrived only a bit more presentable

than normal. She still had an odor about her, and though she'd made an effort, she looked like a stunned animal, searching for something familiar. My father led her into the chapel. She looked at her husband, turned to my father, and said, "That ain't my husband. What have you done with Titus?"

Stunned, the undertaker had never before encountered such a reaction. "Well, Annie, it sure is. It's Titus all right."

"No, it ain't. I don't know who this character is, but it ain't Titus".

Then she became upset and looked all around as if she might find her husband sitting in one of the chairs, or as if he might be standing at the doorway. My father thought she would snap out of it, but she didn't.

He tried to calm her, and when he was sure she was settled in a chair, he ran out to the office where two of her cousins waited. He directed them into the chapel to the plain wooden coffin. They were just as shocked as Annie, but after several moments they recognized him as Titus. One of the ladies sat down with Annie and after a fair amount of cajoling convinced her that the man inside the coffin was indeed her husband.

As I eventually learned of death rituals in other cultures that greatly differed from ours, I realized that our customs were so ingrained in our community that even the poorest among us sacrificed everyday comforts so that they could one day be embalmed and placed in a casket or coffin. A more frugal Annie Bromley might have wrapped her husband in a sheet and buried him on their property. I'm sure it was never a consideration.

Each time Titus had removed his tattered bandanna and deposited his coins on my father's desk, his act mirrored those of thousands who had gone before him. For hundreds, if not thousands, of years people had chosen to incur debt rather than forgo their idea of a good death.

I figured that Titus and Annie were just as stretched to enter our world as we were to be a part of theirs. They had created a life ritual that blurred class distinctions in the face of death, and this, supported by the rituals my father performed, taught me about empathy. Sometimes people who had less, who sacrificed everything to have what many of us took for granted, were the strongest among us, even though they might be in tattered clothes and smell unpleasant.

I believe my father set the groundwork for a specific approach to one of life's mysteries — people. His unspoken message, set by his example, was to examine the person, not his or her social standing. I would flounder, occasionally get it right, sometimes get it horribly wrong, but I tried to follow his example.

CHAPTER 12
SECRETS

On a sunny Saturday afternoon in June, Evelyn would walk down the aisle of a church. To no one's surprise, at eighteen years of age she chose marriage over college. At high noon on the day of this jubilant event, the door to her room was firmly closed. We anticipated that she was busying herself with a plethora of beauty rituals, plucking her brows, teasing her hair. But as I walked by her door I didn't hear the radio, or the rustling and bustling of a nervous bride. Jemma and I panicked; we had to be at the church any minute now. This was a job for my mother. She tapped on the door while the three of us anxiously huddled around it. No response. Finally, my mother opened the door. The sun streamed through the window, the air smelled stale from the previous night, and there was Evelyn, still lost to the world.

"Evelyn Dianne! Evelyn. You get up right

now. Wake up, wake up!"

My mother's voice, filled with frustration, didn't cause much of a stir. Evelyn yawned and looked at us with an I-don't-understand-what-all-the-fuss-is glare, annoyed that we were annoyed. And, oh, by the way, what's a girl got to do to get some breakfast on her wedding day? Jemma and I walked away, staring at each other in disbelief. Evelyn's idea of wedding planning was that she should show up at the church. She'd said something to me about being a bridesmaid. When I'd asked my mother if I had to, she said yes, of course. Jemma was too old to be a flower girl and too young to be a bridesmaid, but our mother insisted that she be included in the wedding party, so she created a role for Jemma, which was to carry the unity candle down the aisle, place it in the candleholder, and then sit down with our parents. Jemma would rather have fallen into an open grave.

Evelyn's choice of husband was curious. Lenny was short and wiry. His voice sounded like Donald Duck's with a Southern drawl. He wore rather large glasses, or maybe they looked large because his head was small. Older than Evelyn by a few years, he was too young to have thinning hair, but nevertheless . . . He didn't look or act like a redneck, but, oh my God, the back of his car was jacked up too high for my comfort. He was an amiable kind of guy, and I wondered what punishment he sought by marrying Evelyn. They had a huge argument a few days before the date and we held our breath, waiting to hear if the wedding was still on. All was forgiven, and this was made apparent when they punched each other in the arms, just for the fun of it. Maybe he was perfect for her after all.

When the pastel mints and the wedding cake were eaten, the fruity, red punch sipped with as much delicacy as the guests could muster, my father laughed when he said to Lenny, "She's all yours now," with a hint of "the joke's on you, kid" in his delivery.

After the wedding, the funeral home grew even quieter. Thomas and Emily had married and moved to another part of the state, hours away, while Evelyn and Lenny stayed in Jubilee. Half of the top floor now belonged solely to Jemma and me, and we settled into a foursome, our lives above the funeral home quieter in the absence of the two eldest.

The landscape of Jubilee's funeral business changed and as if to punctuate the changes in our family — Alfred Deboe finally died.

Though it wasn't exactly a surprise, a short shock of energy permeated our house with the news of the death of our rival and what it would mean for our funeral home. For a while, this left only Sonny's new funeral home and my father's to compete for the loyalty of Jubilee's families. But that competition was just as stiff and more personally acrid. It seemed that whenever Sonny's funeral home won a family over, it stung much more than if it had been Deboe's.

The town was more or less evenly divided between the two and my father stayed busy, and when the funeral home was busy, the only time I could practice the organ was late at night when the house was closed for the evening. The deceased lay in the chapel in a sliver of light that made its way into the room from the foyer. I sat at the organ just outside the entry to the chapel. Of course I knew the corpse was in the other room, but I couldn't see it from my organ bench. Hundreds of nights I'd sat here in my pajamas, my fingers sliding across the keys while the dead slept. One night, when I finished, instead of going upstairs, I felt compelled to walk into the chapel and stand by the casket of an elderly man. As was customary, the top half of the casket remained open. I didn't know him, had never before seen him. I stared at the man for what seemed a long time, then I felt the atmosphere in the room change. It seemed the air became thicker, and time had stopped. I turned to see if anyone had entered the room. Of course not, yet I felt something hovering, even while I insisted to myself that it wasn't possible. I looked down at the man again, half expecting him to move. I became entranced with the hair in his nostrils, willing it not to move with a sudden intake of breath. I stared at his chest, thinking that if it rose, I would faint.

I rationalized that my father and mother were only a few feet away. They were watching the late news in the living room right at the top of the stairs. I could even faintly hear the television from where I stood. It was ridiculous, but the thought of turning my back on the man in the casket and turning out the light in the foyer terrified me.

When I could stand it no longer I forced myself to call out, "Daddy! Daaaaaaddy!" — never taking my eyes off the corpse.

I heard the staircase creaking from his footsteps. "What is it?"

"In here," I managed to say.

"What are you carrying on about?"

I turned to him. "I'm scared."

"Of what?"

"I don't know."

"Well, good grief . . ."

"I don't know what happened, but I got so frightened I couldn't turn off the lights."

I followed closely behind him as he walked through the other rooms and flipped the switches that placed the three of us in darkness.

"I don't believe it," he said. "After all these years."

I could understand his confusion. Although I remained squeamish about the embalming room, I'd never been afraid of anything else in the funeral home before; in fact, quite the opposite.

"That man in there . . . I think he's still around, Daddy."

"Good God. You've lost your mind. Come on, let's go back in there."

He turned the light on again and we walked up to the casket.

"Now," he said with his arms folded, "what are you afraid of?"

It was gone; whatever vestige of mystery I had experienced disappeared with the sound of my father's smooth voice.

"Nothing," I whispered, "I'm not afraid of anything."

"Good. Dead is dead. Remember that."

I thought about the elderly man the next day and surmised that it must have been a fluke, a moment that defeated me. He would be with us one more night and I was determined to summon more bravery than I had previously shown, so down the stairs I went again that night. I entered the chapel and walked toward the casket. I sat down and gazed at the old man and felt it immediately. It felt as if something inhabited the space with me. The force of it was not as strong as the night before, and I don't know if that was because I anticipated it, or because the strength of it had dissipated. I had no feeling of the presence being either good or bad. The thought of a ghost, a spirit, or a personality never crossed my mind. Still, it was queer and I was frightened. This time I didn't call out for my father. I willed myself to turn my back on the casket, and with a fear that crept up my spine, I ran up the stairs as if I were chased by fire.

Before long I no longer needed the added stimulus of night to feel whatever I was experiencing. I found that if I was alone and sat or stood quietly for a short time, I could simply tell the difference when the room was completely clear and void of a presence and when it was not. Without my thinking about it, it became something of a habit.

I began to get the idea that maybe certain people hung around for a while, that perhaps some refused to leave or were confused and could not pass over — a thought by which I was completely flummoxed. The concepts of heaven and hell had been drummed into my head from such an early age that I had not considered that something might exist in between, if only for a short time, a kind of waiting room, or — blasphemy — perhaps there was nothing at all after death. It was a lonely thought, but one I could not shake.

Left to our own devices in a small town with little entertainment, we told ghost stories, consulted the Ouija board, and held séances to relieve the monotony, because it's fun to be scared — but not too scared. There was a line. Not one of us actually wanted a ghost to materialize. We never really hoped the Ouija board would tell us whom we would marry, and if one of our great-grandmothers had actually appeared during a séance, what a mess of terror that would have been. But perhaps even more frightening was the fear of the unknown. Because no one can reveal what it's like to die. It remains the biggest mystery, and therefore one of the biggest fears to face.

I never mentioned my experiences to my father again. It never occurred to me to speak to anyone else about it, either. A rumor was making its way through my classroom that I had seen a dead person sit upright in a casket. And there were always lame jokes: "Hey, wasn't it your daddy who put the *fun* in *funeral home*?" My father's American Express card didn't provide enough space for the words *Mayfield & Son Funeral Home*. Instead, it read *Mayfield & Son Fun Home*. I made the mistake of telling one person, and the next day it might as well have been reported on the local news. So it didn't seem a good idea to try to explain an eerie experience that was true and real to me.

It seemed a small thing at the time, to keep that secret. When something unusual happens and you have no one you may confide in, you are a keeper of secrets. But at some point, when the secrets build and build, you become an outsider. A part of me knew, in a strange and small way, that for the rest of my life there would always be someone who would move to the other side of the room upon discovering that I grew up in a funeral home. It would be distasteful to the person, creepy, even abhorrent.

Those uncanny and inexplicable experiences did make me feel somewhat of an outsider, but an irreversible event of my own choosing was what cemented my creation of another life, a secret one.

It happened in the spring.

I tried my best to find some healthy alternatives to sitting around the funeral home. I sought relief by filling my afternoons, evenings, and weekends with speech- and drama-club activities and various school choruses. I tutored young children, maintained my relationship with Miss Agnes, visited the elderly in the nursing home, and did everything but collect alms for the poor. I ran away from home, but came back every night for dinner and a warm bed.

Despite all the hours swallowed up by ceaseless activities, I remained restless. Jubilee began to feel like a pair of shoes that I'd outgrown. One would think that the ever-watchful eye of a preacher, the threat of being pummeled by a gang of girls, and the risk of causing a riot and ruining my father's business would have been quite enough to keep me off the dark and evil path to interracial damnation. But the more fierce the odds stacked against me, the more compelled I felt to leap over another boundary.

During this unusually hot April, the revival at our church descended on me like a rash. Revivals made me impatient and claustrophobic. Every night for a week a guest preacher, usually a frustrated actor, spread his wings and flew to our church on his spirited ego. He screamed with an anguished face into the dim light of the stained-glass windows, his fists clenched and his mouth spurting saliva. It was enough to strain anyone's nerves. As Southern Baptist congregations go, ours was usually tempered with a less frenetic atmosphere, but this was the final night of the revival and our gusty preacher reveled at a fever pitch. I sat in a pew waiting for the service to end, and I was nervous, nervous, nervous. My palms were sweaty and my stomach turned over at the thought of what I was about to do.

I had carefully plotted my alibi. It was not elaborate or outlandish, just a simple lie: "I'm going to Jo's house after church." I didn't attend to my appearance in any special way that night. After watching my father dress so fastidiously over the years, I trusted that some organic transference had occurred. I possessed a naive confidence that everything in the areas of hair, makeup, and clothing must have been at least passable, though I knew I would never look like Julie Christie, my father's idea of the perfect woman.

I'd planned the loss of my virginity for several weeks. Noah and I had parted ways some time ago — I think he had become frightened of all of the possibilities for disaster our relationship opened up and was secretly relieved. I didn't blame him; I had already found a more daring alternative.

Julian was also black, and older by two years. Whenever I passed him in the hall at school, I felt a rush of prickly energy envelop me. I began to pursue him in a timid, yet, I hoped, clandestine way. I approached him about meeting up, in secret, the only way we could meet. Julian was handsome and Julian was cool. He wore his smile sparingly, which made it that much more appealing. He walked slowly down the halls, as if he were considering every step and might change direction at any moment. He played sports and was known for his talent, yet few knew he harbored a desire to play music and quietly practiced at home. In his room he plucked a guitar and sometimes played and sang to me over the phone. Bluesy riffs poured out of him and I was besotted.

We met secretly for months. My body

responded instantly to his touch. It was electric. We teased each other until we were frenzied, and I believe I grew more frustrated than he. I burned each time I was with him, and whenever I thought of him. I called Julian a few nights before the end of the revival and arranged our Sunday-night meeting. I told him that I had made a decision; he should bring protection. I thought that if hell existed, I was going in a handbasket, and I might as well go on the last night of the revival.

The days were getting longer. By the time I reached the destination, twilight had settled. Another minute would have been too early, the dusk's light would have told on us. Julian and I had been in this spot before. This was where we met to talk, kiss, and fondle. This grassy courtyard was surrounded by school buildings. It was completely private, yet it had a drawback — we would be trapped if anyone came back here. There was only one exit. There wasn't any reason for anyone to come by this area of the schoolyard on a Sunday night. We were as safe as we were going to be.

I waited for him, my back pressed against the brick wall. I almost turned to leave when I heard him.

"I'm worried . . . I'm worried that I won't

know what to do," I whispered out of nervousness as much as necessity.

"Shh. Don't worry. I think you'll know what to do. Just respond."

Julian was kind, and when he knew that I felt safe and that I was wanting, not shrinking, he lost himself, too. He had the strong, firm body of an athlete. He was right. I responded. The sex was great. I walked home in a blue-black night. When darkness fell upon Jubilee, the feeling that anything was possible existed. No judging eyes or wagging tongues were visible, most safely quiescent inside the houses I passed. The air was cool, the night turned liquid around me.

Jubilee was almost unrecognizable to me on this night. Someone's front yard released the odor of a recently mowed patch of wild onions. Mrs. Newman's dog barked. A car passed. Yet everything was different now. I thought of Julian, walking back in the opposite direction. It was sex of the dangerous and forbidden sort and it possessed me. It lapped me up like an unforgiving dry-tongued dog and did not loose its hold for ages. I remembered something I read, I couldn't recall where: "He has taken her to the fire." As I drew closer to the funeral home, the thought of my parents shot through me and a momentary feeling of "What have I done?" descended. Suddenly I didn't know who I was. Was I the high-achieving student by day and the vampire of love at night? The blessings of the non-virginal gods were upon me when I returned, and no one paid much attention to me. I bolted to the bathroom. A grass stain on the back of my yellow dress startled me; I couldn't believe how green it was. A bright red spot of blood glared at me from the white cloth I used to wash myself.

A stack of *National Geographic* magazines sat in the corner of the room Jemma and I used as a TV room. I found the one I was looking for and took it to bed with me. In the issue a journalist wrote of a tribe in Africa in which the girls married at the age of twelve. A photograph showed a bare-breasted young girl holding her baby. It made me feel a little better, a bit more sober. At least one girl out there in the world was younger than me when she lost her virginity. I would be fifteen in a couple of months. Forget the handbasket, I was going to hell propelled down the fastest chute available. The guilt of defying the dictates of history was almost unbearable. I swore I would stop seeing him. And even as I swore it, I knew I would go to great lengths to see him again. It was about a preference, an attraction, that I couldn't ignore or understand. An awful dichotomy presented itself: that of desiring and doing one thing, when society's expectations impressed upon me that it was wrong and would only end in disaster. I had no rebellious thoughts, no secret wish to be discovered, and I did not set out to hurt anyone. It was a private matter.

The next morning Jo and I walked to school together as usual.

"I'm not going to ask you what it was like. That would be stupid. But do you regret it this morning? Are you sorry you did it? How do you feel now?"

"I'm not sorry . . . but I feel guilty. Can you understand that? Not to mention that I'd probably be strung up and quartered if anyone knew. And I'm a little sore."

"Yeah, I get all that."

"Is there something you want to talk about?" I'd noticed lately that Jo had been awfully friendly with one of the black boys she'd met at the library.

"I like Dean."

"You're kidding."

"No, I'm not kidding. Why? Do you think you're the only white girl in the whole world who could be attracted to a black boy?"

"I don't know, I'm the only one I know of at this moment in time."

"Well, now there are two."

Whoa, Jo! Who would have thought? I wondered if she would have been attracted to Dean if she'd never met me. He was three years older than us and that appealed to her. Jo had never showed much interest in boys — this was the first, as far I knew. She was a loner and never had any friends, other than me. But I did have other friends now, although Jo was the only person I trusted. My friends were a mixed group, some popular, some not. We Jubileans ran into each other on every corner, in every classroom, yet we still had fierce cliques within cliques within cliques. I tried to straddle several groups. Jo was not a joiner.

I soon discovered that my secret life was not the secret I'd thought it was. A few of us sat at the public pool one hot summer day. We were wet and oily and lay on our beach towels, smoking cigarettes, eating potato chips, and drinking Cokes with crushed ice. During a moment's pause in our chatter, one of the girls, Fay, began chanting. Softly she said, "Nigger lover." Someone giggled. And then again: "Nigger lover."

I froze. No one else said a word. The

words hung in the air and I couldn't speak. I pretended that I didn't hear. The lifeguard blew the whistle and children ran and jumped into the pool; the noise level rose and the moment was over.

These were the popular girls. They thought they knew something about me, but offered neither details nor confrontation. Once in a while the truth popped out like a bad tooth extracted from its roots. And the truth about me was that I was two people. That truth confused them and made them uncomfortable. They knew me as the person who entertained them from behind the proscenium of the school stage and the church choir loft. They heard my name announced over the school loudspeaker for winning trophies and often saw my name in the paper. I made good grades. They cried when my father walked down the aisle of the school auditorium carrying a dozen roses for me during a curtain call. And when I least expected it, they softly chanted, "Nigger lover," while we sat on our towels at the swimming pool in the summer. They couldn't reconcile the two of us. I was their high-achieving friend with a nasty flaw, one so repulsive to them that I was surprised their suspicions hadn't already led them to ignore me completely. Girls like me did not stray from the straight and narrow, nor make, in their eyes, foolish mistakes. And they never let me forget it.

I invited the same group of girls to a slumber party at the funeral home. We were just a few months shy of getting our driver's licenses and still frustratingly dependent on in-house parties and events to entertain ourselves. Jo wouldn't even consider coming and spoke of the girls with disdain. But I desired to be popular, or at least included. The night of the slumber party was uneventful until we told ghost stories.

"Come on. Someone tell the Bell Witch story."

"No, not that one. We always tell that one."

"What about the girl in the cemetery?"

"No, just heard that one the other night."

"Why don't you tell one about the funeral home?"

They all turned to me.

"Yeah! You tell one," they said.

"I don't know any." Never would I tell any of these girls about feeling the spirits of the dead bodies hanging around, or whatever they had been. That was for me alone.

"Make one up, for Christ's sake. This is the perfect setting."

"Yeah, make one up about the funeral home. That'll be scary."

So I told them a story, but I didn't tell them it was my story, a nightmare I'd had twice already. I let them think I was making it up on the spot. I turned out the lights and lit a candle.

"Okay. There was a girl who lived in a funeral home. One night she snuck out of the funeral home to meet her boyfriend —"

"Who was her boyfriend? Was he a nigger?" It was Fay again.

The silence in the room roared. I shook inside. It had come out of nowhere.

"No," I managed to say. "The girl's boyfriend was the son of a preacher. His father was a snake handler and spoke in tongues. He was a Holy Roller, she wasn't, so they had to meet in secret."

That kept them quiet.

"When she returned from the date —"

Fay interrupted, "What did they do on the date? Did they do it?"

"I don't know, Fay. The damn story's not about doing it. Do you want to hear it or not?"

Finally, silence.

"When she returned to the funeral home from her secret date, she noticed that the hearse wasn't parked in the garage but in the driveway, which was unusual. As she drew closer, she saw that dead people were sticking their heads out of the windows of the hearse. The ghosts looked like real people, except they weren't as thick. You couldn't see through them, but they were kind of like liquid people."

"Did the girl know any of the people?"

"She thought she recognized them, but she'd seen so many dead bodies that she couldn't be sure who they were, they were all kind of blurry. The bodies began to come out of the hearse, but not through the doors. They floated through the top of the hearse and through the side panels. There were other dead people still hanging out of the windows all holding their arms open to the girl, like they wanted something from her. And others were peeking out from under the hearse's underbelly. The hearse was covered in moving, seeing, breathing dead bodies. She had to get away from them. She could have just run away, they were moving more slowly than she was, but that was not what she wanted. She wanted to go inside the funeral home. She knew it didn't make sense, but that was where she felt safe. So she slowly moved to the nearest door. It was locked. She tried not to look back, but she could feel that they were almost upon her now. She banged on the door."

Then, as if I had staged a dramatic effect,

just when I said the word *banged,* lightning flashed outside and thunder cracked so loudly it sounded as if it were in the room. A chorus of shrieks ensued, and one of the girls began to cry.

"This room must be haunted," I whispered.

That was payback for the nigger comment. They formed a line to the bathroom after the fright. I wanted to strangle Fay, but I knew she spoke for all of them. Their fright was but a small victory. They didn't want to hear any more.

The next morning I was in the kitchen helping my mother with breakfast. When I returned to my room, Fay stood at my chest of drawers, rummaging through the top drawer. She quickly shut it and giggled when she saw me. Another girl was in my closet going through shoeboxes. She, too, giggled. I stood in the doorway looking at them, unable to speak. I was embarrassed that they would be so rude and confounded because I didn't know what they were looking for. I assumed they sought evidence of something. Maybe they thought they'd find pictures of black boys, or a diary in which I revealed all.

"Guess it's time for us to go," Fay said.

"But what about breakfast? My mother's

made breakfast for everybody."

"I'm not hungry. Are y'all?"

No. None of them were hungry.

These were the girls I'd been handed. And I, in turn, was handed to them. That's what life in a small town was all about. You live with it, or you leave. My slumber-party days were officially over. I had better things to do at night anyway. Crazy things. I must have been crazy. My parents must have been crazy. When Evelyn left home, I inherited the bedroom with a private door that led outside. A teenager with a private door was a dangerous thing. A crazy thing.

The daylight hours belonged to everyone else. I always did as I was told. Schoolteachers, piano teacher, Sunday-school teacher, preacher, my parents . . . someone was always watching, someone always wanting something. I wanted the night to belong to me. I planned trysts with friends who were old enough to drive. We drove around, drank bad, cheap wine, and felt what it was like to be out in the night when everyone else was sleeping. I planned midnight meetings with Julian. Sometimes I returned only a couple of hours before it was time to get up and go to school. I was terrified that I would arrive back at the funeral home to find the sheriff's car waiting for me, or at the very least I feared that when I reached the top of those rickety wooden stairs, I would find my parents exploding from anger. My father and I could easily have passed in the night. We walked the same path. It was a miracle that I did not run into him when he was out at every hour of the morning, collecting dead bodies.

Jubilee showed its vulnerable side at night. Men rarely seen out of their suits or work clothes walked past their lit windows in their undershirts; women in curlers and their dressing gowns closed the shutters. But outside, anything might happen. A kind of freedom was in that. It was worth the fear of getting caught. And with that sense of freedom came an itch to break away from the confines of Jubilee's ten square miles. I went to sleep in the small hours thinking of that possibility, dreaming of the day when I didn't have to sleep above the dead bodies, when I would be known to people as someone other than the undertaker's daughter.

CHAPTER 13
JUBILEE'S UNDERBELLY

The seventies crept up on Jubilee and settled like a canker sore. Was it possible to hate an entire decade based on a dearth of natural fibers? A single stray match among all the cheap polyester bell-bottoms in Jubilee and that would have been it. One night after dinner, my father strolled into the living room in a black jumpsuit. I thought the world had ended.

"What?" He looked at the stricken expression on my face. "It's just a lounge suit."

"Does the man you buy your suits from know about this?"

"I bought it from him. You don't know anything. This is sharp. I'm only going to wear it at home."

Thank God for that. I feared for his reputation.

Valiant attempts at modernism by the youth of Jubilee fell fallow due to a lack of resources. Beauticians struggled with the demand for Farrah Fawcett hairstyles. Scissoring out of their comfort zone, they were forced to interpret Farrah's look, which was in opposition to the granny helmets to which they were accustomed. The sight was painful to behold. Their efforts to create a carefree, soft, hip look just didn't work. I had a friend whose hair featured wings sprayed stiff to the side of her head in an aerodynamic structure. It took her over two hours to ready it for takeoff. I grew my hair long, but opted out of the rough cut. Suddenly denim was everywhere. We modeled ourselves after characters in television shows. For some unknown reason, the denim that Pete, Linc, and Julie wore in *The Mod Squad* bore no resemblance to the denim we wore in Jubilee. Ours was bad denim, the kind adults wore, adults who had no business wearing denim. Not one of us looked remotely like a member of the Mod Squad.

Middle-aged men put away their ties on the weekend and wore turtlenecks and sports jackets. A few women drove out of town to worship at the feet of a city hairstylist who gave them freedom from the holy trinity — teasing, hairspray, and an hour under the dryer. Girdles and slips were relegated to the back of the drawer, and everything hung freely, more or less.

Funerals didn't change that much. Fresh new preachers arrived in town along with a few more people from the North, who settled into our Southern ways and death practices. Brother Vince got contact lenses and had a devil of a time adjusting. He blinked and teared up so much that the new widows of Jubilee were touched by his obvious display of emotion.

As comfortable as I had always been with adults, it turned out they were pretty comfortable around me as well. By the time I entered high school they let their hair down a little and sometimes indulged their loose tongues. They told me about the cracks, the weak seams, and the dirt that accumulated around the fringes of good society. The doctor's daughter pulled her hair out and banged her head against the wall, and he didn't know what to do about it. The dentist's wife lowered the shades during the day and placed empty bottles in the garbage at night. A preacher's wife drove to Greenville frequently to go shopping, but always came home with a small bag of something she could have bought anywhere. One of the male antique dealers was often seen in the company of young boys. And, oops, out spilled an unlawful number of bottles of prescription medicine when the magistrate's wife dropped her purse at the grocery. Little pills in a rainbow of colors rolled under the refrigerated-meat section. Therefore, I was shocked, but not surprised, when I found myself running away from the adult underbelly of Jubilee.

There was a man. He had the face of a beekeeper's apprentice and the body of a half-cured ham — fat and unsettled. Like a walrus, his body had no definition. The connection of one fleshy part to another was a mystery. His scowl and smile were one and the same. He scratched himself compulsively. Even if he'd broken both of his clammy, nail-bitten hands, it wouldn't have prevented him from breathing on a girl's neck or massaging her back with his bloated arm. He had the look of an old man about him even in his bloom. In a salute to their idea of his testicular fortitude, the boys called him Neddy Numb Nuts. Ned Barker enjoyed an unfettered access to girls, made possible by his position as overseer of several extracurricular activities for boys and girls from the ages of fourteen to eighteen, and his proclaimed importance in Jubilee's pecking order gave him courage. He was a well-known, high-profile member of his church. The first time I was snared by

Mr. Barker's grope was in the nest he created for legitimate club meetings. I drove to the edge of Jubilee onto a country road and turned into a gravel driveway. There was the feeling of seclusion. I recognized three or four other cars and was glad not to be the first to arrive. I was nervous because this was my first meeting and I didn't know what to expect.

Mr. Barker had transformed his basement into a place we called the dragon's den, in which he moved about with a reptilian thud. There were no windows, and his feeble attempts at mood lighting gave the furniture and carpet a sickly yellow glow. The only seating was an oversize sofa, and I thought it odd that there weren't any chairs. Three or four boys and girls sat cross-legged on the floor, and a couple of girls were on the sofa where Mr. Barker sat, or rather where his body spread over the cushions, with a clipboard on his lap and a pen in hand. He patted the seat next to him. Unaware of his predilection for underage, sweet young things, I sat down. I sank into the worn cushion and found that any movement at all made me sink farther into the bowels of the sofa. It felt like being trapped. Each of us was there to receive feedback on our projects, which we were required to present to Mr. Barker. I don't think any of us were particularly thrilled. There was no way around it, though, if you were a high-school-age kid who wanted to do something after school other than booze it up in a tobacco barn. Mr. Barker had a little niche going in the realm of extracurricular activities.

While all eyes were focused on Bobby and his presentation, I felt Mr. Barker's heavy arm creep onto my shoulders as he placed half of it on the back of the sofa and half around me. It was awkward. I squirmed, hoping to signal to him that he'd made a mistake. Nothing. Then I felt one of his fingers on my neck. I jumped, but he pressed me back in the seat again with a firm hand. I was dumbfounded. And his soft, round shoulders were stronger than I'd thought. He'd done this before. I said nothing. I did nothing. I thought about how I could get out of the situation, but I felt I could do nothing until Bobby had finished. Would Bobby ever shut his trap?

"Where's the bathroom?" I asked as soon as he spoke his last word.

When I returned, my seat was still empty and I looked at the other two girls. One of them glanced at me out of the corner of her eyes and then looked straight ahead. I sat on the floor.

"Come on back up here and sit down," Mr. Barker said to me.

"That's all right. I'm fine."

The next time we were supposed to meet I tried to make excuses but was assured that a project short of perfection was not acceptable. I arrived late, hoping that the special seat next to Mr. Barker had already been taken. Hallelujah! A girl sat next to him and I was surprised to see his hairy arm on her shoulders now. She had a blank look on her face, or maybe it was shock. Damn. This guy didn't discriminate. He boldly chose girls from the right side of the tracks. I realized that he must have felt very sure of himself.

Later in the evening, after an assortment of soft drinks had been offered and the laughter of the boys rang in the air from a sophomoric joke, the room cleared and only two of us were left to perform. The boys, who were allowed to do their bit and leave, had no idea what they were missing. Mr. Barker asked the other girl to present her work. I sat on the far end of the sofa. The space that had previously been taken by others was now empty, and before I had a chance to move to the floor, he slid over next to me during the girl's presentation. Within seconds his arm was around my

shoulders and I felt his cold, wet finger sliding into my blouse, then right into my bra. I
moved my body in some way that knocked
his hand away from me. The movement
drew him out of his trance. The girl's voice
droned on. I panted internally, desperate to
find a way not to be left alone with him.

"Gosh," I interrupted. "Would you look at
the time? I have really got to head out of
here."

"But you haven't done your work yet."
Did I detect a hint of temper?

"Sorry, I'll go first next time."

I don't know how many girls found themselves within Mr. Barker's web of fondling
madness, and I don't know why we didn't
report him. We didn't even talk to each
other about it. I was embarrassed by it and
thought that this was somehow punishment
for the other life I led in secret. I thought
that his being after me was a reflection of
whom I had become.

One night I found myself drunk in Mr.
Barker's hotel room. Unbelievably, he was
allowed to take groups of kids on overnight
trips. We were to have a "meeting" in his
room after dinner. I walked in and found
just one other girl there. She was a year
younger than me and I didn't know her
well. He clumped over to the minibar and

began pouring drinks. I waited for everyone else to show up, and by the time I'd downed my third bourbon and Coke, I finally realized that no one else was coming. I was nearly passed out on the bed and the other girl was in a similar state, just inches away from me. Mr. Barker climbed onto the bed and plowed between us. He had concocted a high-school-girl sandwich and was the big, fat filling. I heard a giggle erupt from her. Surely not? I thought. But, no, there it was again.

He said something about being able to watch TV better from the bed. I tried to sit up and focus on the television but became dizzy and fell back on the pillow to stop the room from spinning. I had enough sense to know that I couldn't let myself pass out in that room, but before I could make an effort to get up, I felt his hand sliding down my pants and into my underwear. He was quick and practiced. His toxic hand made me feel sick. I was stunned by the difference between the touch for which the whole body aches and yearns, and the unwanted, feral touch of a predator. I jumped up and staggered out.

In an effort to assuage my guilt for not being the other girl's caretaker, the next morning I searched for her at breakfast. She sat alone, hunched over a plate of eggs, and crunched on a piece of toast as if it were her last. My head was splitting and my mouth was as dry as a dust storm, the very thought of food . . .

"Are you all right?" I asked.

"I'm fine. Why?" She smiled brightly.

"No reason."

I made plans. I would have to be smarter and more alert. There wasn't any way to stay completely clear of him, but I vowed he'd never touch me again. Eventually, he landed on another girl like a beached whale. I guess he kept trying until he found a taker. I was eternally grateful that Sarah let him do whatever he wanted to her. She lived in the doctor-and-lawyer area of town, where we often saw his car parked in her driveway. My friends and I were puzzled that this academically brilliant, good-looking girl could allow Mr. Barker's clammy hands near her. We drove by her house to see how late his car stayed in the driveway. Why did her parents allow him to visit her? Didn't they think it was strange? How did he get away with it? He somehow managed to pull off normalcy with the adults of Jubilee. And still no one reported him.

In a summer ritual on Sunday nights when the sun finally set, a group of us packed into several cars and formed a train to the drive-in. We never watched the movie, but strolled from car to car getting sloshed on Purple Passion or Strawberry Hill. We walked by Mr. Barker's car, and Sarah was hanging out the window three sheets to the wind. He tried to walk her around and sober her up, to no avail. It would be impossible to take her home bombed out of her mind. I felt a little sorry for her and remembered a time when I was so drunk that someone stood me up at my door in one piece. My parents were out this night so I told Mr. Barker he could bring her to my house. But his idea of sobering her up was entirely different from mine. I was thinking coffee. Jemma and I watched with open mouths as Mr. Barker stripped the fifteen-year-old girl and carried her naked into the shower.

"Mr. Barker . . . Mr. Barker," she giggled in a drunken stupor.

We left them to it.

"Damn, those rumors must be true," I said to Jemma.

"Yeah, but I thought she was supposed to be smart. Why would she let him near her?"

"There are different kinds of smart."

The same could have been said about me. I wasn't always smart. I took too many chances and knew that something had to give. If Jo's father hadn't contemplated taking a job in Mississippi, then maybe things would have turned out differently. She felt sure they would move away and began prematurely to wrap up her life in Jubilee. She stopped seeing Dean at the same time that I stopped seeing Julian. The lack of any normalcy in our relationship had left Julian restless.

"I'm tired of all this sneaking around," he told me. "Jubilee is too backward, it won't ever accept mixed relationships."

I could say nothing to that. He was right. We'd never go to the movies together. We'd never walk into a restaurant together, or go to the Beacon Dipper for ice cream, and he would never meet my parents. The fear of getting caught would always haunt us. It ended amicably and with great relief. I walked away feeling as if I'd just been saved from some terrible disaster that I couldn't name, one that had hovered over me for a long time.

CHAPTER 14
A CASKET IN RED

I avoided boys, young men, old men, any kind of men except dead ones, for a long time. I tried to focus on my schoolwork. I planned to embalm a cat for my science project. *This will be unique!* I thought. I could position it on a wooden platform and source a glass dome to cover it. What a visual display! I drove my science teacher and my father crazy until they agreed to a meeting.

I arranged for Mr. Whitlock to drop by the funeral home after school. The day the three of us met in my father's office, I was so excited that I paced back and forth while the two men sat in leisurely calm.

"So, she wants to embalm a cat, does she?" my father said to Mr. Whitlock, as though I weren't in the room.

"Looks that way."

"Okay, well, first we have to find a cat," my father said.

Oh. I hadn't thought of that.

"Yep, then she'll have to kill it." Mr. Whitlock sat comfortably with his hands in his pockets and his legs crossed.

"Kill it?" I asked.

"Of course. You can't embalm a cat unless it's dead." My father looked conspiratorially at Mr. Whitlock.

"Can't we just find a cat that's already dead?" I asked.

"Why, sure. There's one on every corner," my father said.

"I know of a big ole stray cat. She's pregnant though," said Mr. Whitlock.

"There you go. You can kill a pregnant cat." My father sounded serious.

"How could I do that? I can't do that. Can't you find a cat and kill it?"

"Oh, no. You have to kill it. I'll help with the embalming. But you have to kill it."

"Can't we just find a possum or squirrel or something that's already dead?"

"Roadkill? You want to embalm roadkill?" My father laughed.

"Maybe you can run over the pregnant cat," suggested Mr. Whitlock.

"I can't run over a pregnant cat! Just forget it."

Meeting over.

I borrowed someone's ten-year-old butterfly collection that year for my science project. The butterflies were so old that a few of them disintegrated into dust.

If I ever had any lingering doubts about following in my father's footsteps, the unsuccessful cat-embalming project put paid to that. Though their approach was lighthearted, clearly I was being tested. And this test, at any rate, I had failed.

The ritual of visiting Miss Agnes remained constant and I found it comforting. I still dressed up for our visits, and for once conservatism and fashion merged congenially. I slipped out of the bad denim and tossed a maxi dress over my head, grabbed a crocheted shawl, and arrived at Miss Agnes's doorstep a seventies belle. Out of long-standing habit, my father continued to direct the visits. "Show her this, show her that . . . and tell her about the time . . ." Her eyes told me that she could still hear a little, and shouting at her no longer bothered me. She displayed clippings from the newspapers of various articles in which I was mentioned, and a few about her. I had grown fond of her over the years. We were content to be in each other's company without the need of many affectionate reassurances.

By the beginning of the 1970s her squat, red figure was still an acceptable eccentricity in Jubilee, but outsiders found her too odd. She was curious to see the first indoor shopping mall, recently built in a town near us, and asked my father to take her. Miss Agnes meandered through the mall in her big red hat with her yellow hair sticking out at the sides, her arms and neck laden with red beads. She had not changed her appearance in any way for at least forty years. My father was sad and uncomfortable that people pointed and gawked at her.

Thirteen years ago he had taken her to the Jubilee hospital for the first time, and now, when she became ill in her old age, she would only be content in a hospital that was a forty-minute drive away. He drove back and forth every day, twice a day, to see her. He resolved issues with her nurses and doctor, brightened her room with flowers, and arrived in the evening with a plate of her favorite foods.

When she asked for me near the end, I entered her hospital room wearing the dress she had requested. The high collar and long sleeves were virginal looking, and the white, eyelet cotton fabric floated to the floor. I came as close as I ever would to resembling an angel, and that was no small achievement. At the end of this frigid November day on which the sun never bothered to appear, I shivered in the thin dress. I fervently hoped that I wouldn't run into anyone who knew me because I looked ridiculously out of season. Her private room was bright and sterile and quite large. She sat up in bed waiting for our arrival. It was the first time I had ever seen her without her aura of red. The white hospital gown softened her features and stole a little of the power the other, vibrant color had given her. A nurse rose from a chair and left the room. I stood beside Miss Agnes and held her old, spotted hand. During this final meeting it seemed strange to yell into her ear, but I bent down as my father had and raised my voice.

"Miss Agnes, you're looking real well," I lied.

"Why, honey, thank you so much for coming such a long way to see me."

"I've brought you some cookies."

"Let's have one then, honey. Frank, you want a cookie?"

"No, thank you, Miss Agnes. Those are for you."

She asked me to sit in the chair and I pulled it close to her bed.

"Your daddy's taken real good care of me."

"Yes, ma'am."

Her hair spread over her shoulders like a curly broom, and I thought she looked like a child who had deep folds in her skin. The cookie crumbled on her blanket; she only nibbled a bit. I wiped the crumbs away. I asked her if she wanted me to read to her; she said no, it was too much of an effort. We talked a while longer until she was noticeably tired, and my father led us in our farewells.

At home, I scrambled to find something she'd written, something to which I'd paid little attention at the time: a piece of paper upon which she'd typed a few words about Poe and death. The tingle of my first regret rushed through me. Now I wished we'd discussed her favorite story after the Christmas visit when she'd asked me to read "The Fall of the House of Usher." Now I wanted to know why she was so attached to the story. Now, it was too late. I found the paper with her words typed neatly across the page; oddly, the ribbon had just begun to fade as she typed the last of them.

I read her words: "Somehow, I feel that I shall continue to hear the hushes, until the hush of death closes over me, as silently as the waters of the tarn over the House of Usher."

What were *the hushes*? I hoped to discover the meaning of these words at the library. I sat in a corner in the back and read the story again, scanning for *hushes,* but found no mention of the word in Poe's story. The hushes were hers alone. It occurred to me that she must have been talking about silence. Miss Agnes lived alone all of her adult life, most of it in the big house, roaming from room to room, the beloved antiques her only companions, except for the friendship of my father. The hour or so he spent with her every day in that house, the hour that I sometimes begrudged her, was the only time her house was not filled with silence.

A few nights later, the crunching of the tires of the ambulance on the gravel under my window woke me. The windowpane was ice-cold and frosty. It was so cold that the exhaust from the ambulance rose up in a fury and bathed both my father and Rex in a thick fog. The night had deepened; it was too late for anything but death. They opened the rear door and pulled out the gurney. I knew it was Miss Agnes even though a sheet covered the body. My father's nightlong vigils at the hospital had ended. Then, as they lifted the gurney onto the ramp, I heard a loud thud.

'"Ah! Oh my God, he's dropped her!" I shouted to no one.

I put my fist up to the window and hurriedly wiped my breath from the cold glass. They scrambled to put her right. I couldn't believe it. Never, in all of the years, with all of the bodies that had passed through our doors, had my father dropped anyone. But he sure did drop Miss Agnes.

The next morning I rushed downstairs to the office, where he sat staring out the window.

"I saw you bring her in last night, Daddy. You dropped her, didn't you?"

"Never dropped anybody."

"I know. What happened?"

"I don't know." He paused. "I don't know. She just slipped off."

He'd already laid her out. He must have worked into the early-morning hours. I don't know how he managed to embalm her. I wondered how he could. It would be like trying to embalm his own mother.

Inside the chapel I placed a chair close to Miss Agnes and waited to see if she was hanging about. Perhaps she'd be confused, or ornery about leaving us, but I didn't feel her. As far as I could tell, she was gone. So engrossed was I in Miss Agnes's change of state that I didn't notice that Rex had entered the chapel. I jumped.

"Sorry . . . I forgot," he said.

Rex was the most sensitive of men. He noticed all manner of things that most young men never noticed. He knew not to sneak up on me in the funeral home, since he knew I jumped when people didn't announce themselves, even in daylight. He'd recently become a partner in the business. He was a self-motivated man. Once, when we were away, he stripped the embalming room wall of its tired and faded wallpaper. He admitted he couldn't stand to look at it another moment. He painted all weekend, and upon our return we were welcomed by the embalming room's dazzling white walls.

Helplessly addicted to Cokes, Rex already held one in his hand this morning. His glasses slid down his nose and with his free hand he pushed them back up.

"Your daddy's hurting. I can see it," he told me.

"Yes, I know. He's going to bury his best friend."

"You know, before Frank made our partnership official, he asked me to go meet Miss Agnes." Rex already had an undertaker's voice, soft, with genuine reverence.

"Frank told me that he wanted to hear Miss Agnes's opinion, he said it meant a lot to him. So I met with her at the hospital. I was a little nervous; she was such a legend and all. But even in her illness she was a genteel Southern lady."

"Genteel? Never heard her described in that way."

"I know she was a hard-nosed business-woman, too, but she was very cordial with me, very soft. It was a short visit because she was severely ailing at that point."

My father walked into the chapel then. He had taken his jacket off, and in his white shirtsleeves he looked industrious. He held the familiar palette of lip colors in one hand and his long, thin brush in the other. He touched up her lips with just a faint hint of color. I'd recently been wondering about the purpose of all of this. Was it really neces-sary to see Miss Agnes lying in what increas-ingly seemed to me an unnatural state? I watched as he made her lips come to life. He'd called upon a small casket company to make Miss Agnes's bespoke casket. I'd never seen a red casket before. It was hand-painted and made of steel.

"Is that velvet?" I asked him.

Inside, the casket was lined in white velvet, and a strip of red velvet bordered the pillow and the interior band of the casket.

"This was what she wanted."

"Where did that dress come from?"

"Aunt Ruby made it."

I smiled at the coincidence that my aunt's name was that of the color of Miss Agnes's life. "She would have liked that."

My mother's sister sewed the red velvet dress by hand and trimmed the empire waist with a red satin ribbon. Many people asked my father if he would make a replica of her casket for them. Could they place a special order for one? they asked. But he refused.

"There will never be another like it while I'm alive," he told them.

During visitation, Beacon County's farmers filled the funeral home in their Sunday best, and Jubilee's citizens came by the droves, a few to pay their respects, most out of curiosity. Her lawyer, who served as a pallbearer, wore scarlet trousers. Red flowers of all types filled the chapel. Large and small arrangements were delivered in no other color. The room became a crimson garden, and flowers spilled into the hall and to other sitting areas.

My father graciously spoke to people who had never cared about her, who only stopped by to see what kind of send-off she would receive. Some were sympathetic toward my father and knew that when you spend that much time with people, they are your family and you grieve for them when they are gone. After the last visitor departed that night, he locked the doors, pulled a chair up to her casket, and sat with her for a while. Then he drove to her house as he had done every night for almost thirteen years and turned on the lights to deter vandalism.

The next day at her funeral many of the town's aristocracy who had snubbed her and been snubbed by her were noticeably absent. Those Old Clan members who had tried so hard to gain entry to her home to cast their eyes over her antiques stayed at home that chilly afternoon when Miss Agnes was lowered into the ground beside her beloved brother and parents. At her burial my father placed a blanket of red carnations on her casket. That was the way in which their relationship began, and that was how it ended.

Jubilee's opinion was divided as to how Miss Agnes should have handled her affairs. The gossip began immediately.

"Frank Mayfield got the whole thing."

"Did you hear? She left him the whole estate."

"That's the only reason he did what he did . . . just so he could get everything."

"If anyone deserved it, Frank Mayfield did."

"Your daddy worked for everything he got, and more. Shoot, I wouldn't have wanted to be at her beck and call."

"What's a man want with an old lady like that?"

"Nobody else would have done what he did for her. No one else would have left his family's Christmas dinner table to take a cantankerous old lady a plate of food."

"That Frank Mayfield is a con man."

I was incensed that even one person in Jubilee could believe that my father had actually planned to inherit. Anyone who knew Miss Agnes was well aware that she could not be coerced into anything. Years later, I learned that she had been clear with him about her intentions early in their friendship. Fearful that it might fall into the wrong hands if something happened to her, she secretly deeded her house to him. Perhaps it was also her way of keeping him loyal, I don't know. I cannot imagine that he would have behaved any differently toward her whether or not she left him her estate.

After the will was made public a curious number of people wanted to be our friends for the first time. Others, not extremely talented at hiding envy, were uncertain if they would ever speak to us again. One thing was certain — after thirteen years, we were moving out of the funeral home.

My father drove me to Miss Agnes's house early one evening and coasted slowly in front of it. With the same conviction that he said Julie Christie was the most beautiful woman in the world, he told me, "Here is the most beautiful house in Jubilee. I hope you appreciate it."

It was a prime example of American-colonial-and-Palladian-style architecture. Two-story columns fronted a brick facade and flanked one-story wings. Here were marble statues and massive urns from which red zinnias sprouted. This was our new home. It was too much of a house to talk about all in one breath. The house had nothing of the appearance of a museum because everything in it was personal. It contained a few things a little more worth talking about than others.

German furniture designer John Henry Belter had originated the method of laminating rosewood in his New York workshop in 1844. He kept his method secret for many years, until 1858 when he finally took out a patent for it. The process made it possible to create elaborate designs, and with it he could carve concave backs to his chairs. Before he died in 1863, he destroyed his patterns and smashed his pattern molds so that his ornately carved furniture could never be reproduced. Five Belter pieces, grand and rare, occupied the center of Miss Agnes's parlor. The sofa and chairs of a three-piece drawing-room suite were upholstered in red satin, as were an additional armchair and a smaller side chair. Candelabra and miniature glass slippers sat atop tier tables inlaid with French ormolu. Miss Agnes had been particularly fond of her satin ruby and ormolu parlor lamp known as a *Gone with the Wind* lamp, a misnomer because the use of the lamps in the movie was an anachronism; they were not produced until after the Civil War. She didn't care; it was still valuable. Red-and-white china plates lined the shelves of a cupboard. Copper pots that rested on trivets by the fireplace appeared ready for the boil. There were Duncan Phyfe chairs, a serpentine chest, vases, candlesticks, framed prints, walnut tables, and a bellpull. A thick Oriental rug covered the beautiful wood floor. There was more.

In the spacious entry hall a French crystal chandelier glistened from the high ceiling, and a heavily carved piano graced a corner. Another Oriental softened the walk across the foyer. The house had been remodeled in 1880, and the Victorian influence was evident in the winding staircase in the entry hall. The staircase led to the room that was to be my bedroom. In it, a large, floor-to-ceiling Palladian window divided into three parts dominated one wall. My new view looked out upon shade trees that stretched high above the house, a manicured green lawn, and shrubbery that met a slightly raised front porch supported by two elegant columns. The porch extended the length of the house and was partially framed by the black wrought iron from New Orleans.

A few months after her death, I stood on the concrete floor of a building site in the back of Miss Agnes's house.

"What's all this?" I asked my father. "Aren't there enough rooms in this house for us?"

"There are, but we're not going to live in all of the rooms. We can't sit around on Victorian furniture and watch television. And there's no kitchen in the house to speak of."

A two-story addition was built in the back of the house, not visible from the street, designed so that the facade was not affected.

As my father spoke of the new kitchen and his walk-in, cedar-lined closet, I noticed a small brick structure at the back of the property.

"What's that?" I pointed.

"Slaves' quarters."

We stood before a windowless building, which from the outside had the deceiving facade of a cozy, little brick cottage, the only sign that remained of Major Bibb's one hundred slaves. My father and I stepped into a close, dark space so small that no more than three people could lie next to each other without touching. I inhaled stale air as my eyes adjusted. The walls and floor were achingly featureless, without even a hearth to lend them character. This was the kind of historical structure of which Jubilee was so proud.

The slaves' quarters were a reminder to me that ancestors of Noah and Julian had been kept behind the houses of Jubilee in buildings not fit for animals. I was sickened by the very thought. Neither of us spoke and I was glad of it. I had nothing to say that he would understand.

My father didn't sling the word *nigger* around like many people I knew, and he never hesitated when the black funeral home needed help, but the division remained. In fact, the funeral business was the most segregated business in Jubilee and the whole of the South.

The line between races in the 1970s was as severe and noticeable as it had ever been. Nothing much had changed since that day at school when Ophelia first entered the classroom in my red plaid dress. My father's attitude was much the same as that of many in Jubilee. Our black community were to know their place and stay in it. Our schools may have survived integration, but our churches, restaurants, and our relationships — governed by the largest unspoken taboo — were still glaringly separate.

This was neither a family nor a town in which I could lay down the burden of my secret lovers. As my father closed the door of the slaves' quarters, I closed the door to the notion that I would ever be able to confide in him. This was one of those moments when I drew a silent breath and told myself to have patience, that I only had to finish high school and then I could leave Jubilee.

CHAPTER 15
THE HOUSE THAT
RICHARD BUILT

Miss Agnes's house creaked and made
noises at night that only I could hear, for
while Jemma and our parents slept in the
new wing, my room kept a solid foot in the
old. Oddly, after living in the funeral home
for thirteen years, I thought this was the
sort of house in which one could be, well,
properly scared. The winding staircase in
the spacious entrance hall led directly up to
my bedroom. At the other end of my room
a heavy door opened into what had been a
children's playroom. Beside my bed was yet
another door, behind which a venerable
stairway led to an attic room. The grandfather clock at the bottom of the stairs
ticked loudly. At night, in the dark, a presence lingered in the baronial rooms downstairs. It may have been age itself. The house
seemed to groan under its 155 years. Perhaps the people who had lived here before
us left traces of themselves, and the old

timbers swelled and sighed in the summers and shrank in the cold of winter, creaking their accompaniment to the house's watchful spirits. Some were benign, I felt. Some not so. I wondered if Belle minded working in this house with its loathsome history. She would never say.

Things went missing from my bedroom. Sometimes I phoned her in the evenings.

"Have you seen my blue spiral notebook?"

"I can't find my red pajamas."

Every week it was something different. Jemma swore she wasn't playing games. The items I sought, a pair of socks, a book, disappeared, and items I didn't particularly need cropped up regularly, such as the red diary Miss Agnes had given me years ago. I wanted to keep a diary, I wanted to record everything, but I couldn't possibly. The girls at my slumber party had taught me that it wasn't safe for anything about my life to be written on paper. The risk of discovery was too great, so I tucked it away in a drawer. I found it under the bed one night. The pages were still blank.

In spite of these mildly perturbing goings-on, I fell in love with the house. Just as the funeral home was a house for both living and dead, this house seemed to exist somewhere between the past and the present. If

Miss Agnes had suddenly walked in the front door again, she would have been able to pick up right where she left off. Nothing was changed or disturbed; our modern possessions didn't mingle with her ancient collections. The design of the new addition was clever. It was possible to leave modernity behind simply by walking through a door.

I often wandered through the old part of the house when no one else was home. It felt like eavesdropping on another era. The big, cavernous rooms filled with solid, heavy furniture seemed to suit me. I read while sitting in the Belter chairs and woke from naps with marks from their carved wood impressed into my face. The ornate piano was sorely off-key but I played it anyway; my father seemed in no hurry to have it tuned. My repertoire contained no hymns or funereal music. No mourner's crying was to be heard and no dead people were in this house, at least, none we could see. Instead there was silence of a different kind. Miss Agnes was still here. In every corner, in every room bathed in red fabric, she was here. By not occupying her bedroom, by not using her drawing room or her kitchen, we kept our memories of her alive. On our first Thanksgiving in the house we gathered in her dining room, a place that had not been the scene of any human visitation for over thirty years. My father carved the turkey and sliced the ham, and for the first time in over a decade, he didn't leave the table to go to her.

Not long after we'd moved in, in the middle of dinner, we heard a determined knock on our back door. My mother sighed, my father ignored it, and Jemma looked at me.

"You go," she said.

"No, you go," I said.

"No, *you* go."

"All right, all right, I'll go!"

I found a young teenager, someone from Jemma's class whom she barely knew, and a couple of other girls, huddled together giggling.

One of them boldly stepped forward. "We want to see your house," she demanded.

"I'm sorry, we're eating supper and now's not a good time."

"We'll come back later."

"No, please don't." I sought for an excuse. "We're really busy tonight."

Interruptions like this became a recurring feature of our life. Young, old, middle-aged, people known to us, absolute strangers, anyone and everyone knocked on our door at all hours and expected *le grand* tour.

Many people believed stoutly that now that the strange, old chatelaine was dead and buried, they had every right to demand entrance into the mysterious place from which she had barred entry for so long. Miss Agnes had, of course, known that after she was gone the deluge would begin, this being one of the reasons she'd left the house to my father, to prevent such trespasses. So there we were, bound to respect her wish that her things not be disturbed, trusted to behave as caretakers who lived in a certain way; in the same way, in fact, as we had lived above the funeral home — quietly and respectfully. We had no parties, no large gatherings, and certainly no tours. Our close friends, who had never minded being entertained in the funeral home, were the only people we invited to our new home. Tamales, fried chicken, and barbecue tasted the same wherever they were served. When Jemma and I refused classmates' requests to sneak them into the house when our parents weren't home, we became known in certain circles as snobs. I'd unwittingly made the lateral move from being a nigger lover to a stuck-up irritant. I was exasperated when a classmate, who'd never expressed any interest in visiting the house before, told me, "Everyone is jealous of you now."

There it was, that piercing, clear bell — a warning that eyes would cut away from me and whispers would continue. Under the stifling Southern politeness of this community was a pettiness from which I wanted to flee so badly that I thought my brain would explode. It seemed that my parents accepted the roots they had planted and were absorbed in the minutiae of their chosen spot on the map. But if there had been a small part of me that still found any comfort or sentiment for this small-minded town, it now crumbled to dust like the old bones in the cemetery where I once played.

My last year of high school was made memorable for me by a woman who seemed to care little for antebellum mansions or racial slurs. Mrs. Flanders stood at the door of the classroom as we entered, silently relaying the message that we were on her turf now. Occasionally she grabbed my arm, looked straight into my eyes, and quoted Keats and Byron without explanation. She was our Senior English teacher, her glasses so thick that her saucer-size, brown eyes seemed to have a separate existence. They remained slightly moist when she beseeched us to always remember that Robert Burns was much more than "Auld Lang Syne." When we were required to read *A Tale of Two Cities,* I thought she might be something special, but when she announced that our next book was to be Bram Stoker's *Dracula,* we couldn't believe our luck.

I had no rational explanation for my subsequent search for a string of fresh garlic, and no excuse, except to say that I was frightened stiff by that book. Ours was not the perfect house in which to read *Dracula.* Or, actually, maybe it was. I read late at night when everyone else was asleep. The windows in my bedroom unsettled me. Set high up beneath the portico, they rattled from the lightest breeze. These were windows a bat would love, I was sure of it. I thought, *Here I am with two sets of stairs in my room . . . a front door below me.* No one would ever know if I was taken away. What if Evelyn had told the truth that time and I really was a sleepwalker? What if I began sleepwalking again? Mr. Stoker's Lucy found herself a heap of trouble walking in her sleep. The brave and daring person who had sneaked out at night from the funeral home was reduced to nursing a morbid fear of bats.

Then the thing we'd all been fearing arrived. The Senior English term paper was dreaded for the entire four years of high school. This obstacle was similar to the nauseating dissection of frogs or the rote recitation of Brutus's speech by every member of our class, one after the other. I was enthralled by Dickens, but thought he would be pure hell to pin down. Hoping better to understand Miss Agnes's obsession, I chose to write about Edgar Allan Poe — a different kind of hell.

I thought it would be easy, but I was wrong. Old Poe worked his dark magic on me, and the night before the paper was due I still hadn't completed it. I was no closer to unlocking his secrets than I was those of Miss Agnes. I coerced a friend to help me, and we sat at a table piled high with books. Someone made coffee. I wrote, he referenced, I read, and he typed.

When it was all over, Mrs. Flanders asked me to stay after class. "Do you think that creativity must be fueled by alcohol or drugs?" She never bothered to lead into her searching questions. She threw them straight.

"Oh, God, I hope not. I mean, I don't know, but . . ."

"It doesn't work like that. People think it does. It's tricky, because at first you'll think you have the tiger by the tail. But it will tire you out. You'll lose and then those substances will kill creativity stone dead. Kill it, kill it, kill it. Mr. Poe was not a party animal. He was a *very sick man.*"

"Mrs. Flanders, I don't do drugs."

"I know that." She sounded as if she wanted to add the word *silly.*

"I mean, to tell you the truth, I've tried, but I'm naturally too paranoid."

Although she didn't flinch or raise her eyebrows, her saucer eyes grew sad. "I never thought I'd see the day when so many of our young people would arrive in school wacked out of their brains."

She was right. Drugs of all kinds had infiltrated our community. The fields surrounding little ole Jubilee were rife with a homegrown variety of marijuana guaranteed to sneak up on you and rob you of your equilibrium. Several of the girls who'd made such an effort to make me uncomfortable became druggies and confided they had serious addiction problems. That's how it worked in our small town. In a moment of weakness, a flaw was laid bare.

"Do you think Mr. Poe was mad?" Mrs. Flanders asked.

"I'm not sure, but I think he must have known someone who was."

"You should have written more about his influences. Form an opinion next time and allow yourself to be wrong."

Shortly after Dracula's demise, I grew my own set of fangs. My father's former lover slipped back into town, hopefully chastened by her banishment to Louisville. Viv smiled and nodded to me at social events in Jubilee. In a show of loyalty to my mother, I ignored her and developed what I hoped was a smoldering look. Once, we couldn't avoid one another and her eyes dogged me whenever I moved across the room. Jubilee never felt so stifling and small. I wondered how my mother could stand it.

I never saw my father share a public space with Viv, although I'm sure they must have run into each other from time to time. He had other things on his mind. One morning he sat at the breakfast table, his shirt collar unbuttoned and tieless.

"What's the matter?" I asked.

"Your father's not feeling well." My mother spoke for him — another peculiar sign.

Later that day the principal announced my name over the loudspeaker right in the middle of a class.

My mother stood inside the office, waiting for me. "Your father's had a heart attack. He's been taken to Greenville."

"Is he all right?"

"Yes, but get your things, we're going there right now."

He was fifty years old. The doctors told us that the heart attack had been mild. He didn't need surgery, but they wanted to keep him there for a week or so to watch over him. He recovered brilliantly, but was frightened by the experience, which brought him face-to-face with his own mortality. The doctors advised him that it wouldn't be a bad thing to lighten his workload.

Competition had become tougher in Jubilee. My mother kept her ear to the radio, listening to the funeral announcements, keeping a tally of which families had moved over to Sonny's camp. A small group of men remodeled Alfred Deboe's former premises and began an entirely new funeral business. The population couldn't support three white funeral homes. My father respected these people and liked the way they conducted business. Without even consulting Rex, he sold his business to the new consortium.

My father, Rex, and Fount were all invited to work at the new funeral home, and that seemed to suit my father and his new lifestyle. A lighter schedule without the headaches of ownership left him free to do a bit of traveling and enjoy his new home. Before everything began to wind down at the funeral home, my mother asked me to deliver a package to Fount's wife, Martha; the couple now occupied our former residence upstairs. I felt disoriented climbing the stairs, strange to be the one visiting.

"Martha?" I called to her. "It's me."

Nothing.

I entered the room that was once our dining room and found it transformed. It looked like the interior of a Gypsy's wagon. Lampshades covered in dark-colored handkerchiefs shed minimal light. A large cloth in muted hues draped a sofa that was oddly placed in the middle of the room. The faded fabric of a couple of easy chairs lent the room a tired parlor look. I found Martha nearly concealed from view but for an arm dangling down from the back of a wingback chair. She usually had a glass in her hand. I moved in front of her to avoid startling her. Slowly, she tilted her head and with some effort fixed her gaze upon me.

She immediately began speaking to me as if I were her closest friend, confiding in me as if we were not more than a few years apart in age. I didn't mind at first that she rattled on because she made fun of herself in a breathless stream of words. Then I noticed that these words, this story, had come round before. Her voice, and its slow, deep drawl, began to grate; there seemed to be no end to the sentence, the story, or the day. Then I noticed what I'd not seen before. The ice in her glass was trembling a little. Her chocolate-colored eyes, which I'd at first admired for their directness, were glazed over and out of her control — they didn't move because they couldn't. Her lipstick, upon further scrutiny, had missed the mark, and the faded color revealed the true line of her thin upper lip. When she occasionally ran her hand through her dark red hair, she exposed half an inch of white at the roots. A whiff of the sweet odor of bourbon and Coke, heavy on the bourbon, inflamed my nostrils. By the time I began to retreat from her, it was too late. Her bony hand had fastened on my arm and I was hers for the rest of the hour.

She was not going to make a précis of her story. No, she had me now and I was ensnared by whatever she desperately wanted to share. She spent some time talking about the place she was from without ever telling me where it was. Of course it was much farther south, easy to tell from her single-syllable words that picked up two or three more in her drawl. Then she switched gears and made me her confessor.

"Fount, ya know, spent some time in the pen." She held an unlit cigarette. "Your daddy didn't care. He hired him anyway." Tap, tap. Tap, tap. Maddeningly she tapped the cigarette on a coffee table littered with pink cellophane wrappers and overflowing ashtrays.

"Fount had a lot of difficulty in his life. Did ya know he used to be a policeman in another county?" She didn't wait for an answer. "Yeah," she slurred. "He worked at a car dealership, too." She put the cigarette to her lips, but took it away. "The man he worked for got himself involved in a car-theft ring. But Fount took the rap."

She closed her eyes and I thought she was gone. I made a move, but as soon as she heard the floor creak, she sat up, wide-eyed.

"He was innocent." She finally lit the cigarette and sucked on it as if it were her last. "They sent him to the federal pen in Atlanta. He loves the funeral business. He adores your daddy." She threw back the rest of her drink. "Sonny, that sorry-ass son of a bitch, he found out."

She used the tip of her ring finger to remove a speck of tobacco from her tongue. "Sonny let it out of the bag. About prison. Fount wanted to get his funeral director's license, but that son-of-a-mother-whore told them about Fount. What did he care? He's got his own rotten funeral home now. Told them about Atlanta. So Fount can't get his license. Because of the conviction."

"I know, Martha, you told me before. Remember? And I'm so sorry. I've got to go. My mother asked me to give you these fresh tomatoes from the garden."

Her lips curled up into a half smile and her head moved in slow motion, as if to say thank-you. We both knew she didn't care about the tomatoes. She tried to cadge a few cigarettes off me before I left, but I didn't have any.

Even though my father seemed content with his decision, it was the end of an era. After Fount and Martha moved out, the funeral home fell abandoned. I felt an emptiness whenever I drove by.

Wrapped up in a hundred senior-year activities, at first I didn't notice the change in my father's behavior. I knew he was spending more time "checking the garden," and at times when I stopped by to see him at the new funeral home, Rex or Fount told me he was out. Sometimes at breakfast he was quiet and moody. I asked him once if he was mad at someone or something and he shook his head no. Then, out of the blue, he'd act angry.

I'd been rehearsing long hours for our high school's first musical-theater production, a big event for our little town. I came home late one afternoon to grab a quick bite before heading out to another rehearsal. After a shower and a change of clothes, I sat at my place at the table opposite him. My mother always sat beside him and Jemma sat on the other side. He put his fork down and, with elbows on the table, folded his hands and stared at me. Angry disapproval was on his face.

"What?" I asked.

"You think you're so damn pretty, don't you?"

Nothing could have been further from my mind.

"Don't you?"

His voice was accusatory with something bordering nasty thrown in. It was unlike him. I was embarrassed by his glare and looked down at my food. Suddenly I had no saliva to wash down the steak I chewed. I was the little girl again who had walked through the kitchen, innocent and unaware of the spanking to come. He might have smacked me, his words stung so. I glanced at Jemma out of the corner of my eye, and she looked down at her food and pushed her fork around on the plate. I thought my mother would come to my rescue, but she too was angry and accused me of the high crime of never being at home. Then, within their silence, they both grew distant from me and from each other.

On another night, after he returned from the funeral home, I broached a subject with as much subtlety as a wrecking ball.

"I don't want to go to college. I want to go to New York to study acting."

My mother said nothing. I think she held her breath, waiting for the explosion. My father acted as if I'd told him that I was going to throw myself in front of a train.

"New York?" He raised his hands like a hellfire preacher. "New York! Do you know what you'll be in New York? Another pea in the pod, that's what you'll be. Just another pea in the pod. Well, you can forget that. You'll go to college or you'll get a job."

Cigarette-smoking, alcoholic, adulterous, and now leash-holding Big Daddy — Tennessee Williams made a fortune off men like my father. We had reached the stage that so many Southern daddies and daughters approach — the time for letting go. I was a teenager who was too much like him, and he was having trouble with his loss of control.

I didn't mention New York again. Instead I approached Mrs. Flanders for a written recommendation to her alma mater, a university within the state. When I dropped by her classroom to retrieve it, she asked me to close the door.

"You know I'm happy to give you this." She licked the envelope.

"Yes, ma'am, I appreciate it."

"But really, you need to go far from here. Not to some little university forty minutes' drive away."

I don't believe any adult had ever spoken to me so honestly before. Not even Miss Agnes.

"You're different," she said matter-of-factly. "And I mean that in the nicest way possible. You just don't belong anywhere near here."

Hearing her drop this soft bomb so simply, so bluntly, was a relief. Her words hit me at the core and I knew she was right. But my father's hold on me was still too strong. New York would have to wait until I was more capable — if that moment ever arrived.

Mrs. Flanders, tall and buxom, was known to be a little different herself. She was emotionally exuberant, and color spread easily across her face in moments of high flush. People used the word *unstable* to describe her. But like Totty, she was simply different. She invited me to her home the summer before I left for college. When I told my mother I was going, her sarcasm sparked my temper.

"That woman's crazy. I don't know why you want to go see her."

"Why is it that everyone I like is crazy? Totty's crazy, Mrs. Flanders is crazy, everyone that you don't like for some reason is crazy. They like me — is *that* why they're crazy?"

"You shut your mouth or I'll tell your father."

"Tell him!" I shouted. "What are you going to tell him? He's not perfect. I know what he's done! I know who he is!"

"You don't know anything! Don't you dare say a word about your father! Don't you dare! After all he's done for us. You don't appreciate anything. Don't you dare say one word against your father!"

Baffled and numb, I drove to Mrs. Flanders's house. Why my mother had defended him was beyond my comprehension. I could only assume that she had some kind of crazy love for him that was so great and so unconditional that she would endure almost anything.

Mrs. Flanders and her husband lived in a lovely, old farmhouse on the edge of the county. I drove down a winding gravel road, and from a quarter mile away I could see the skirt of her bright, flowered dress billowing in the breeze. I was calmer now.

Mrs. Flanders's dark hair and open face had none of their usual teacherly seriousness about them, quite the opposite. Her house was sparkling and airy and filled with her "mother's pieces." To her good fortune her mother had had quite an eye for antique furniture. Mrs. Flanders served cake and iced tea on her veranda and told stories of her college days. She sat in an aged and weathered rocker and nearly toppled it over in her high spirits. Her humor was wild and irreverent, but completely innocent. She laughed with a throaty depth and spoke like a woman who might have lived farther South. I imagined that she would meld nicely with well-to-do women from Georgia. I felt that she wanted me to know that there was more to her than I'd witnessed for an hour a day between four concrete walls.

As I prepared to leave this woman who wove enchantment out of the written legacy of dead poets, she leaned against the post that supported the roof of her veranda and rested her head upon it. "I'm glad you're going to college, but someday you've still got to go far away."

I wondered if she was thinking of what might have been in her own life.

Her gentle command was perhaps also a caution to me. Go. Go while you can. Go while you're young and have the world before you.

No other words passed between my mother and me about Mrs. Flanders or Viv. A few nights later I arrived home to find my father sitting alone on the sofa watching television.

"Where's Mother?" I asked.

"I guess she's upstairs packing. She says she's moving back to Lanesboro."

"What are you talking about?"

He turned back to the television and said no more. He wasn't concerned, just annoyed.

I found her lying across the bed crying.

"What's wrong?" I asked. She wasn't a scene maker.

"Nothing." She turned her face from me. She wouldn't say what he had done this time to move her to tears. I'd rarely seen her cry. I backed out of the room, uncomfortable that I had invaded her privacy.

She wasn't leaving. She would never leave.

I couldn't wait to.

■ ■ ■ ■

On my first day of college, the day hundreds of freshmen awkwardly milled around the gymnasium where we signed up for classes, I sat on a bleacher in an effort to make sense of my schedule. In a moment of insanity I had signed up for an 8:00 a.m. class called Agriculture. Pondering the wisdom of this, I had a feeling of dread that I was in the wrong place entirely. Mrs. Flanders's advice lingered, fresh from our meeting, while I desperately sought to fill space in a curriculum that currently held only English and theater classes. Geology was next. Lord. What was I doing?

I chose the local university because it was known to have the best theater department in the state. I won a small theater scholarship and thought I would be far enough away from Jubilee to lead my own life, whatever that was going to be, without the town gossips breathing down my neck. Instead, it was like moving to the suburbs of Jubilee. At every corner I turned, a face from home greeted me. I ran into them in the grocery stores and restaurants, and on the weekends my dorm was empty because everyone lived close enough to spend the weekends in their hometowns. Freshmen weren't allowed to have cars on campus, so many weekends my father drove to college to pick me up. During one of those drives he spoke of his old nemesis Fletcher Hamilton, and how he had the feeling that the lawyer was going to cause trouble for him again.

From the moment we moved into Miss Agnes's house an underlying, unspoken taint of disapproval always came from Fletcher. Whatever happiness or enjoyment any in our family received from living there was tainted by the niggling thought that the town's kingpin didn't approve of our good fortune. The gossip about our inheritance never died down. We had Fletcher to thank for that, as well as the editor of the local paper, who ran the same article on the history of our house, over and over. Fletcher was now Jubilee's brilliant star attorney who dominated the local news with his championship of old buildings and lost causes. A controversial lawyer, he took up the plight of the Mennonites in the county who wanted to hold on to their ancient ways. He crusaded for the purchase of the buildings the Shakers had built in Beacon County. History and its preservation was the very air that he breathed. In his only murder case, he defended a man accused of killing a policeman and won him a surprisingly light sentence. If he was on your side, he was your hero; if not, he was a vulture who picked your bones clean and dry. He was reputed to be ferocious, sometimes insulting, and always quarrelsome, sarcastic, and lacking in tact. He enjoyed being a local character, just as Miss Agnes had. Now he turned his attention to us, soon after we moved into Miss Agnes's home, when so many "friends" knocked on our door demanding admission.

Fletcher phoned my father and asked him to open our home for tours. My father explained that he had two children who still lived at home and that while he was working full-time, it was not convenient. He further explained that someone had to act as a "tour guide" and he was not in a position to be that person at this time.

Fletcher knew well how Miss Agnes had felt about tours through her home. Item twelve of her last will and testament clearly expressed her wishes: "I demand that NOBODY be permitted to come into my house after my death and paw over my belongings."

During her lifetime Miss Agnes herself conducted a handful of tours through her house, always for small groups of invited guests. She held only one tour during the thirteen years my father knew her, and even with both Miss Agnes and him present and watchful, at least one of the fine ladies of Kentucky slipped several valuable items into her large handbag. Miss Agnes had remained intensely bitter toward the people whose families had abandoned her in her time of trial and regularly reeled off names of those whom my father should never allow in the home after her death. One of these was Fletcher Hamilton's mother.

"Don't you ever let old Mrs. Hamilton into my house after I'm gone."

But Fletcher Hamilton was not interested in the needs of our family or the wishes of a dead lady. He had a bee in his bonnet about the historic house and regularly phoned to ask us to open our home to the public. My father always said no. He'd walked this path before with Fletcher and had the uneasy feeling that his refusal to comply with this pesky man's wishes wasn't the end of things: Fletcher was even more powerful now, and this matter concerned something dearer to him than a few concrete vaults.

The summer after my freshman year in college, four years after the death of Miss Agnes, my father's bank filed a friendly suit against him to receive the court's interpretation of Miss Agnes's will. The bank and my father wished to clear the cloud that hung over the title of the mansion, upon which the bank held first mortgage rights. Confident that this action was a formality, in reply to the suit my father also asked for the court's guidance in interpreting Miss Agnes's will. In the same month that the bank filed the friendly suit, Fletcher Hamilton contacted Miss Agnes's closest living relative, a nephew who lived in another part of the state — a man Fletcher had never even met.

"Frank Mayfield has that house," Fletcher told the nephew. "If you're not going to get it, don't you think it should go to the Historical Society? Don't you think we should put a stop to this?"

At the time of her death, Miss Agnes had not spoken to her nephew in over ten years. Her will attests to her dislike for him: "My nephew is my closest relative. It is with ample and adequate reason that I eliminate him from participating in my estate or the proceeds thereof, and he shall take no part of my real, personal or residuary estate or property of any nature or description. He has been extremely rude to me and has annoyed me in many ways. He was a cruel and

431

ungrateful son of his deceased father. I have the right to dispose of my property as I wish, and it is my express and long-considered desire that he have none of it."

On behalf of Miss Agnes's nephew, George Davis, Fletcher Hamilton filed a motion to intervene in the bank's friendly suit. The battle began.

Jemma made a few unwelcome discoveries while I was away at school. She was outside feeding her pet skunk one day when she saw a gin bottle nestled within one of the big, decorative urns. She thought it belonged to the gardener. Like a temperance evangelist, she emptied it and threw the bottle away. Another bottle appeared. Jemma thought the gardener was playing a game. She threw it out. Another one appeared. This time as a joke, she filled the bottle with tea. She had a grand old time playing the game with the gardener until one afternoon when our father was present and watched, stunned as she fished out the next bottle.

"You little shit! It was you all this time?"

"These are yours?"

"That's none of your damn business!"

"I'm going to throw them away if I find them again. You have to stop this."

Jemma was adamant about cruelty to

animals and her father's drinking habit.

Meanwhile he quashed the outrage and distress he felt about the legal proceedings until the end of each day, when he tried to drink himself oblivious. He, Rex, and Fount, this trio of morticians, shared a thousand private cocktail hours, relocated from Main Street to the new funeral home. For years Rex had watched over his mentor and friend and thought that he handled his booze fine. But when the litigation began, Rex noticed that what had once been a couple of drinks after work became three or four, and then more and more. One night, after my father had already knocked back a few, he returned to the funeral home after supper. Rex was still there that evening, a concerned witness as his friend poured gin down his throat with abandon.

"Frank, you just need to go home now. Come on, I'll give you a ride."

In the ensuing months my father lost himself to bottles and bottles of gin. He waited for the evening and found excuses to return to the funeral home or concocted reasons to stay late. He never appeared as a bibulous sort of drunk. Rather, he was deeply ashamed and made a gigantic effort to hide his dependence from everyone except Rex and Fount. As painful as it must have been to witness, Rex became even closer to my father, the way loyal friends do who remain by your side when things are at their worst.

Sometimes my father didn't hide it well and the anger burst through, as I had found to my cost. He was lost in some subterranean realm of pain we could not fathom, though we lived with its effect. He couldn't help it or be helped. There was nowhere to go. He had witnessed Fount's wife's rapid descent. Martha's doctor occasionally sent her to the state mental hospital to dry out. Each time she came back a little less the woman she had been. No thanks. Not for Frank Mayfield.

One weekend I brought my friend Jack home with me from college — I borrowed him from all the boys in the theater department who were in love with him. He was well dressed and extremely congenial and polite. His dark good looks, which included a meticulously trimmed, thick mustache and black, curly lashes, lent him an air of old-fashioned masculinity. Only when he settled into a chair and began a good gossip session did the old woman in him come to the fore. When he crossed his legs, the leg on top swung furiously, he lit a cigarette with a limp wrist, and he suddenly became an old broad.

"Well, Miss Mayfield?" He never addressed me by my first name. "Tell me what to expect. Is your daddy gonna string me up by the gonads and tickle me with a feather so I'll tell him all of your deep, dark secrets?" He chain-smoked and poured all his energy into lighting fresh cigarettes.

"No, but he may want to know what your secrets are."

"God Almighty, I swear, these Southern daddies, Miss Mayfield, they are somethin' else, somethin' else. My daddy's meaner than hell. I thought he was going to beat the shit out of me when I told him I was queer. Jesus Christ, Miss Mayfield, I was ready to fight him."

Jemma and I could never figure out if my father knew that Jack was gay, but we took pleasure in watching for signs of such knowledge. Homosexuality was the second great taboo in Jubilee. If anyone in town at that time were actually gay, then they hid in deeper caverns than I did. What amazed me was that only thirty miles away in our small college town the whole world of gay life existed in a discreet but noticeable way.

Jack and I drove from school to Jubilee on a Friday evening, and as soon as we pulled into the driveway, he jumped out and headed straight for my father, who stood outside at the barbecue grilling his famous bacon-wrapped filets mignons from Omaha Steaks. Jack offered him a firm handshake and commented on the house, my father's car, and the "best aroma in the world coming from your grill, Mr. Mayfield." He was in.

Jack then went inside to meet my mother, whom he charmed in less than five minutes. My work was done. Everybody was happy. I'd greeted my father at the barbecue for twenty years. He had a habit of opening his arms in welcome with a kitchen towel in one hand and a pair of tongs in the other. He wrapped his arms around me with the instruments of his chefhood protecting my back. It was a good habit. A smiling man with his arms open — that is how I remembered my father just before he became ill.

No one could put a name to his illness. The doctor performed exploratory surgery; I thought it was an ungodly term for a look around inside. Whatever they were looking for, they didn't find. They told my mother it was neither his heart nor, surprisingly, his liver that was making him ill.

And like *Bleak House's* Jarndyce vs. Jarndyce, the lawsuit over the house droned on and on.

The judge overruled a motion that George Davis could intervene. Immediately, Fletcher Hamilton filed another suit, this time including the state attorney general as a defendant. The decision was reversed and the judge ruled that George Davis could indeed intervene and sue my father over the will. In his suit, George Davis, under the guidance of Fletcher Hamilton, asked that the house be kept open to the public as a museum, and that if it was not, Davis should be declared the owner. It was incomprehensible to us that Miss Agnes's express wishes could be ignored in this way.

My parents' first choice to represent them was Charles Markham, a man who had been practicing law in Jubilee even longer than Fletcher Hamilton. My parents thought that dipping into the town's resources was wiser than hiring a stranger from a larger town. But Charles Markham was busy on another big case and persuaded my father to put his trust in Charles's son, Henry Markham. Henry performed well. He was smart, knew the law, and was not complacent, ever aware of the prevailing wind of his foe. But Fletcher was patient, and he continued to move forward with appeal after appeal.

In the midst of all this, my father began to fall apart.

Chapter 16
She's Come Undone

The summer my father became ill I decided that if I didn't go to summer school, I would never pass college math. I sublet an apartment from a guy in the theater department and lived next door to an alcoholic married couple. They were always sunburned and somehow managed to exist without many teeth. The flow of drink into those yawning mouths was ceaseless. My impression from a few drunken remarks was that they were cousins.

Another reason I didn't want to live at home that summer was because Evelyn had divorced and descended upon the house with her two children. The youngest, a beautiful boy still in diapers, was fathered by Jerry, Evelyn's postdivorce relationship. At the time it was a disgrace to be unwed and pregnant, and to further her humiliation, Jerry bolted as soon as he was made aware of her pregnancy. For the first time in my life, I felt sorry for Evelyn. However short-lived those feelings would be, I gained no satisfaction in her predicament.

I didn't like the idea that Jemma was left at home with her because they'd never gotten along, but then, no one ever got along with Evelyn.

My father spent the summer in the hospital in Greenville, and my mother stayed with him twenty-four hours a day. She found a room somewhere near the hospital. I never saw it, but I think it was soulless. She drove the hour and a half home every three or four days, just long enough to grab clean clothes and take care of any pressing business. I drove home from college on the weekends to collect Jemma and then went on to Greenville so that we could spend time with our parents. This was our flight pattern.

One weekend I stopped by my friend Gus's house in Jubilee before I collected Jemma. The phone rang; Gus answered and handed it to me: "It's Jemma."

"I'll be home in a few minutes to pick you up," I told her.

"You've got to come now." She was sobbing. "Evelyn is trying to kill me!"

I hung up and looked at Gus.

"What?"

"I've got to go. I think Jemma's in

trouble."

"Call me if you need me. Okay? Call me."

But I was already running to my car, sensing that Jemma wasn't exaggerating.

She met me at the door, her whole face swollen. She looked at me through eyes that were not just frightened but anguished and set in bruised red-and-purple skin. I thought I would be sick. Then I was driven to act, not by courage, because I didn't seem to be in control of my voice or my thinking. I simply took over the situation as if I had always known this day would come.

"Where is she, Jemma?"

"Upstairs."

"Are you all right?"

"No."

"Ice, you need ice . . ."

We raided the freezer.

"Check your teeth. Are any of them loose?"

Jemma started to cry and said she didn't think so. "She knocked me down the stairs. She's crazy! I swear, she's psychotic."

I didn't hear her. I was already on my way up the stairs. "Stay down here."

I found Evelyn in the upstairs den.

When she saw me, she stomped over to the telephone. "I'm going to call Mama."

This completely threw me. "What?"

"I'm going to call her at the hospital." Evelyn held the receiver in her hand.

"No. You are not going to disturb our mother." I grabbed the phone from her and put it back on the hook.

She snatched at the phone.

Again I tore it out of her hands. "You are not going to bother her. What are you going to tell her — that you just beat Jemma to a pulp?"

"I'll tell her that you and Jemma ganged up on me."

Understanding now that Evelyn was already concocting an elaborate cover story and that she wanted to reach our mother before I did, I held the phone away from her.

Her son toddled by and she scooped the poor boy up in her arms and shielded herself with his little body. "You wouldn't hit me with a baby in my arms."

I had no intention of hitting her, but I wanted her to know that I was not frightened of her, either.

"Try me. You are not going to call our mother."

Evelyn put the child down and went barreling down the stairs. "I'll just use the phone down here then."

"Jemma!" I panicked. "Jemma, go up-stairs!"

Our younger sister scurried past.

"Go to your room and close your door, Jemma. Put a chair in front of it." I turned to Evelyn. "Don't touch her."

"You fucking sissy! You're both fucking sissies." Evelyn laughed.

Downstairs, she picked up the phone. I grabbed it from her and we tussled until I won.

"Who do you think you are?" She had such venom in her voice that for the first time I wondered if I was doing the right thing.

Evelyn walked over to the kitchen drawer and pulled out a knife. She pointed the knife's serrated blade at my stomach. "I should have killed you a long time ago."

I can't say that I wasn't frightened. I didn't move or say anything. The room, a large, open-plan kitchen and living room, suddenly felt cramped.

"I should have killed you the night you got caught with Jerry."

Oh, for Christ's sake, I thought. For a moment I forgot about the knife and her fists and answered her from an angry memory. "Evelyn, I was never 'caught' with Jerry. I just gave him a ride home. You're an idiot. I was never remotely interested in him."

"You're a liar. He told me you kissed him."

"*He's* the liar," I shot back.

"You're a goddamn nigger lover. Don't think I don't know about that." She still held the knife. "You fucking mother of a cunt-faced whore!" she screamed.

She moved forward with the knife and I backed away.

"Don't touch Jemma again. And put that knife away."

She came toward me again, but bizarrely, this time she seemed to be using the knife to protect herself. Later, I realized that she must have thought I was going to hit her, even though I'd made no move toward her. If that was the case, why she moved in closer was a mystery. She ranted on for a few more minutes, spewing out the kind of language that might be heard in a prison brawl. I guarded the telephone and thought how insane it was that I was protecting a phone.

Suddenly, Evelyn turned and barged up the stairs. I ran after her again, thinking that she was going either for the phone or for Jemma. But this time she grabbed her son like a football and came back downstairs and went straight out the door, cursing under her breath. I locked all of the doors, including the inside door, to which she had no key, and the front door, to which no one had keys except my parents. She couldn't get back in unless we let her in, or unless we left the house.

Jemma. I ran upstairs to tell her it was safe. She was vomiting. We didn't know if it was a reaction from fear and nerves or whether it had something to do with the blows she'd received from the fists of our crazy sister. I should have called the doctor, but shamefully, I didn't even think of it. Neither of us could think of anything other than staying safe and keeping this from our mother, who was already exhausted and anxious from the vigil she kept at my father's bedside. Jemma stopped throwing up and ran from door to door, checking the locks. She couldn't stop shaking.

Now that Evelyn was gone, I began to tremble, too. "They're locked. She can't get in," I assured Jemma.

"What if she breaks the door down? She's crazy. She'd do it."

"Then we'll call the police."

"No, don't do that. They'll let her in." Jemma started to cry again.

"Okay. Okay. We'll just sit here for a while. She won't get in, I promise."

"I was home alone when Evelyn came in with her friend Valerie and the baby. I think

Michael is with his other grandmother," Jemma explained through cut lips.

We sat on her bed. It wasn't even dark yet. It felt strange that something like this could happen without the cover of night.

"I was watching TV when they came in. I turned around and saw that Valerie was wearing one of my tops. I made a comment about it, and Evelyn . . . she was on her way up the stairs . . . turned and just starting cursing at me in the most horrible language. You've never heard anything like it. I followed her because I didn't want her to go into my room. When we got to the top, she . . . she reared back and knocked me down the stairs."

"You fell down the stairs?"

"I went down every single one of them."

"Are you all right? Oh my God, you could have broken your neck."

"No, *she* could have broken my neck. She came running down the stairs after me. I don't know. She just lost control. She started beating on me with her fists." Jemma spoke between little whimpers. "She wasn't hitting, or slapping. She punched me like a man. She punched with enough power to knock me down. And every time I tried to stand up, she knocked me down again. I tried to hit her back, but it was useless. What do I weigh? About a hundred, a hundred and ten, something like that? Evelyn's built like a refrigerator. She was punching like a crazy, psychotic person and cussed like an insane sailor."

"Where was Valerie? What did she do?"

Jemma looked at me, tears streaming down her face. "She left. Didn't try to help me. She slipped out the door while Evelyn was beating me."

I didn't know what to say to her.

"I saw a Coke bottle on the counter. I picked it up and told Evelyn that if she hit me again, then I would hit her back with the Coke bottle. But I changed my mind. I thought that if I did hit her with it, she would kill me. So I put the bottle down and backed away. I grabbed one of the kitchen chairs and held it in front of me. I couldn't stop crying and I begged her to leave me alone."

Jemma told me that Evelyn abruptly left and went up the stairs. Before she reached the top, she turned to face Jemma and warned, "I'm not finished with you." Then she disappeared upstairs.

That was when Jemma called me.

"She did one more thing." My younger sister shook her head. "You won't believe this. I went into the bathroom while Evelyn was downstairs with you. The top that Valerie had been wearing, my top . . . it was in the toilet and Evelyn had peed on it."

Neither of us said anything for a long time.

"What's that? Is that her? Did you hear a car drive up? Go downstairs and check."

"I didn't hear anything, Jemma."

"Go downstairs and check!" she screamed. "Please. Go see if she's back!"

No one was there. It was going to be a long night.

"I think you'd better pack some things. You can come back to my apartment and stay with me after we go to Greenville. We'll have to think of something to tell Mother."

"Really?"

"Yeah, you can't stay here. We still have to go to Greenville tomorrow, but then you'll come back with me."

"What are we going to tell everybody when they see my face?"

"We'll tell them you fell down the stairs. It's the truth."

"No, it isn't. I was pushed."

Later, I thought we should eat something but was surprised to find no food in the house. "Why is the refrigerator so empty? There's always something in the refrigerator."

"Mother leaves cash for groceries and

emergencies, but Evelyn steals it."

"Jesus Christ, Jemma, you should have told Mother!"

"I couldn't. I couldn't do that to her right now."

"Well, do you feel like going out? Let's go get something to eat." I looked at her face. "You can stay in the car. We'll just pick something up."

"Sure we will. You forget you're in Jubilee. There's nothing here except the Beacon Dipper."

"Then we'll go to the Beacon Dipper and I'll get out of the car and order and you can keep the doors locked."

"What if she comes back while we're gone?"

"Then we'll just drive to my apartment. We've got to eat."

Suddenly the simple task of eating had become complex. We were held hostage by the thought of Evelyn's returning. I couldn't talk Jemma into leaving the house. But that was okay because every time I looked at her bruised face I felt sick and lost my appetite.

That night, for the first time since we were young girls, we slept together in Jemma's bed. We were both frightened and found something, a bat or a broom, I'm not sure, to put beside the bed, and I placed a knife under the mattress. Just in case.

Evelyn didn't come home that night. I don't know where she and her children slept, probably at a friend's house. Jemma and I left early that morning for Greenville. For sixty miles on a two-lane road, we practiced our story, our lie about Jemma's face.

"What happened to you?" my mother asked immediately.

"I had a really bad fall down the steps," Jemma said. "But I'm okay. It's not as bad as it looks."

And that was it. No more questions, not even a second glance. Clearly our lie had been accepted. My mother didn't want to think about us right now. When she was not with my father, she was thinking about him, and we held her attention for only moments before she looked at her watch.

Rex had just delivered a patient to the hospital and stopped by to see us before he drove back to Jubilee. He looked at Jemma and said nothing until our mother left the room. "What happened to your face?"

"I fell," Jemma said a little too quickly.

"Jesus. You better take care of that."

"I'm fine."

I changed the subject.

That night at the hospital Jemma and my

mother took a break from my father's bedside while our friend Billy and I stayed with him. The hospital room blinked and bleeped with lights and sounds from a bank of machines. After all that had happened the day before, I had almost forgotten about my father. I still didn't know what was wrong with him. I hadn't seen my mother long enough to question her, and we put on happy faces while in his room. He couldn't sit up. Even when the nurse came in and removed the oxygen mask, he still didn't speak. He was restless and his legs wrestled in continuous movement under the blanket.

He lay with his chest bare, that long, pitiless scar on his stomach fully exposed.

Billy read my mind. "Just think, if your daddy hadn't been guarding that building, he wouldn't have that scar. And who knows, maybe he wouldn't be sick today?"

"What building?"

"Well, the building where he was shot. When that soldier came out the door and shot him."

"But I thought . . . I thought he was in a jeep, transporting a prisoner?"

We stared at each other, not knowing what to say about these conflicting stories.

My father reached for his groin.

"What's he doing?" I asked Billy.

"He's trying to remove his catheter. It's probably uncomfortable." Billy reached for my father's hand and gently moved it away from his groin.

I felt terrible. Evelyn had served up twenty-four hours of hell and it wasn't getting any easier. I held my father's hand. He stared at me with glassy, wild eyes and slowly guided my hand toward his lips. I thought he was going to kiss my hand. I was so touched that tears streamed down my cheeks. But when my hand reached his mouth, he opened wide, too wide for a kiss, and I saw his teeth. I noticed they had accumulated saliva. Before I knew what was happening, those teeth came down hard upon my hand. The weakness of his illness temporarily disappearing, he held on to my wrist while he savaged my hand, and I was trapped by his unnatural strength.

"He's biting me!" I turned to Billy, my hand gripped in my father's mouth. "He's biting me! Make him stop! Why is he biting me?"

Billy calmly took my hand and gently pried it from my father's grasp. "He doesn't know what he's doing."

"Then why is he doing it to me? Why didn't he bite you?"

"He doesn't know who we are. It's the

451

drugs. It's just the drugs. They've pumped him full tonight. He won't even remember this tomorrow."

Eventually, I would discover after hours of combing through records that this was not the first time my father had been treated with powerful drugs, but it would be the last. For now, refusing to face the inevitable, I held his hand while he slept.

CHAPTER 17
THE DEAD TAKE THEIR
SECRETS WITH THEM

The next day I drove Jemma back to college with me, but she couldn't stay for the rest of the summer without alerting my mother, so we devised a system in which a couple of Jemma's friends rotated staying with her, so that she need never be alone with Evelyn. Our elder sister kept an erratic schedule after the day of her insanity. We didn't see her again for a few weeks. My fear of facing her slipped away when a big, walloping dose of anger took its place. I chose to ignore her. It was much easier to pretend that she didn't exist than to risk another confrontation. Jemma erected an invisible brick wall around herself whenever she was in Evelyn's presence. We had inadvertently adopted the old Amish habit of shunning and put all of our energy into it. Jemma and I neither knew nor cared about Evelyn's response to this. She never mentioned what she'd done or approached either of us with anything resembling an apology. She was so absorbed in herself that it took her a while to figure out we weren't speaking to her. She finally got the message when I ran into her in front of the drugstore in Jubilee. She was speaking with a friend of our family's and called out to me, "Hey, Mrs. Dale and I want to ask you something."

I stopped beside them. People meandered around us in the early evening, socializing while shopkeepers locked their doors for the night. It was still hot, and Mrs. Dale fanned herself furiously with a small paper fan, a tropical scene on one side and a tractor advertisement on the other. I realized for the first time that I had never seen Evelyn sweat, and today was no exception.

"Mrs. Dale wants the phone number at the hospital. I can't remember it. Do you have it?"

I watched my sister's brown eyes grow wider as I silently stared her down.

"What?" She looked at Mrs. Dale and back to me. "What?"

I turned around and walked away in silence.

It was a small, but very public, gesture. Mrs. Dale would rush home and tell her best friend that the Mayfield girls weren't getting along, how terrible, with Frank so sick and Lily Tate running herself ragged. And then Mrs. Dale's best friend would tell her friends at the beauty parlor. That's the way it usually went. I might have wanted that result, I'm not sure.

Evelyn rarely visited the hospital, and when she did, she arrived with an entourage of seedy-looking characters, stayed for a few minutes, then left. Jemma and I developed sudden hunger pangs and quit the room, not to return until she was well on her way. Oddly enough, my mother did notice this, even though Jemma and I thought we cleverly disguised it.

"What's going on with you two and Evelyn?" she asked me.

"Nothing."

"I wish you'd make more of an effort to get along with her."

"Oh, well, don't worry about it."

"You all need to get along right now. I don't have time for this."

"We will."

But we didn't.

This proved to me that our mother really did swallow the lie we'd told her about Jemma's swollen face. Thomas was the only person we told about Evelyn's day of madness. His and Emily's first baby, the first granddaughter in the family, was less than a month old. They lived almost a four-hour drive away, which made it difficult for him to visit the hospital, so Jemma and I didn't expect him to drop everything to caretake us. And I didn't want him to do anything. Thomas was too much of a diplomat; we weren't eager for him to referee and try to patch things up. Jemma and I became quite comfortable avoiding Evelyn. Forgiving her was out of the question.

At the end of the summer semester the university's theater department gave performances of Edgar Lee Masters's *Spoon River Anthology.* When I auditioned, I thought the production might be a big yawn. But during rehearsals I discovered I felt at home in the play. Postmortem autobiographical epitaphs slid easily off my tongue. Spoon River's residents were able to tell the truth about their lives in the small town for the first time, with honesty and without fear. The production was dark and somber, and we moved slowly around the cemetery like phantoms compelled to speak. The director added little-known, melancholic folk music, and a few of us sang these old ballads woefully. The thing was, I forgot to tell Jemma that the show wasn't going to be a barrel of laughs. She'd never heard of Edgar Lee

Masters. On the night of the last perfor-
mance, I invited her and her friend Percy to
the cast party afterward. They came back-
stage, and when I saw their faces, my smile
disappeared. Jemma looked as if she'd seen
a ghost.

"What's wrong?" Surely the play wasn't
that depressing.

"We've got to go."

"Yeah, I know, we're all going to the party,
right?"

"No," Jemma said. "We've got to go to
Greenville . . . to the hospital."

"Now? It's late. Why do we have to go
now? We can't see him tonight, visiting
hours are over."

There were people everywhere, jostling
around, looking for their friends and family,
speaking to me, pulling on me.

"We have got to go right now! Mother
didn't want me to tell you before the perfor-
mance. It's not good there. She wants us to
be there tonight," Jemma insisted.

"Okay, okay. Let me change and we'll go."

We left Percy to drive back to Jubilee on
his own. By the time we were in my car and
on our way, it must have been eleven
o'clock. I knew what was going on, but I
couldn't say it or face it. Jemma and I had

never said the words: *He's dying. He's going to die.*

"Well, that was really an upper," my sister said as I drove.

"What?"

"That play. A bunch of people in a grave-yard."

"The play was about their lives, not their deaths."

"Yeah, but that song you sang. I was . . . I couldn't hold it back. When you sang those words, 'He's gone, he's gone away,' I'll never forget that. I lost it. How did you do it? How could you sing that without breaking down?"

"I was acting, Jemma, it wasn't real."

Acting was the only thing that kept me sane that summer. Immersed in the summer theater program, I fell into the rhythm created by each production. We became an intimate family that discovered each other's characters' lives as we rehearsed night after night. After rehearsals our late-night dinners were rich with theater talk and evenings faded with bottles of wine at someone's apartment. It felt grown-up and artsy, and after each production ended we began the same rituals with a new play and a new family of performers and production staff. I was so engrossed with the work the world and all of the dead of Jubilee could have dropped away and I would not have known.

My father was in the intensive care unit. We took up our usual seats in the waiting room, a room in which we'd spent many nights trying to doze in its uncomfortable chairs. I'd lost track of how many days he'd been there — long enough for us to become intimately familiar with the cafeteria, hallways, and elevators.

The next morning we began the familiar routine. Ten minutes each hour would be divided between the three of us. My mother took six minutes and Jemma and I had two each. The ICU was full of hospital beds with no uniformity. Machines were everywhere keeping people alive. I maneuvered between the chaos of the machines and the beds to reach my father. Everything was bright — the lights, the sheets, the walls, all were glowing, permeating the room. Yet with all the clear, clean brilliance, life here seemed dark and won by narrow margins.

My father was awake. He couldn't move for all of the equipment, the needles in his arms, the tube in his mouth, and his face was almost completely covered with an oxygen mask. The bed, normally raised up, was almost flat, and in that position he looked like a constrained mental patient. His hand was all that was left free to hold. His eyes told me he wanted to say something and I could sense his frustration. This was no way to die.

I looked up at the infernal clock; I had a few seconds left. He looked at me again with either fear or fight in his eyes; I don't know, maybe both. I bent down to him and whispered in his ear, "Everything is going to be all right."

He made eye contact with me, then slowly moved his head to say no. *No, it won't.*

So much was unsaid between us, and I did not see how we would find a way through it. One tear slid down his face. Just one. I had never before seen my father cry.

Later that morning Jemma and I were on our way to the cafeteria when one of the ICU doctors walked briskly toward us. He didn't bother to pause, but kept walking as he looked ahead of him. To the air he announced, "Your father's finally died."

Jemma and I looked at each other, turned on our heels, and almost ran down the hall to beat the doctor to the waiting room. We couldn't allow this man in his perfectly pressed white coat with his heartless attitude to approach our mother on his own. We skidded into the waiting room with the doctor on our trail. My mother was talking to a friend and stopped in midsentence when she saw the three of us.

"He's gone," the doctor said.

My mother opened her pocketbook, fumbled through her change purse, and presented us with two dimes. "Call your brother," she said to me. "Call Evelyn," she said to Jemma.

We nodded and immediately went back to the hallway.

Jemma stopped before we reached the telephones. "I'm not calling Evelyn. You call for me. I can't do it. I'll call Thomas."

Then we exchanged dimes, as if hers were contaminated.

When we returned to the waiting room, my father's surgeon was speaking with my mother, his hand on her shoulder. His golfer's tan glared above his expensively tailored three-piece suit, and the dazzle from his shiny gold watch nearly blinded us. A gold bracelet on the other wrist tipped over the taste boundary for me, and I wondered what my father would have made of it.

"We'd like to do an autopsy. We'd just like to make sure for you."

My mother, still seated, looked up at him and shook her head. "I'm sorry. I can't. I promised Frank."

The surgeon wanted to confirm that my father had died of pancreatic cancer. There had been no way to tell for certain that the small organ hidden behind the liver was cancerous.

In his working life my father had seen dozens of bodies cut open and crudely stitched back together. He'd witnessed autopsies in which the facial skin was pulled back and then sewn onto the neck with thick, black stitches. Many years ago he'd told my mother, "When I die, don't let them do that to me. I want you to promise me that you won't let them do that to me." Even though my father had taken out a "cancer insurance policy," my mother would not let them perform an autopsy, which was the only way to claim the insurance.

When Rex and Fount arrived in Greenville to take my father's body back to Jubilee, they tried to convince her to let the doctors perform the autopsy.

"We say things today, Lily Tate, but we don't know how they're going to pan out in the future. There won't be any other way to prove that he had pancreatic cancer," Rex told her.

"I'm sorry, Rex. You may be right, but I can't."

The death certificate read "pancreatitis" as the cause of death. My father was fifty-two years old.

I left the room to get some air and ran into Fount in the hall. He looked as if he'd kill for a Pall Mall. The crumpled red pack bulged out of his shirt pocket.

"Looks like there aren't going to be any more scars on my father, Fount. Just that one big one from the war."

"Aw, Missy" — he sometimes called me that — "you don't need to think about that right now."

"Did he ever tell you how he got that scar?"

"Oh, sure. It was right after the war ended. He was still over there, part of the MP. He was walking around on patrol and a German soldier got him."

"On patrol? Not guarding a building? And not in a jeep?"

"No. No jeep. And I don't know anything about a building."

A weariness settled in as I prepared for the drive back to Jubilee with Jemma. I sat for a moment with my head in my hands and asked myself what kind of secrets my father had just taken with him.

The daughter of a woman who had committed suicide stood at the front door of the funeral home one dismal autumn morning. I was a child when I stood at the door behind my mother on that rainy day. The girl stood in the rain, her hair dripping, her clothes soaked, and pounded on the door seeking entry to the funeral home before opening hours. The woebegone girl, with fresh misery on her face, thrust a gold necklace at my mother when she answered the door.

The girl raised her voice above the rain, which was beating down harder and heavier. "Please, please put this on my mother."

The mother had drowned herself in a large pond, and now the daughter stood like the ghost of her, pale and sodden. The necklace hung from her hands, the only bright and shiny thing to be seen this gray morning. At that moment, the necklace was more important to her than anything else in the world. The relief on the girl's face when my mother took the necklace from her helped us believe that the daughter would survive her grief.

The living are often concerned with what material thing the dead should take with them and often feel compelled to consign something of value to the coffin. I became quite worried about what kinds of objects were buried with the dead and barraged my father with questions: "Will that man be buried with his wedding ring?" "What will happen to that woman's brooch?" "What does a child take with them?"

My father answered with a calm certainty, "Mostly, what the dead take with them are their secrets."

CHAPTER 18
MEMENTO MORI

Rex and Fount removed my father's body from the hospital and drove back to Jubilee. By the time they reached the funeral home, a small band of men had gathered to help. After the handshakes and comments about the occasion, Fount and Rex assumed their professional roles and kicked the well-intentioned men out of the funeral home. Rex knew it was his job and his alone to embalm the man he had loved as much as his own father. Fount helped him move their friend to the embalming table.

My father lay under the white sheet in the presence of two men who knew a few of his secrets. These men had covered for him when he slipped away on one of his trysts. How many times had they been ready with an excuse, a story for my mother? How many of his gin bottles had they secreted away? But now was not the time to speak of flaws, or insatiable appetites.

"Fount, do you remember one day when you and Frank were messin' around with the water hose? I was standing at the door of the funeral home, listening for the phones, and you and Frank started wrestling with the hose," Rex remembered.

"Yeah, we were acting silly." Fount wasn't one for oratory.

"Frank grabbed the hose from you and sprayed you with it. Then he took off with it, ran the length of the hose. It snapped on him and he fell to the ground. When he got up and brushed himself off, I'll be damned if he had only a small grass stain on his shirt pocket, about the size of a quarter. If it had been us who'd fallen, we would've ripped the knees out of our pants, scuffed our shoes, and had bloody noses. But Frank got up and laughed. He had the most infectious laugh. . . . I'll leave you here, Fount, so you can have your time alone with him."

Later, Rex went back into the embalming room and asked Fount to leave. Then he shut the door and locked it. He told Fount and the other employees who'd shown up to leave him the hell alone and he'd be fine. Before he began, he thought back to what his former boss, partner, and friend would have wanted. "He would want me to come in and flip that switch, put my professional hat on, and do what I had to do, to the best of my ability, regardless of who it was."

It took him two hours to prepare himself mentally to perform the task before him. Weeks later, Rex said that he knew that after doing that, he could embalm anyone in his own family. It was like stepping out of his emotional attachments. As Rex set out to perform the task at hand, men from the funeral home continued to knock on the door.

"Everything all right in there?"

"Can I get you anything?"

"Sure you don't need some help?"

"Hell, no," he said, "no one's going to do this but me."

Then he embalmed my father, one undertaker in the hands of another. It was late when he turned off the light.

Rex and I never discussed the details of how he managed to perform his duties that day, the day my father died. Many years later we spoke about it. The images of my father's death emerged and took my breath away. I ended the phone call and sat silently as a new wave of grief tremored within me. With a little gasp I realized that the grief wasn't new; it had never really disappeared.

The next evening our family arrived for the

private viewing before the funeral home was opened to the public for visitation. Rex wore his impassive undertaker's expression when he opened the door to the chapel. It was one of those stifling-hot summer nights; lightning flashed through the sky, and inside the air-conditioning was on full blast. Rex walked on one side of my mother and Thomas was at her other side. Jemma and I held hands, and Evelyn walked along behind us. It was an interminably long walk.

As we approached and my mother caught the first glimpse of her husband lying in a casket, her knees buckled underneath her and her head tilted back into a near faint. Her knees hovered only inches from the floor as Rex and Thomas held her by her elbows and lifted her to standing. My mother was not the fainting type and was not given to dramatics, but I think she must have suppressed an overwhelming urge to wail, for some strange sound came from her. At that moment the lights flashed and went out completely. The roar of the air conditioner stopped and the room was plunged into darkness and silence. We stood frozen like ice sculptures in the black air until, just as suddenly, the lights came sputtering back on and the air conditioner revved up and broke the terrifying silence. I think someone involuntarily cursed, and a collective gulp of relief filled the air. We looked at each other incredulously and began walking again as if Moses had just parted the sea.

Poor Rex, I thought. A blackout at my father's viewing. Was it his last little prank? My father might have been saying, "Are you on your toes there, Rex? Remember what I taught you? Remember that day in the church?"

He and Rex had been setting up casket trucks in the front of a church, preparing it for a funeral. After they placed the casket on the trucks meant to hold it, they noticed the casket wasn't perfectly centered. The church's casket trucks weren't as long as they should have been, and the casket teetered enough to make Rex antsy. My father called him into the vestibule and told him, "If the casket falls off the trucks, just calmly walk down there and look at your watch as if to say, 'Yep, right on time.' Behave as if you planned it that way all along. Whatever occurs, just let it happen, and don't show that you're nervous. Deal with it and then move on."

Rex said my father was always calm on the surface. "He might have been as nervous as he could be, but you never saw Frank sweat. You never saw anything throw him off his game."

Now he lay in a fifteen-gauge casket shaded to look like bronze. It had a brownish edge around it and a brush finish. The velvet interior was a light taupe. Fount and Rex had dressed him in a brown suit that my mother had chosen, though I thought he had looked better in black. The enveloping scent of mortuary cosmetics rose from his casket.

I was afraid that someday, some year, I would walk down a street far from Jubilee and would not be able to recall the face of my father. So on this day, the last one that I would see him, I tried to memorize his face. I traced the line of his strong jaw and made a note that his face held traces of both his father's and his mother's. He was more handsome than his brother and darker than his sister. In him, I saw his family and the new one he'd made in ours.

He had not been ready to die. The doctors told us he fought and fought and held on for as long as he could. He died not knowing what would happen to us; our inheritance was still in litigation and two of his children not yet established. And he died before he made complete amends to his wife, although she had begun to feel his contrition. There wasn't enough time for a complete life.

Evelyn stood beside Jemma and reached for her hand. Jemma, cold and brave in her grief, moved away, but not before she whispered, "Don't *ever* touch me again." Her first and only words to Evelyn since what we had begun to call "that day."

Evelyn then moved beside me and linked her arm in mine. I removed her arm and, without taking my eyes off my father, felt my feet slowly step away from her, as if in a dream. His death had only strengthened my resolve. I'd still not said a word to her. I felt her neediness and it was pitiful, but it didn't move me enough to allow her in. She sniveled and moved over to our mother, the one person who always stood by her.

When Rex opened the doors that evening, people poured in. Streams of men and women from all four corners of the county formed a line to pay their respects. Many were disappointed that Frank would not be there to bury them. They seemed as stunned as we were. When people thought of my father, they thought of their own deaths. They couldn't help it; it was an unconscious reaction to the sound of his name. And somehow it didn't seem right for an undertaker to die young.

Then Fletcher Hamilton strolled in. I

watched as he scanned the chapel thoroughly, slowly making his way through, shaking hands. *Oh, yes, of course,* I thought. *He wants to be seen.* The light on the registry podium cast a yellow glow over his face and I wished at that moment that I could read his mind. *What a chilly old soul he must have,* I thought. I avoided him so that I wouldn't say anything that would later embarrass my mother, or myself. When he entered the chapel, I stood at the door behind him as he walked down the aisle toward my father's coffin. He lent the scene a surreal aura and I wanted to demand that he leave, and then I saw my mother's red-rimmed eyes glance toward him. She drew in a breath and sagged a little. I could think of nothing better than relieving my waist of a rather beautiful black patent belt and wrapping it around his neck until his face turned purple and he begged for his life. He soon left, his show of concern duly registered by the town.

I breathed in the heady mix of flowers and the cheap perfume in which someone near me seemed to have bathed. I stared at the carpet and wondered who chose dark green. I tried not to look at the casket, but it wouldn't be ignored. An inner dialogue took over as I shook hands with people whom I had lived among for so many years. I listened to their condolences as a suffocating fear lodged in my throat: *What a fine mess you've left us with, Daddy. What are we going to do now?* As if it were his fault that he died, that somehow he could have prevented this big black void of unknowing. I consoled myself with the thought that I could leave this place now. A calm, clear prospect of freedom pulled me around as I faced friends from college, who had surprised me with their presence.

When the public went home that evening, I had less than two minutes of private time with the undertaker in the casket. It's hard to look at people you love lying there in their final house. I knew that already, but now, the evening before his funeral, my experience, layered by all those years of intimacy with the dead, deepened. There's something to be said for a closed-casket service. There's something to be said for not embalming. I sat down and closed my eyes. The room was full of something, but I had no idea what it was. Maybe I'd lost the ability to feel anything.

Rex came into the room. He looked awful; he'd been up for over twenty-four hours and his eyes were pink and swollen.

"There were not many things that your

daddy and I didn't talk about. When you spend as many hours of the day and night with each other as we did, especially when we weren't busy, we just got to know each other real well. We developed a very close, meaningful relationship that I never will forget. I've said on many occasions that I was closer to Frank than I was to my own dad. I wouldn't ask my father for his opinion of anything much, but I spent a lot of time talking to Frank about things. He was a real mentor to me. I got to the point where I won his confidence. He knew that I could do the job without a problem or concern about my ability to handle anything that came down in the funeral business. And that came from him. He taught me well."

For a second — just one short second — I thought I should forget all my plans, go back to college, and marry Rex. After I recovered from that moment of moral cowardice, I realized from Rex's soliloquy that my father had created some sort of relationship with his partner that he'd never had with Thomas. I felt an overwhelming sadness for my brother then. It was the first moment during the last twenty-four hours that I'd felt anything at all.

"Do you need anything?" Rex asked. "Can I get you anything?"

"Just my daddy, Rex; just my daddy. Can you do that?"

"No. I'm sorry."

"I know."

The morning of the funeral, a wagonload of food arrived early at our house. Belle came into my room with her arms folded. She always folded her arms when she was ill at ease.

"I'm real sorry 'bout yer daddy."

"I know you are, Belle. Are you coming with us today?"

"No, no, I's gonna stay here and gits things ready for later. I'm real sorry. Jest real sorry 'bout yer daddy."

August is not my favorite time of year. My father was buried in August; the sun was bright and it was humid and steaming hot . . . so hot that I refused to wear black. A long-sleeved, deep-wine-colored blouse and a heavy, khaki cotton skirt were not much help deflecting the sun's harsh glare, and at once I regretted not wearing the black silk dress destined for this occasion. I think it was an act of rebellion.

The premature funeral left me numb. The preacher intoned the service with a monotonous chant I'd heard so many times. Now, when I needed them, the words had lost their meaning. I had a sense that we'd done this a thousand times before, and I felt ashamed for feeling it. I couldn't believe that this time, this service, this ritual, was for my father. Totty played "Nearer, My God, to Thee." I looked over at her glistening eyes. One of my father's friends sang a hymn; his face turned beet red as he strained and stretched for the high notes. We had tissues in our hands, but mine was dry. I scanned the arrangements of gladioli, their smoky stems stretching, stretching like crooked claws. They were the most popular choice because they were the least expensive. I was weary of them. I hoped to never see another gladiolus.

After the service, the cortege made its way down Ninth Street, and in the polite, respectful tradition of some places, passing cars pulled to the side of the road as we crawled to the cemetery. None of us spoke. Groomed all of our lives to be comfortable with the death of others, we were naturally uncomfortable with the passing of one of our own. We didn't grieve more or less than anyone else just because we knew the rituals better than most.

At the cemetery, Rex stood at the head of the casket just as my father used to. I didn't hear the preacher's words, finding solace instead in the images around me. The coveys of women who looked like fluttering blackbirds gave credence to the old belief that black garments were thought to bestow invisibility upon the grieving, thereby protecting us from vengeful spirits. I'd always felt comfortable in this necropolis. I remembered days of skipping happily along the roads of this cemetery, and realized I would never do that again. The crape myrtles normally gave shady rest in the abominable heat. But on this day the sun in the cloudless sky spilled into every dark corner of the cemetery. The light struck the tombstones that stood near the freshly opened earth. The granite sparkled. I wondered if Bobby and Luther had dug my father's grave. I forgot to ask. So this is how you buried an undertaker — just like everyone else. The difference was that our family knew each step, each station, in the ritual. We knew that Rex had excelled. After the brief lapse of the power outage the night before, every movement today was seamless, the attention to detail faultless. Our family sat on chairs in front of the casket, and others stood behind us, around us, beside us. Here we were then, the undertaker's women, sitting in a row in front of him.

Few things are so broken that they can't

be fixed. However, as I looked at Evelyn with her head down, and Jemma with hers focused straight ahead on our father's grave, I wondered if something here was broken that would never be repaired. I thought that without him the odds on reparation being made were slim.

My mother thought that because he never laid a hand on her or her children, and never denied us anything he could afford, he was basically a good husband. The alcohol and women weren't enough to scare her away. She had loved him unconditionally.

The other women who'd been his for a night, a week, or several months were not here today. We were his last audience. Patsy and Viv, and who knew how many more, might think of him with . . . what? Nostalgia? Perhaps a grimace of regret, or a satisfied smile? Would any of them remember the crispness of his shirts, the way he smelled, or how he lathered his face with soap in the mornings?

Before they put him in the ground I had the sudden urge to know all of his secrets. I wanted to know if anything important remained unsaid. Maybe something that he forgot to tell us because he was too sick and too frightened. Could there be something, some small thing, we should know that he didn't think was important, but that to us would be of overwhelming significance? Didn't he trust us enough to tell us?

The day after the funeral, shortly before noon, Jed, a friend of our family's, came over.

"What are you doing here?" I asked. "Shouldn't you be at work?"

He looked at me and without a word quickly climbed the stairs to my mother's bedroom. The cause of his unease was revealed when he made several trips down the stairs and out to his car laden with my father's beautiful suits. Armload by armload, my father's shirts and ties, shoes and belts, passed before me in some kind of forlorn fashion show. Jed couldn't look at me and I didn't offer to help. I wished my mother had warned me. But she never consulted any of the females in our family about anything, only Thomas. Why so soon? Why look at an empty closet? I knew why. She didn't want to bury her face in his clothes and weep or smell his scent and not be able to come up for air.

Rex did a bit of housecleaning, too. My father's favorite toy, the Buick Roadmaster, needed an exorcism. During those last months, my father used the trunk of the Roadmaster as a receptacle, a place to hide his empty bottles. The trunk, the size of a small boat, held enough glass to build a wall. Rex, who was determined that no one else find the stash, cleaned out the trunk, drove out to a friend's farm, and tossed the bottles in a sinkhole. He thought he was burying a secret.

I had sorting of my own to do as well. I spent the next days packing my things for a journey from which I would never entirely return. At the beginning of the summer I had written to an acting school in New York. I didn't tell my mother until I received a letter of acceptance. I never told my father. Two weeks after the funeral, I loaded a U-Haul truck.

"Comes and sees me sometimes when you're back for a visit." Belle rubbed her arms nervously and hit me on the back several times in a display of affection.

"I will, Belle. You know I will."

Jemma looked small and miserable. There wasn't much for us to say. We'd traveled an ugly road together that summer, and I felt I was abandoning her now by leaving her before she'd found a calmer path.

My mother stood in the driveway crying as I climbed into the truck. I forced myself not to look back at her. In a span of sixty seconds I felt pain from leaving her and Jemma, relief to be leaving Jubilee, and joy at the thought of New York. I felt the house around me — felt it almost enveloping me — and the lawn, the statue of the lady, and the beautiful, tall columns were the last things I saw before I drove away.

I was told that people couldn't believe I left my family so soon after my father's death. At times I couldn't believe it either, but if I had waited a day, an hour, or a moment later, I might not have been able to make that journey. No one understood that I had to go, except the farmer's wife who had quoted Keats at me and whose words were continuously in my thoughts:

"You've got to get away from here."

EPILOGUE

In February 1978, three years after court action began, and one year after the death of Frank Mayfield, the circuit court ruled that the heirs or devisees of Frank Mayfield were the owners in fee simple of the real estate. The judge ruled that the will of the late Agnes Davis did not create a public charitable trust and that the property transmitted by that will to Mayfield was the result of the express desire and intent of Agnes Davis. The ruling stated that the personal property was to be maintained as part of a memorial, and that the Mayfield family could maintain and plan that memorial as they saw fit, and they should not be limited to the use and occupancy of the residence.

George Davis and Fletcher Hamilton appealed the decision. In July of 1979 the Court of Appeals duly reversed part of their decision by saying that the personal property formed a public charitable trust and was to be used to maintain the grounds and the exterior of the home, so that people who walked by could see the home as a memorial. Fletcher Hamilton and George Davis appealed again. The case moved to the state Supreme Court.

In June of 1980 the decision on Fletcher Hamilton's appeal came down. The state Supreme Court overruled the lower court's actions. The justices ruled that Miss Agnes did not intend to leave her estate to Frank Mayfield as a private residence and did indeed create a public trust. The opinion stated, "Clearly, the purpose of the trust is that the house and grounds and the furnishings of the house be preserved and maintained as a museum and be kept open at reasonable times and under reasonable conditions for public viewing." The decision was unanimous. In November of 1980 the Kentucky Supreme Court denied Mrs. Mayfield's petition for a rehearing on the case.

Mrs. Lily Tate Mayfield was requested to leave the premises.

The people of Jubilee displayed a variety of reactions from genuine astonishment and confusion that matched our own, to whispers of satisfaction from those who couldn't wait to get their hands on it or to finally be awarded a gawking session inside the house after all the years of being denied.

A succession of caretakers has since been appointed to occupy the home and maintain it. In June of 1981 five hundred people toured the Bibb House Museum in one afternoon.

The house can now be rented for business and private functions. It is open for both public and private tours. Fashion shows have been held indoors in the winter at which ladies modeled clothes from local shops. Outside on the lawn the Summer Pops Picnic is popular, as is the Fall Gospel Concert. Occasionally, throughout the year, various women dress in red clothing and red hats and greet visitors as they enter the home. Miss Agnes would die a second death to learn of these events that smack of provincial tastes and ignore her specific instructions. How hurt and angered she would be that anyone would think that my father somehow inveigled his way into her life to steal her estate from the people of Jubilee.

The most recent reports of October 2013 from a Jubilee online news journal state that Miss Agnes donated the house to the public in 1978. An amazing feat of resurrection, considering she'd been dead since 1972.

A few years ago I visited Jubilee for the first time in many years. I drove down a graveled back road in Bibbtown territory, a place I'd never been before. There is no town in Bibbtown, and the only sign of modernity on this aged land was a few telephone poles that disappeared entirely as I approached the home of Miss Alberta Foulks. The spry ninety-six-year-old lived on the land bequeathed to her great-grandmother, Catherine Bibb Arnold, a former slave of Major Richard Bibb.

Miss Alberta lived without running water, electricity, or a telephone in a small trailer on her property. An educated woman who was once a teacher, Miss Alberta fell upon hard times when the family farmhouse burned to the ground. Although mentally alert, she was no longer able to work the fields her ancestors had plowed or to raise tobacco or tend the large vegetable garden she once loved. Yet still she relished caring for a small, white clapboard church a few feet from her home, the 150-year-old Bibbtown African Methodist Zion Church, also called Arnold's Chapel, which her people had helped to build. We sat together there on a shiny wooden pew hidden from the searing August sun.

"Catherine, my great-grandmother, was the daughter of Major Richard Bibb," she told me. "Catherine's mother was a house slave in the big house. You know what that often meant back then."

Suddenly the impeccable character of the abolitionist major lost its sheen. The position of a female house slave brought dangers impossible for the younger ones to avoid. It is not known whether this cruel inevitability between Catherine's mother and the major occurred one time or one hundred times. All that is known is that the unholy union produced a child.

"Did your great-grandmother ever speak of it?" I asked as gently as I could.

"No, you didn't speak about such things back then." The slender fingers of Miss Alberta's light-skinned hand repeatedly smoothed her skirt.

At the time of my visit, a great deal of hoopla concerned the establishment of an African American Heritage Museum in Jubilee. I asked Miss Alberta what she thought about it.

"There is something lacking in the attempt, and showiness. There's something inauthentic about it."

"Might you compare it to throwing a

ravenous dog a small bone, then?"

"Yes, something like that. Too little, too late."

Before we parted Miss Alberta told me that many years ago another woman had come to her property seeking a connection to the history of the house in which she lived. She said the lady wore red and was named Agnes Davis. I was quite struck that I had unknowingly mirrored Miss Agnes's journey. I understood her longing to put a face to history, and flesh and blood to the bones of that house. The house that came to represent a great sweeping epic of turmoil, battles fought, won and lost. There was the sense of a massive turning wheel and that Miss Alberta, Miss Agnes, and I had each given it a spin.

On this same visit to Jubilee, the house that was formerly my family's funeral home was for sale. The house was fairly recognizable from the outside, although it looked badly run-down and was probably the most unattractive house on the street. The current owner had run ugly cables and wires in front and had clumsily incorporated an extra window. I called the real estate agent and asked her if she would help me gain access. She explained that the house had been divided into apartments and wondered if I still wanted to see it. I asked her to bring all of the keys. I wanted to see every single one of them.

I lost count of how many apartments there were, perhaps four or five. The rooms that were left unchanged were smaller than I remembered. The original tiles surrounding the fireplaces were now cracked and yellowed. Amazingly, the claw-foot bath had not been replaced. We climbed the very same steps to my bedroom, from where, without thinking, I looked out the window, as if I'd catch a glimpse of my father again making his way to the garage.

Most of the apartments were filthy and had the feel of drug dens. Clothes were strewn everywhere, ashtrays were full of butts, and empty beer cans littered the rooms. We repeatedly went outside to gain entry through a different door to a different apartment. The real estate agent performed admirably; the jangling of her clunky keys drowned my sighs. Each time a door opened, I experienced something familiar, but it was like walking with a veil over my face.

The downstairs area, where the business of death had taken place, was the most changed. One of the apartments downstairs was newly renovated and empty. I stepped onto the new carpet and admired the fresh paint job, then walked though a door into a closet or storage area, a small, narrow room with no windows. We couldn't find the light switch and stood in almost complete darkness. In the silence a sudden shiver rippled up my spine, and then I knew. This was the embalming room. I was sure of it. I could scarcely breathe. As chilling as it was, it was the most peculiar and familiar feeling, the closest I had yet come to reexperiencing my childhood home.

The sound of the real estate agent's keys brought me out of my trance and we left. I was shattered.

Years after the death of my father and the loss of our home, many miles from Kentucky, I sought to discover as best I could what had happened to him to make him the man he was. My mother, the executor of all of his wishes, broke a promise she'd made to him decades before, in an attempt to help me. She handed me an envelope. "Here, read this. He told me to read it, put it away, and never show it to anyone else. But you should see it."

My father's neat handwriting filled pages of thick, white paper, the kind they don't make anymore. This was the only letter of his my mother had kept from his two years in Europe.

The hardest three days of battle I ever saw or took part in was two days before Thanksgiving, and Thanksgiving Day 1944. We were on the move, taking close to five tours a day. Have just crossed the Maginot line. There were snipers, machine guns, mortars, shells, burp guns, airplanes and teller mines and it seemed as if every one of them were aimed straight at you. Hungry and nothing to eat, cold and could not get warm, sleepy and was afraid to go to sleep. We had about 1000 yards of open ground to reach the small town, was about 4:00pm. That was our objective. So here we go. I ran as fast as I could, trying to miss all of those guns. I was sneaking about, it was hard, but by luck I did. When I reached the first house I pushed the door open, just as I got inside an 88mm shell fell on the porch, which killed 5 of my men. So there I was, lost again. Well in war, you may know we don't stop to grieve over the dead.

We went from house to house clearing the Germans. Now it is just about dark. Thought maybe things would be quiet. But orders came down that we had to take the next town, which was about one half night away. We started out of town when all of a sudden we were caught in machine gun fire. We laid in cold muddy water for hours. When it got full dark we slipped into a field and were on our way. They were waiting for us. Of course you want to know how we could see to fight after dark. It was not much trouble, they used flares, and then too, the towns were set on fire by shells. I again made it to the first house and there were about ten of us that got into the house. We were waiting until we could get a chance to push a little further, when all at once a shell came through and set the house on fire. So you can see by now we were trapped. Either we burned to death, or take a narrow chance of getting through the gunfire. Staying just as close to the ground as we could, we made it to the next house about two of us at a time and in different houses.

From where I was I had a good view of the Germans and they could not see where I was hiding. I was picking them off pretty good, so they began backing up. By the time we all got set and began firing they really got on the move and we had a pretty good night. By daylight here we are on the move again. The town was about three miles away and I knew it would be rough. We had a company on our right helping us. We started up a long hill, walking with our guns set and ready to fire. When all at once machine guns open on us. I hit the ground and moved over to a shell hole. Just before I got there a bullet went over my head and hit a very good friend of mine. So I took a chance and slipped over to give him first aid. By the time I got there he looked up at me and said, "Well, Mayfield, this is it. You take care of yourself and keep up the good work." By now maybe you understand why we drink. Sometimes that's what it takes. But anyway, later we found it was our own men shooting at us. Bad mistake, what do you think.

Thanksgiving Day! About 8:00am orders came down to take one company and go over the hill and clear out a small town and then come back and have a good Thanksgiving dinner, and we needed it too. We all left our packs there, just had our rifles and four bandoleers. However, I was carrying the automatic rifle, which fired like a machine gun and of course the man who carried that was the boy that they tried to pick off first because it has so much firepower. I had not reached the top of the hill when a shell landed about 15 yards from me. A piece of shrapnel hit my ammo belt. It went through two clips of ammo but just nipped the skin. It turned me a good flip but I was not hurt.

We got to the top of the hill at last. They told us there were only about twenty-five Germans in the town, but we knew better. So the captain called back and told the Commander that with just one company of men we could not take the town. But our orders were to take the town. So here we go. We could see tanks moving around in the town and they set up and began firing point straight at us and I mean that is rough. I was running toward the town like a storm. I saw that I could not make it — men were falling all around me dead before they hit the ground. Then about 20 yards away I saw a little stone stile block about 2 feet wide and about 3 feet high. So I made a dive for it and lucky me made it. Well I stuck my BAR out around one corner and began firing but was not doing any damage. So I laid there and wondered what would happen, because I knew that we did not stand a chance.

I turned around and saw about ten of our men running for the same stone I was behind, only about five got there, the rest were shot down. I knew it would not work with six behind the stone and it didn't because they began cutting it down. So I took off again. How bullets missed me I will never know.

So I got into this little wood building. I was the only one in the building, in fact I was the first one to get to the town alive. I was tired, hungry and afraid and anything else you could think of. The Germans saw me go into the building but they did not try to get me right then. I think that is why I am living today. If they had gotten into the little building I think I would have been shot. Then here comes the Captain too, men were covering him. He was shot in the right hip. Then that made four of us in there and I knew it was not safe. So I started to climb out of the window when the Germans opened up on the little house. So I got flat on the floor. On that go round one of the boys was hit in the chest, in fact it went through him. I gave him first aid even though I knew it would not do any good. While I was doing that, a German Lieutenant came to the door with a pistol. I started to grab my rifle, but saw that it was too late. He came in and took everything away from us and smashed our guns, kicked us and then walked to the door. One of our men saw him and took good aim and shot him through the head from across the street.

I knew what would happen after killing the Lieutenant because they thought one of us did it. I saw several mattresses just piled in one corner and I got under them and stayed. It was about 11:00am. I really don't think I moved or got my breath. I could hear the Germans talking, then I heard four shots. I knew they had killed the Captain and the other men and that they could do me the same way if they found me. This went on the rest of the day and part of the night. About 11:00pm I slipped real easy from under the mattresses and got out where I could hear, but there was only one boy still living and he was drowning in his own blood. So there was not much I could do. I waded through the stiff bodies to the door. When I got there I did not see or hear anything. I then stepped outside, looked all around and started real easy toward our lines.

I didn't have any rifle or protection at all, but I knew it was the only thing to do. I came down through the orchard on a slow run; it was darker than hell. Just as I got into the open field I was shot at by a tracer bullet that missed me by about 4 feet. I had gotten about 200 yards from town and I began stumbling over dead bodies, so I slowed down a bit in order that I might see them in time to step over them or go around.

I got back to the company, went on to my Sergeant and found only one man with his head hanging down, crying. When he saw me he came running and said, "Mayfield did you make it?" I said, "Yes, but this looks like all of us." So out of my company of two hundred and fifty men there were only four who got back alive. So that's it, just a small piece of what went on in the war.

I have since discovered, through a helpful and committed network of World War II veterans, that one of the battles my father described was at Hilsprich, France. All of the officers and almost all of the noncommissioned American officers were killed or captured on that Thanksgiving Day. It was the most costly battle of the entire war for Company C, of the 137th Infantry Regiment. After Hilsprich, the company consisted almost entirely of new troops. The soldiers of Company C were also the first members of Patton's army to set foot on

German soil, and my father was still with the company on that day in December 1944.

On July 12, 1973, the entire sixth floor of the Military Personnel Records Center in St. Louis, Missouri, was destroyed by fire, along with over 16 million military service records. Anyone in search of a family member's records will know how disappointing it was to me to discover this.

Thanks to an invaluable tip from a veteran, I was fortunate to retrieve one hundred pages of my father's medical records from the Veterans Administration. The reports and charts compiled by doctors and nurses in France, Belgium, and Germany relayed in clipped medicalese the experiences that so deeply affected my father. They told me the story of what happened to him after the battles he described, the story he withheld from his own family afterward, including my mother.

After the battle on Thanksgiving Day, my father developed a nasty tremor in his limbs. The records state that he woke up panting from nightmares, and the fear of being captured again immobilized him. On Christmas Day, he snapped.

He was suffering from battle fatigue, then diagnosed as "neurosis due to combat." Drug abreaction was used on "neurotic" casualties, to generate intense excitement by first relaxing the patient to a highly suggestible state and then coaxing him into a frenzy in order to relive the horror and, hopefully, discharge — or abreact — the blocked emotions. Initially barbiturates were used to produce a semidrunk state, but ether was also introduced since it released a higher degree of explosive excitement compared to barbiturates. Ether was considered especially effective on hard-to-crack cases.

My father was administered ether for three days before he began five days of abreaction with sodium amytal. Abreaction was meant to be only one stage in the treatment; the narcotic therapy should be followed by a total integration, both emotionally and intellectually. Nagging feelings of survival guilt had to be dealt with, not to mention lingering rushes of fear and anger. During the abreaction, my father described screaming on the battlefield under shellfire, the terror he'd felt of being captured. He spoke of the mutilated bodies he had stumbled over and cried for the dead he'd left behind without a decent burial. He told the doctor that before Thanksgiving Day he had been as calm as anyone could be in combat. But since then, the fear had possessed him. He shook uncontrollably in a hospital far from home, and he screamed and screamed and screamed.

His breakdown and the effect of the amytal itself necessitated his evacuation to a hospital in Toul, France, for one month. He was never reassigned to his company or to the front line. Doctors eventually ceased prescribing abreaction therapy — it seemed that reliving the trauma of the battles so soon after the experience made the men's suffering worse.

My father was then assigned to Belgium, where he became a military policeman. When I began asking my family members to tell me their version of the day my father was shot, which occurred during his service as an MP, no two people told the same story.

The medical records clarified most of the mystery. My father had lied to all of us. The wound that eventually sent him home was inflicted on him in a civilian café in Huy, Belgium, while he was still an MP. At midnight on January 20, 1946, while attending a dance in the café with a few of his buddies, he "engaged in a fight" with a civilian, who shot him in the abdomen with a .25 German automatic pistol. The documents don't specify whether he was on duty at this time. It is not clear whether the civilian was German or Belgian or who began the fight, what it was about, or if it had anything to do with the war or the military. No one else was shot or harmed. I can only guess and entertain strong suspicions of too much alcohol or an altercation over a woman. Or, more innocently, he was simply in the wrong place at the wrong time. The first two explanations would be reason enough for him to lie about the wound that eventually led to his return to the States. The third, that it was just his bad luck — not so much. The secret is ultimately his.

I am certain that those two years he spent in Europe dictated the pattern of the rest of his life. I believe he became an undertaker partially because of his experiences on the battlefield; men falling horribly injured around him, my father perhaps trying to save them but impotent to help, stumbling upon the dead and learning to walk respectfully around them, the very thing he taught me to do. I believe his elder brother, who did not survive the war, made an indelible impression upon him when he expressed his desire to honor the fallen by becoming an undertaker. As soon as my father was healthy enough to work upon returning from Europe, he served his apprenticeship at a funeral home in Lanesboro. When he faced his first body in the embalming room, the embalmer, his mentor, pulled the sheet off the deceased. Lying on the embalming table was a man with one leg. Not having been told in advance, my father had a startling beginning to his career.

At one time I thought my father's well-concealed alcoholism stemmed from his years in the death business. There may be some truth to that, but he also seemed strangely comfortable around death, happiest when he was busy and the funeral home was teeming with people. Only when I happened upon him when things were quiet did I find him sullen and melancholy, and the stress of the court case at the end of his life made his thirst unquenchable. There is no history of alcoholism in his family, or in ours now. With this knowledge and hindsight, it all began to make sense to me.

Jerry Melnyk, a former marine and a highly respected peer counselor, ran group therapy sessions for veterans for the Veterans Administration in Culver City, California. I met with him to try to understand more about the effects of war upon my father.

"You have right there, in just the little bit that you've told me, a classic case of post-traumatic stress disorder. It's pretty obvious. He's got everything we need for a diagnosis of PTSD. He had a life-threatening situation in battle and a breakdown. He returns home with remorse and survivor guilt. He'd be asking himself how he escaped when everyone else perished. If you are one of the fortunate ones to survive that event, you go through a depressive state. Normally, if you have a support network, you would come out of the depression and become angry. You're then motivated by the anger to assist your move into resolution. That's the best scenario. There was no help at that time for veterans who came home after the war. The VA dealt with their medical disabilities, but no one ever asked them about their war experiences."

I asked Jerry if he had any thoughts about why my father might have lied about being shot in the café.

"Of course we can never be sure, but it may be because it wasn't honorable. It's only honorable to be shot in battle."

Along with the alienating and often violent behavior, alcoholism, and drug abuse that results from the repression of traumatic war experiences, my father's behavior was a shoo-in for the "you're either for me or against me" polarity that existed in the world of a World War II infantryman. I would hear those words echoed by my father's eighty-four-year-old army buddy whom I tracked down in North Carolina.

At first, he laughed when I asked him about my father. "Frank had the cleanest, shiniest shoes in the entire army." He told me my father was the kind of guy who "if he liked you, he liked you, and if he didn't, he didn't." This attitude was the very thing that later led him into disagreements with Jubilee's elite Old Clan network — especially when he knew he was right. It was also what Miss Agnes found so attractive in him, for she was very much like that herself. They stood united against perceived injustice. In letters to her dying brother she writes of putting on a smile so that the townspeople wouldn't see the pain that lay underneath. This is exactly what my father did, and, from what I've learned, what so many other veterans continue to do.

I squeezed one last conversation out of my mother about life with my father before I felt the shutters close between us, a clear sign that she'd had enough of my questions and of thinking about the past.

"Isn't it good to be able to talk about this?" I asked her.

"Well, I just never have been one to air my troubles."

"I know, but most people have one or two others they can talk to, just to get a little support."

"I guess I felt like I never needed any."

"If you had it to do all over again, would you?"

"I probably would."

"So you also had good times with Daddy?"

"Oh, yes. There were good times. He wasn't all bad."

"As fathers go, he was really fun."

"Sure he was. He didn't mistreat anybody."

Of course that isn't true. He hurt her over and over. But she fought for him and won him back. She was the most faithful of all the undertaker's women. In spite of everything, she loved him. She never remarried.

My mother lived in Jubilee for fifty years before she moved to northern Kentucky where Thomas and his family made their home. She remains a passionate bridge player.

Today, Thomas is a devoted family man who has a successful career in communications, one that couldn't be further from the funeral business.

Jemma married an undertaker and has a daughter.

Evelyn is the only member of our family who still lives in Jubilee. One day, midlife, she checked herself into a psychiatric ward.

She repeated this several times before she was diagnosed with severe bipolar disorder.

I haven't seen Noah or Julian since high school.

Fletcher Hamilton died long ago, suddenly, and in a public place.

Rex remained in the funeral business. He continues to be a Southern gentleman of the best kind.

Whenever I passed through Jubilee, I always dropped by Belle's house, where she fed me pecan pie and kept me informed on all manner of things. She lived into her eighties and died in her sleep.

After years of indulging my wanderlust, I settled in London with my British husband. For many years he designed and sold exquisite men's clothing to high-profile customers, from his retail premises in London's West End. I wish my father could have crossed the pond again to play the dandy in a more European way. It is no effort for me whatsoever to imagine him reveling in a softer cut, a finer fabric . . . wearing the kind of suit that only the Europeans have mastered. The quality of the clothes they produce would have fascinated and gladdened my peacock father.

I wish he could see and experience the London I've come to know. Perhaps then I could have helped him replace the vision he held of England, which, through the eyes of a terrified teenager, was only a brief stopover on his way to war, the first stage on his journey to an uncertain manhood.

And I wonder what he would have made of the London walking funeral cortege. It doesn't occur often nowadays, but twice I've stood silently on a busy London street to witness a carriage drawn by horses wearing ostrich-plume headdresses. The undertaker who preceded them was dressed as if he'd raided a Victorian costume department. He strode solemnly in his black top hat, eyes straight ahead. Hanging carriage lanterns rattled in the wind, and flowers pressed against the glass sides of the carriage through which a fleeting glimpse of the coffin somehow brought me full circle. I know the sight would have stopped my father in his tracks.

Recently there's been a surge in people who seek to demystify death and its history and rituals. Global explorers of death come together at Death Cafés and Death Dinners in social and educational gatherings to persuade the taboo subject out of its darkness. There is a growing desire for green burials and the formation of Natural Death Centers and Societies. Collectors continue to unearth antique and historical items of mourning. Cemeteries and their exquisite monuments are being restored. In the tradition of Bram Stoker and others, vigilant artists in all mediums entertain us with the tantalizing idea of immortality. A Death Movement is out there. I participate with a curiosity and a perspective that is laced with a good dose of life. And so it comes back to my father. . . .

He could have chosen to declare the funeral home off-limits to my childhood. But he didn't. How fortunate I was that he allowed me to follow him downstairs each day to occupy his world. He welcomed me with open arms to an environment where I learned to explore, observe, and use my imagination in the midst of death. What a generous gift it was. For when it was time to leave Jubilee, I did so with relish, wide eyes, and an eagerness to test the thumping breast of life. For that, I will always be grateful.

ACKNOWLEDGMENTS

Grateful thanks to my brilliant agent, Oli Munson, at A. M. Heath, without whom this book would have remained in a dark crypt.

Many thanks to my US editor at Gallery Books, Abby Zidle, whose gentle probing, clarity, and decisiveness have made this a better book; publishers Jennifer Bergstrom and Louise Burke for their enthusiasm and encouragement; the inventive Regina Starace for the original publisher's jacket cover; Steve Boldt, an extraordinary copyeditor; my publicist, Mary McCue, and all the Gallery team, including Michele Martin, John Paul Jones, and Liz Psaltis.

I'm grateful to my wonderful UK editor, Suzanne Baboneau, at Simon and Schuster UK for ushering this book to readers in the UK with an incredibly experienced and elegant hand. Kudos and thanks to Mel Four for the original publisher's cover design and to publicist Elizabeth Preston, Dawn Burnett in marketing, and Gill Richardson in sales.

Further thanks and appreciation to fellow Southerner turned Londoner, Jennifer Custer, International Rights Director at A. M. Heath.

Special thanks to, Denise Stewart who generously and tirelessly contributed guidance and expertise beyond the call of any duty; Randy Stuart, Paul Cripps, Brenda Mountjoy Sorkin, Larry Sorkin, and Nita Shah for generous help in numerous ways.

Posthumous thanks to Keith Bullock, 35th Infantry Division, for helping me locate the truth.

Heartfelt thanks to my friends in the writing and publishing community in the UK for their exuberant support and on whom I have leaned.

Thank you to my family and friends afar who have offered more of their memories, time, and patience than I thought possible.

Last but not least, I am deeply grateful to Malcolm Levene for his unswerving belief and support. Thank you, Malcolm.

ABOUT THE AUTHOR

Kate Mayfield is the coauthor of *Ten Steps to Fashion Freedom* and *Ellie Hart Goes to Work.* She attended Western Kentucky University before moving to Manhattan, where she graduated from the American Academy of Dramatic Arts. She now lives in London.

Visit her on the web at www.katemayfield .com.

The employees of Thorndike Press hope you have enjoyed this Large Print book. All our Thorndike, Wheeler, and Kennebec Large Print titles are designed for easy reading, and all our books are made to last. Other Thorndike Press Large Print books are available at your library, through selected bookstores, or directly from us.

For information about titles, please call:
  (800) 223-1244

or visit our Web site at:
  http://gale.cengage.com/thorndike

To share your comments, please write:
  Publisher
  Thorndike Press
  10 Water St., Suite 310
  Waterville, ME 04901